D1996548

Europahauptschule
Johann Heinrich Pestalozzi
Sekundarstufe 1
Pestalozzistr. - 52477 Alsdorf

08/2010 - E10 - 23/60
GHS Johann Heinrich Pestalozzi
Alsdorf
Benutzer Kl. Schj.
1. Mervetcan Resadiyeli
2. Mustafa Rezi 10 A1
3. Kevin Beier 10 A3 15/16
Christian Rinau 10 B 16/17

New Highlight 6

Cornelsen

New Highlight
Band 6

Im Auftrage des Verlages herausgegeben von
Frank Donoghue, Nenagh, Irland

Erarbeitet von
Sydney Thorne, York

Verlagsredaktion
Susanne Döpper (Projektleitung) • Silvia Wiedemann (verantwortliche Redakteurin)
Eva Baumgart (Bildredaktion)

Anhang
Redaktionsbüro Birgit Herrmann, Freudenstadt

Beratende Mitwirkung
Hans Bebermeier, Bielefeld • Dr. Johannes Berning, Münster • Hartmut Bondzio, Bielefeld • Annette Bondzio-Abbit, Bielefeld • Gisela Feldmann, Haltern • Prof. Dr. Liesel Hermes, Karlsruhe • Ingrid-Barbara Hoffmann, Böblingen • Dagmar Höffner, Ingelheim • Petra Klein, Villmar • Martina Kriebel, Brigachtal • Inge Kronisch, Flensburg • Christa Lüdemann, Hannover • Konstanze Stöckermann-Borst, Leimen • Ellen Wiegard-Kaiser, Bielefeld • Herbert Willms, Herford • Gunhild Wolf, Unna

Illustration/Grafik
Adrian Barclay, Bristol • John Batten, London • Carlos Borrell, Berlin • Christian Görke, Berlin • Michael Teßmer, Hamburg

Umschlaggestaltung
Leonardi.Wollein, Berlin

Layoutkonzept
Christoph Schall

Layout und technische Umsetzung
Klein & Halm Grafikdesign, Berlin

www.cornelsen.de

Die Internetadressen, die in diesem Lehrwerk angegeben sind, wurden vor Drucklegung geprüft. Der Verlag übernimmt keine Gewähr für die Aktualität und den Inhalt dieser Adressen und Dateien oder solcher, die mit ihnen verlinkt sind.

1. Auflage, 1. Druck 2010

Alle Drucke dieser Auflage sind inhaltlich unverändert und können im Unterricht nebeneinander verwendet werden.

© 2010 Cornelsen Verlag, Berlin

Das Werk und seine Teile sind urheberrechtlich geschützt. Jede Nutzung in anderen als den gesetzlich zugelassenen Fällen bedarf der vorherigen schriftlichen Einwilligung des Verlages.
Hinweis zu den §§ 46, 52 a UrhG: Weder das Werk noch seine Teile dürfen ohne eine solche Einwilligung eingescannt und in ein Netzwerk eingestellt oder sonst öffentlich zugänglich gemacht werden.
Dies gilt auch für Intranets von Schulen und sonstigen Bildungseinrichtungen.

Druck: CS-Druck CornelsenStürtz, Berlin

ISBN 978-3-464-34475-0 – broschiert
ISBN 978-3-464-34348-7 – gebunden

Inhalt gedruckt auf säurefreiem Papier aus nachhaltiger Forstwirtschaft.

1⊙2 Als Hörtext oder Song auf der Audio-CD vorhanden; die Track-Angaben beziehen sich auf die Vollfassung (Bestellnummer 344762): 1⊙2 = CD 1, Track 2.

W ⊙ Zusätzliche Aufgaben auf der CD-ROM im Workbook

Kann dem Portfolio-Ordner hinzugefügt werden

Aufgaben:

○ leicht ◑ mittel ● schwierig

Interkulturell

Wiederholung

MORE HELP! p. 110 Im Anhang auf S. 110 findet man Hilfen zur Lösung der Aufgabe.

Begleitend zum Schülerbuch finden sich unter www.new-highlight.de interaktive Online-Übungen, die am Ende jeder Unit bearbeitet werden können.

*** Fakultativ (wahlfreie Bestandteile des Lehrwerks)**

Unit 1

Rainbow Nation

1 What do you know about South Africa?

a) Work with a partner. Look at the photos and the map.
Then read these sentences and pick two correct answers in each sentence.

1 South Africa has big cities, for example **a)** Cape Town **b)** Nairobi **c)** Johannesburg.
2 Two of South Africa's most popular sports are **a)** baseball **b)** soccer **c)** cricket.
3 South Africa is called the *Rainbow Nation* because it has many **a)** rainbows **b)** cultures **c)** languages.
4 South Africa has **a)** modern city centres **b)** the highest building in the world **c)** townships where poorer people live.
5 South Africa has national parks with **a)** lions **b)** elephants **c)** tigers.

b) Now listen to the radio advert for South Africa. Check your answers from exercise 1a).

1 ◎ 2

▸ WB 1, p. 115

H

I

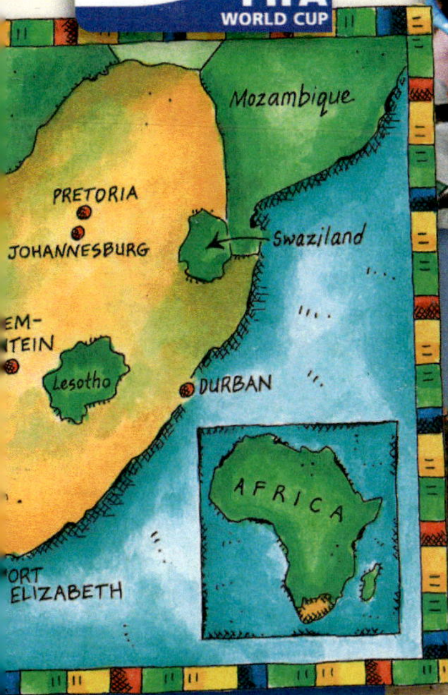

J

K

2 AND YOU?

Work with a partner and choose a) or b).

a) Look at the photos and tell your partner three things that you have learned about South Africa.

- South Africa has … . I didn't know that.
- In South Africa people speak …

b) Imagine you spent a holiday in South Africa. Look at the photos and tell your partner five things that you did or saw.

- One day I visited … and I saw …
- On another day I watched …

▸ W 3, 1–3 ▸ WB 2, p. 115

FROM COWS TO CRICKET

1 Look at the title and photos.
What do you think the text is about?
Which paragraph is about:

a) Ntini as a boy
b) how he joined the national team
c) Ntini and his fans
d) how he helps young people?

Makhaya Ntini is South Africa's most popular sports celebrity. Why? The reason is simple. Although 80% of South Africans are black, before 1998 all the players in the national cricket team were white. Then, in 1998, when he was only 20, Ntini became the first black player in the national team – a symbol of the multicultural Rainbow Nation in one of the country's most popular sports.

"As a kid I was very poor," says Ntini. "I lived in a big family of seven children and had to fight for everything." The family lived in a small village and spoke Xhosa, an African language. During the day the boy looked after the village's cows. But he had no shoes. When he wanted to keep his feet warm early in the morning, he stood in fresh, warm cow dung.

One day some people from town came to the village. They were looking for young cricket players with talent for the game. They gave the boys cricket balls – and Ntini threw the balls better than the experts! Ntini's friends weren't surprised. They knew his talent, because they had often thrown stones and had tried to hit the cows' horns. And Ntini had always won.

The cricket experts now encouraged Ntini to go to college, where he soon played for the South Africa schools team. Then he was picked for South Africa's national cricket team for their tour of Australia. Some people said that the team had only picked Ntini because they wanted to have a black player – not because he was a good player. But Ntini played brilliantly and quickly showed his critics that they were wrong.

Ntini is not only a brilliant international player – he's also great with his fans. "People know him and love him," says national team manager Goolam Rajah. "I have seen more than a hundred fans waiting for his autograph. He gives every person in the queue a hug."

Ntini also does a lot for children who are as poor as he once was. "I believe there are other Makhaya Ntinis out there," he says. He has worked for example for an organization that helps children with HIV/AIDS. He has also given money to a home for poor children and for a cricket training centre not far from his family's village. His message to children is simple: "Live your dream," he says. "Don't be afraid."

One day Ntini will write a book about his life. He hasn't started yet, but he already knows that its title will be *Ubulongwe* – and in Xhosa that means "cow dung".

Based on: *India Times Cricket*

2 *True (T), false (F) or not in the text (NIT)?*

1 Makhaya Ntini is famous in South Africa.
2 Before he joined the national cricket team only white people had played in it.
3 He had a big family.
4 His family lived in a poor part of a big town.
5 He is married and has children.
6 Ntini was only picked for the national team because he was black.
7 His fans write messages on his blog.
8 Ntini has written a book about his life.

3 WORDPOWER

Find the words or phrases in the text.

1 liked by lots of people (line 1)
2 a famous star (line 2)
3 easy, not difficult (line 2)
4 opposite of *rich* (line 9)
5 not old (line 19)
6 opposite of *worse* (line 21)
7 was chosen (line 25)
8 opposite of *right* (line 28)
9 near (line 38)
10 be frightened (line 40)

4 Copy and complete the sentences.

1 Ntini had no shoes because ... *(paragraph 2)*
2 He stood in fresh cow dung when ... *(paragraph 2)*
3 The cricket experts knew that Ntini had talent for the game because ... *(paragraph 3)*
4 Ntini has helped children in South Africa – for example, he has ... *(paragraph 6)*

5 AND YOU?

a) What do you think? Why is Ntini so popular in South Africa? Write 2–4 full sentences.

Tip:
Find different reasons, for example: successful in sport, his life story, how he helps people.

MORE HELP! p. 108

b) Imagine you're Makhaya Ntini as a boy. Write an article for your school magazine and describe:

- **your life at home**
- **the day when the cricket experts came to your village.**

I live in ... . We don't have much money and I don't have ... . During the day I ... . Last week something special happened. Some people from town came ...

▸W 4–5, 4–5

CHATTING WITH PEOPLE

1 At a rugby match

1◉4 **Jacob is at the Green Point Stadium in Cape Town for a rugby match against Australia. He starts talking to a girl who is sitting next to him. Read the dialogues. Have Jacob and Sarah met before? Do you think they will meet again?**

Before the match starts ...

JACOB Hi. Do you mind if I sit here?
SARAH No. It's free.
JACOB Thanks. – Do you often come to rugby matches here?
SARAH No, I'm from Pretoria. I've come to Cape Town for this match. My name's Sarah, by the way.
JACOB And I'm Jacob. – Well, let's hope it's a great match! I'm looking forward to it.

After the match has finished ...

SARAH What an amazing match! I'm so happy that I came!
JACOB Yes, me too. But I've got to go now. It has been nice talking to you, Sarah. Enjoy your stay in Cape Town!
SARAH Thanks, Jacob. See you again some time maybe?
JACOB I hope so. You can text me on 079 582 4063.
SARAH Thanks, I'll do that. Well, see you, Jacob.
JACOB Take care, Sarah. Let's keep in touch!

2 Starting and finishing conversations

a) Complete the phrases.

Starting a conversation

Do you mind | come to ... here?
Do you often | by the way.
My name's ... | if I sit here?

Finishing a conversation

Well, it has been | your stay in ... | care.
See you again | in touch. | go now.
I've got to | Take | nice talking to you.
Let's keep | Enjoy | some time maybe?

b) What could you say?

1 In a cafe the only free seat is next to a man and woman. What can you say to them?
2 You've met a boy at a football match, but now you have to go. What can you say to him?

MORE HELP! p. 108

c) Imagine you meet a boy or girl at the cinema. Write dialogues:

- **when you sit next to him/her**
- **when you say goodbye after the film.**

►W 6, 6

3 ROLE PLAY

PARTNER A: You have these tickets for a rugby match. Answer your partner's questions.
PARTNER B: Look at your card on page 66.

Tip:
R225 is the price: 225 rand.
How many rand is a euro?
Find out on the Internet.

4 MEDIATING

Now you'd like to watch a rugby match at Newlands Stadium with your friend Felix. He can't speak English very well.
Pick A or B and tell Felix in German what is/isn't allowed in the stadium.

A

Please note that the following items are not allowed in the stadium:

- cans, bottles, alcohol
- cameras with zoom
- video cameras
- helmets

B

Newlands STADIUM REGULATIONS

- Refreshments are on sale inside the stadium, including alcoholic and non-alcoholic beverages.
- Alcohol is sold to over 18s only.
- No alcohol may be drunk during matches.
- No alcohol, cans or glass bottles may be brought into the stadium.
- Small digital cameras are allowed, but cameras with zoom and detachable lenses and video cameras are not allowed.
- Bags are allowed, but may be searched on entry.

5 INTERPRETING

1◉5

Just before the rugby match starts, a girl would like to sit next to Felix. Can you help?

Tip:
You don't have to translate word for word.

GIRL Sorry – do you mind if I sit here?
YOU Sie möchte …
FELIX Kein Problem. Frage sie doch, ob sie hier oft bei Rugbyspielen zuschaut.
YOU Do …?
GIRL As often as I can! Have you seen a rugby match before?
YOU …
FELIX Nein, noch nie. Es ist mein erstes Spiel, und ich freue mich darauf.
YOU …
GIRL You'll love it. Rugby is so exciting – much more exciting than soccer!
YOU …

▸W 6–7, 7–9 ▸W ◉

SOUTH AFRICA – PAST AND PRESENT

1 Before 1994, life for black people was hard in South Africa.

a) Work with a partner. Look at the photos: What was not fair for black people?

1 Black people were / weren't allowed to use the same buses or taxis as white people.
2 The police were fair with / used violence against black people.
3 Black people lived in poor townships / modern city centres.

A

B

C

b) Mrs Lungile Mfeka recorded some of her experiences of life before 1994 for her grandchildren. Listen to her and check your answers in 1 a). 1 6

c) Listen again. What's the right answer?

1 White people had all the good flats / houses / land.
2 The government were all white people / black people / men.
3 We weren't allowed to live in the big cities / capital / country.
4 Our house had no garden / kitchen / running water.
5 All black people had to have a job / pass / boss.

d) Work with a partner. Guess the five missing words. Then listen for a third time and check your answers. 1 6

1 When white people left school, they got better ...
2 Sex ... black and white people was a crime.
3 The police officers were all ... people.
4 We black people had bad schools and ...
5 My father was ... unemployed.

MORE HELP! p. 108

e) What do *you* think about apartheid and life for black people in South Africa before 1994?

In my opinion, life was not fair because ...
White people had ..., but black people didn't have any ...
The police ... . The government ...

2 Life for young South Africans today

1 7 **a) Listen to Delani, who has recorded a message for a radio station in Britain.**

1 Does he like kwaito music?
2 And you? Do you prefer kwaito or gospel music?

b) Listen again. Are these sentences *true (T)* or *false (F)*?

1 Kwaito music started in the rich suburbs of Johannesburg.
2 The words in kwaito music are only in English.
3 50 % of South Africans are under 21 years old.
4 Delani lives in Soweto, a poor area of Johannesburg.
5 The Soweto Gospel Choir started in 1982.
6 They won a Grammy award in Los Angeles in 2007.

3 Thembi's radio diary

1 8 **a) Thembi is a young woman who has the HIV/AIDS virus. Listen to Thembi and her boyfriend Melikhaya. Does Thembi sound sad or happy?**

b) Listen again and pick a) or b).

1 When Thembi heard that her first boyfriend had died, she **a)** went to his house **b)** cried.
2 Her boyfriend's sister said he was sick and couldn't **a)** walk **b)** talk.
3 In the clinic Thembi had HIV/AIDS tests. She had **a)** two tests **b)** five tests.
4 The doctor told Thembi that she had been HIV positive for **a)** six months **b)** many years.
5 When Melikhaya plays music Thembi wants to **a)** dance **b)** sing.
6 Melikhaya **a)** is angry **b)** isn't angry with Thembi because she has HIV/AIDS.

Tip:
Thembi speaks with a South African accent and uses some words that you don't know. Don't worry!
You just have to answer the questions on the left.

c) What do *you* think of Thembi and Melikhaya? Write your opinion.

I think	Thembi Melikhaya	is	brave. very self-confident. amazing. a great person. a good boyfriend.

Although	she has his girlfriend has	HIV/AIDS	he she	isn't stressed and ... loves her and ...

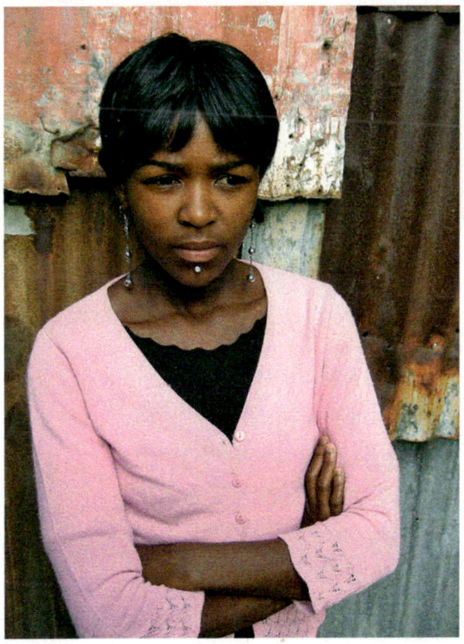

▸W 8, 10–11 ▸W

A WINDOW ON SOUTH AFRICA

The Kruger Park

- How big?
- Where/near which countries?
- What animals live there?
- How can you visit the park?

Apartheid

- "No Blacks" "Whites only"
- The Sharpeville Massacre
- The Soweto Riots
- End of apartheid in 1994

The music scene

- What is kwaito?
- Soweto Gospel Choir
- Some singers and bands, their music and life stories

World Cup 2010

- Where did the teams play?
- The best match(es)
- A good World Cup? Why (not)?
- Successful for South Africa?

South Africa

Nelson Mandela

- Family and education
- 1942–1962: fight against apartheid
- 1962–1990: in prison
- 1994: first black president of South Africa

Languages and cultures

- The Rainbow Nation (How many languages?)
- English and Afrikaans (What do ***lekker***, ***bru*** and ***takkies*** mean?)
- Some African cultures: Zulu, Xhosa, ...

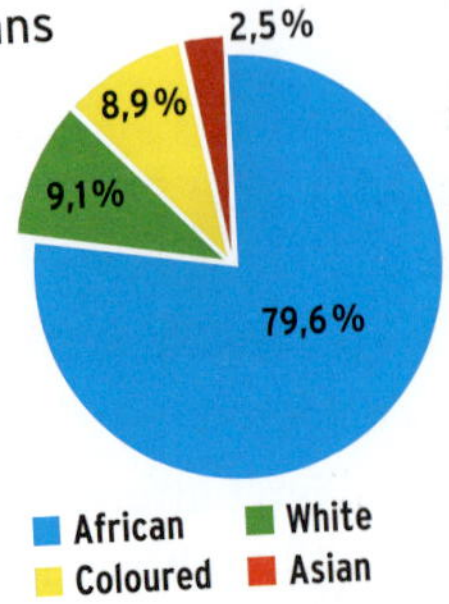

Visiting South Africa

- Big cities
- Sightseeing: Table Mountain, Soweto, Robben Island, national parks
- Things to do: adventure sports, wildlife activities, water activities
- Some problems: crime, HIV/AIDS, poverty

In this project you're going to find out some information about South Africa. Write what you're going to say, prepare pictures and labels, and then give a talk.

STEP 1 Choose one of the topics on page 14.

STEP 2 Find the information.

- **Do some research and write the information that is asked for.**
- **Find out extra information around your topic.**
  World Cup 2010: other sports in South Africa (sandboarding, cricket, ...)
  The Kruger Park: other national parks and animals (whales, dolphins, ...)
  Languages and cultures: the South African flag, national anthem, ...

Tip:
On the Internet, go to: **www.new-highlight.de**
Find the window for the webcode and put in: **NHL-6-15**

Tip:
Go online and use a search engine. Put in keywords, for example: *South Africa + languages*.

TRAINING Using texts from the Internet

- **Websites in English: Don't just copy Internet texts! Give the information in your own words and write your opinion. If you find a text like this ...**

Situated at the coastal town of Betty's Bay on the east coast, 100 km from Cape Town, it is considered to be one of the best dunes for sandboarding in South Africa. The dune is situated between the Hangklip and Blesberg mountains and stands a whopping 250 m tall with a potential run of 400 metres.

... you could write:

About 100 km from Cape Town are dunes which are 250 metres high. You can sandboard for 400 metres. It must be awesome!

- **Websites in German: Mediate in English – don't translate every word! For example, if you find a text like this on a website ...**

Der Addo Elephant National Park bei Port Elizabeth
Dieser soll durch den Zusammenschluss mehrerer Parks der einzige Park der Welt werden, der die *Big Seven* beheimatet. Die *Big Seven* bestehen aus den *Big Five* (Löwe, Elefant, Büffel, Leopard und Nashorn) sowie dem Buckelwal und dem weißen Hai.

... you could write:

The Addo Elephant National Park has lions, elephants, buffaloes, leopards and rhinos – and sea animals too (whales and sharks).

STEP 3 Write the text of your talk – with the extra information.

STEP 4 Plan your talk.

- **Prepare pictures, labels, maps or diagrams for your talk.**
- **Work alone or in a group with students who have prepared the same topic.**
- **If you work in a group: – read and compare everybody's information**
  – plan your talk so that you don't use the same information.
- **Practise your talk. The presentation phrases at the back of the book can help you.**

STEP 5 Now give your talk.

- **Don't just read your sentences. Look at the class when you talk. Good luck!**

▸W

DICTIONARY SKILLS

1 Signs

a) Look at the three signs and guess: Which two signs are warnings?

A

Boulders Penguin Colony, Cape Town

In 1983 a pair of African penguins were spotted at Boulders Bay. Since then the colony has grown rapidly, and by 1997 there were 2350 adult birds. The area has now been taken over by Cape Peninsula National Park and wooden boardwalks allow visitors to view the penguins in their natural habitat. Boulders Bay still remains the only place in the world where one can actually swim amongst the penguins.

B

C

Tip:
- First guess the new words from the context.
- Then check in a dictionary.

b) Pick the right answers – but don't use a dictionary.

Sign A

You can see the penguins when you are
1 in a zoo
2 in a building
3 in the sea and on the beach.

You are
1 allowed to swim
2 not allowed to swim
3 only allowed to swim if there are no birds.

Sign B

The penguins sometimes
1 travel in cars
2 go under cars
3 lie on cars.

Sign C

Here you shouldn't
1 walk near the water
2 feed the animals
3 eat fruit from the trees.

c) Which keywords helped you to find the answers in exercise 1b)? Pick the right words.

Sign A: spot, wooden, view, habitat, actually, amongst?
Sign B: look for, underneath, drive off?
Sign C: baboon, dangerous, attracted by?

Tip:
If you pick the right keywords, you won't have to look up so many words in the dictionary.

d) Look up the keywords in the dictionary. Check your answers in exercise 1c) and correct them.

Tip:
You can use an online dictionary. Put *Wörterbuch Englisch* into your search engine. Choose a dictionary and put in the word that you want to look up.

MEDIATING

2 Robben Island

Imagine you're in Cape Town with your parents. They don't speak English. You've found this website about Robben Island and would like to go there.

a) Tell your parents in German why the island is so famous and how you can visit it.

b) You've also found a brochure about a tour to Robben Island. Read the text and answer your parents' questions.

ROBBEN ISLAND

- 3000 political prisoners were in prison here between 1961 and 1991.
- Nelson Mandela was in prison here from 1963 to 1982.
- The island has been a museum since 1997.
- The tour of the island is 3.5 hours long, including the boat trip.
- Ferries leave at 9 a.m, 11 a.m., 1 p.m. and 3 p.m., weather permitting.
- Tickets cost R200 (adults) and R100 (children under 18).

Robben Island, Cape Town

During your 45-minute guided bus tour of the island, you'll see the lighthouse and a monument to a Muslim prince who was in prison here in 1740. You'll also see a cave where prisoners taught others to read and write, and gave lessons in history and politics.

The tour of the prison is with a guide who was once a political prisoner on the island. He will tell you what life was like for the prisoners: they had to work (for example, they had to break rocks into small pieces), they were often beaten and they were only allowed visits from their families twice a year.

Refreshments can be bought on the island. Allow 3½ hours for the trip and book in advance.

Was werden wir während der Bustour sehen?

Gibt es eine Führung durch das Gefängnis?

Wie waren die Zustände für politische Häftlinge?

Kann man auf der Insel Getränke kaufen?

Tip:
First work without a dictionary. Try to guess the meaning of new words from the context. Then use a dictionary. Look up keywords and check your answers.

▸ Extra Reading, pp. 100–101 ▸W

WHEN YOU WANT TO COMPLAIN

1 Reasons for complaining

a) When do people complain? Write five examples.

1 When they have ordered something and ...

2 When they stayed in a hotel and ...

b) Group work. Pick the five best ideas in exercise 1a).

2 Two e-mails and a letter

a) Read the e-mails and the letter and find out:

1 Which is the most informal? Why?
2 Who ... **a)** ordered something on the Internet? **b)** spent a few days in a hotel?
3 What ... **a)** never arrived? **b)** was broken when it arrived? **c)** was wrong in the hotel?

A

Dear Sir or Madam,

On May 5th I ordered an XN02 laptop computer from your website. It arrived on May 8th, but the screen is damaged and the power cable is missing.

Please tell me what I should do. Should I send the computer back? When can you send me a replacement?

Please let me know as soon as possible.

Corinna Philpott

B

28 Ringwood Road,
Pretoria 0181

SaSa Holidays
Manager

December 8th, 20...

Dear Sir or Madam,

I want to complain about our stay in the Penguin Palace Hotel in Cape Town from November 30th to December 6th.

When we came into our room, the shower was dirty and the TV didn't work.
Also, the brochure says that the hotel is near the sea, but the sea is two kilometres away!

When we complained to the receptionist, he said that we should write to you.

Yours faithfully,
Emily Jackson

C

Dear Karen,

Five days ago (on May 10th) I bought a digital camera and a memory card from you online.
I still haven't received anything. Have you sent them? Please let me know asap.

Thanks
Mike Hemmings

b) Read the the e-mails and letter again. Find the phrases which mean ...

1 broken **2** isn't there **3** a different (computer) **4** they haven't arrived **5** tell me
6 as soon as possible **7** write angrily that you do not like something **8** not clean

►W 9, 12

3 WORDPOWER

Complete the sentences with phrases from the green box. What do they mean in German?

as possible • replacement • send it back • digital camera • was missing • damaged

1 A week ago I ordered a ...
2 When it arrived, it was a bit ...
3 Also, the cable to the camera ...
4 Should I ...?
5 Let me know as soon ...
6 And please send me a ...

4 Missing parts

You ordered a new computer online. But when it arrived, the keyboard and mouse were missing. Write an e-mail and complain.

Tip:
You can use phrases from letter A on p. 18 and from exercise 3.

5 A bad day at the theme park

Complete the letter. Use some of the words in the green box – you won't need all of them.

already • always • at • on • complain • didn't • faithfully • long • says • sea • should

Dear Sir or Madam,

I want to ... about our visit to your theme park on Saturday October 26th.

When we arrived at the park at 9.30 a.m. the car park was ... full. There were ... queues for the rides and one of the roller coasters ... work. Also, the brochure ... that the cafe is open all day, but it was closed ... 4.30 p.m.

When we complained to an assistant, she said that we ... write to you.

Yours ...,

F. Saban (Mrs)

MORE HELP! p. 109

6 A terrible holiday

On a holiday in South Africa you stayed in the *Magic Campsite*. It was terrible. Write a letter to the manager, Mrs Petra van Wyk, and complain. Write 80–100 words.

loud (who?) – dirty (what?) – broken (what?) – pool (what was the problem?) – shop (why was it terrible?) – unfriendly receptionist (what did he say?) – ...

LOOK AT LANGUAGE

1 *Tsotsi*, South Africa's first international film hit

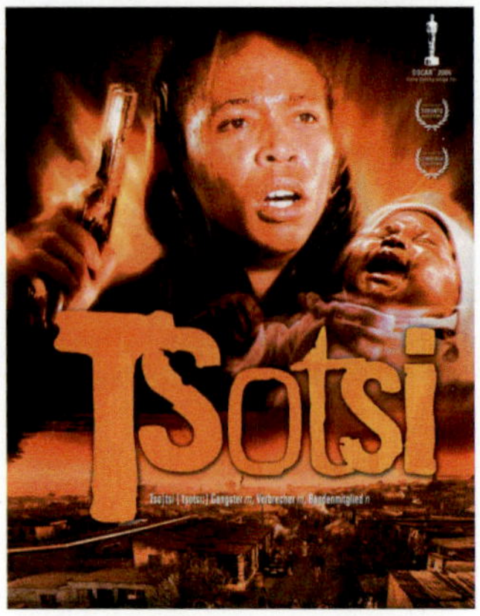

a) Have you seen the film *Tsotsi* – or heard of it?

The film *Tsotsi* is about six days in the life of Tsotsi, a 19-year-old gang leader in Johannesburg. Before Tsotsi joined his gang, he had lived alone on the streets. His life as a child had been very hard. One day, after Tsotsi had stolen a car, he found a baby in it and took it home. Tsotsi then forced a young woman to look after the baby that he had found. Miriam, the young woman, was at first frightened of Tsotsi, but in the end she made Tsotsi think about his life – his past and his future.

A lot of the music in *Tsotsi* was written by kwaito musician Zola who had been South African Artist of the Year in 2002. But the lead actors hadn't had experience in the cinema before. Terry Pheto (Miriam) had acted in the theatre. Presley Chweneyagae (Tsotsi) had acted at school and had had a role in a TV film. But their acting was so great that *Tsotsi* won an Oscar for the *Best Foreign Language Film* in 2006. And everybody in South Africa was happy because the country had never won an Oscar for a film before.

b) Find a sentence in the text for each photo.

A

B

C

2 OVER TO YOU!

a) Read these sentences and say which action happened first.

1 Before Tsotsi joined his gang, he had lived alone.
2 After Tsotsi had stolen a car, he found a baby in it.
3 The woman looked after the baby that Tsotsi had found.

first action *(past perfect)*	**second action** *(simple past)*
had lived	joined
...	...
...	...

b) Now finish the checkpoint and make the rule for the past perfect.

Tip: You can find *past participles* in the *List of irregular verbs* on pages 190–191.

CHECKPOINT

Past perfect

Wenn zwei Handlungen in der Vergangenheit passieren, steht die frühere Handlung im ...

Das *past perfect* bildest du mit ... und dem *past participle* (Partizip Perfekt).

Beispiel:
Before he joined the gang, Tsotsi had lived alone.

▸ W 10–13 ▸ W ⦿ Weitere Übungen: www.new-highlight.de ▸ Extra Practice, pp. 68 ff. ▸ Summary p. 121

TEST YOURSELF

Do these tests and check your answers on page 192. Look again at the new words on pages 127–130. Look at the *Summary* on page 121. Do the tests again after a few weeks.

TEST 1 Pick the correct definitions.

1 Nelson Mandela
2 Rainbow Nation
3 Kwaito
4 The World Cup
5 Rand
6 Kruger

a) a big international football competition in South Africa in 2010
b) popular music that started in South Africa
c) a language in South Africa
d) the money that is used in South Africa
e) a group of people who live in South Africa
f) South Africa's most famous national park
g) South Africa's first black president
h) a popular name for South Africa

6 POINTS

TEST 2 Pick the right word.

join • keep • spend • text • throw • win

1 A good singer can ... an award.
2 It's cold and I want to ... my feet warm.
3 ... the ball to me, please!
4 I like cricket and I'd like to ... a team.
5 Did you ... the holiday at home?
6 You can ... me on 0772 294 2334.

6 POINTS

TEST 3 Pick the right word.

1 I'm interested in / for / on music.
2 He had to fight on / around / for food.
3 She played very / good / brilliantly.
4 Bye, Sarah! Let's keep at / in / with touch.
5 We had no running light / water / electricity.
6 Let's meet during / for / under the holidays.

6 POINTS

TEST 4 Meeting and leaving people
Write the two missing words in each sentence.

1 Do ... ... if I sit here?
2 ... you often come ... rugby matches here?
3 My ...'s Sarah ... the way.
4 I ... ... to go now.
5 It ... ... nice talking to you.
6 See ... again ... time maybe?

6 POINTS

TEST 5 What's the past participle?

Before Nelson Mandela became president ...
1 he had (**work**) in Johannesburg,
2 he had (**have**) six children,
3 he had (**fight**) against apartheid,
4 he had (**be**) in prison for 27 years,
5 he had (**become**) famous and popular,
6 he hadn't (**stop**) fighting for his country.

6 POINTS

TEST 6 Say it in English.

1 Sehr geehrte Damen und Herren ...
2 Ich möchte mich beschweren.
3 Der Fernseher war kaputt.
4 Die Dusche funktionierte nicht.
5 Die Managerin sagte, dass ich Ihnen schreiben sollte.
6 „Mit freundlichen Grüßen" *(Schlussformel)*

6 POINTS

Unit 2

Teenage kicks

Police question teenager

A teenager who was questioned by the police on Tuesday morning said that they were biased against young people. The teenager complained

1 Young people in pictures and newspaper articles

a) Work alone. Pick one of the pictures. Imagine one of the people is your friend. Describe him/her. You can use the phrases in the boxes or your own ideas.

I'm talking about the boy/girl in picture A / ... / one of the boys/girls in picture B/...

My friend looks quite ... → relaxed • aggressive • friendly • provocative • nervous • ...

He/She ... → often hangs around in a gang/with ... • has a problem with ... • is often in trouble with ... • likes wearing ... • doesn't like ... • often relaxes with ... • has driving lessons • does voluntary work

● He/She is ... → usually relaxed because ... • sometimes nervous because ... • often bored because ... • ...

b) Tell a partner about your friend.

c) Talk about your friend in a small group.

► W 14, 1–2 ► WB 3, p. 116

Invitation
to the school prom
at 7.30 p.m. on June 26th
in the Royal Hotel

D

E

F

Alcohol main reason for teenage crime

A survey shows that 25% of teenagers who commit a crime had too much alcohol

G

2 A survey: Life for young people in Britain

1 11 **a) Listen to Loren, Kevin and Ellie. Pick the topics for each teenager.**

A clothes + looking aggressive
B unemployment + exams
C the media + voluntary work

b) Listen again. Do they say this – yes or no?

1 Loren: More young people do voluntary work than commit crimes.
2 Kevin: You can't find any weekend jobs.
3 Ellie: Too many adults are biased against young people.

3 AND YOU?

MORE HELP p. 110

Do you think adults are often biased against teenagers? Write at least five or six sentences.

I think that the media/teachers ... are
sometimes/quite often biased against ...
They often think that all ... In my opinion ...
But I also agree that ...

4 SONG *Teenage kicks*

1 12 **Do you like the song? Why / Why not?**

The song is old / slow / loud / ...
The music sounds angry / sad / ...
I like / don't like the singer's voice /
the rhythm / the words / ...
The music is good for dancing / ...

▸ Extra Reading, pp. 102–103 ▸W 14, 3

SORRY, I CAN'T COME

1 The school prom

1 13

The school prom is a party for the students who have finished their last year at school. Read the two dialogues. Why do Kevin and Ellie say sorry?

LOREN Oh, hi Kev. I wanted to ask you – can you come to my birthday party at about 8 p.m. on June 10th?
KEVIN June 10th? Oh, I'm really sorry, Loren. I'd love to come, but unfortunately I'm going to our school prom on that evening.
LOREN Oh, that's a pity! Can't you change your mind?
KEVIN I'm sorry. It's a pity that it's the same night as your party, but I've already bought my ticket for it.

KEVIN Are you coming to the prom, Ellie?
ELLIE No, I'm not. £35 for a ticket? You must be joking! It's much too expensive! Everybody is buying dresses and suits. It's a waste of money, if you ask me.
KEVIN Oh, come on, Ellie! You don't have to buy a dress if you don't want to. Please!
ELLIE It's really kind of you to ask, Kevin, but I'm sorry, I can't come now anyway. Loren has invited me to her birthday party, and I've already said yes.

2 Saying sorry

a) Read the dialogue with a partner.

TOM Can you ... to my barbecue ... June 15th?
EMILY Oh, I'm ... sorry, Tom. I'd really like to come, but ... I'm ... to the school prom on that evening. It's a ... that it's on the ... night as your barbecue!
TOM Oh, ... on, Emily. Can't you change your ...?
EMILY Look, it's really ... of you to ask, Tom. But I'm sorry, I can't come now ... I've ... bought my ...
TOM Oh, that's a ... . I think school proms are ... too expensive. They're a ... of money!

b) What do you say? Use phrases from the dialogues and/or use your own ideas.

1 **You meet your friend Ann. Invite her to your party: 6.30 p.m., October 1st.**
– Oh, hi Ann. I wanted to ... – can you ... 6.30 p.m. ... October 1st?
2 **You're Ann. You have a ticket for a football match on October 1st. What do you say?**
– I'm really... . I'd ..., but unfortunately ...
3 **React when Ann says that she can't come to your party.**
– Oh, come ... . Can't you change ...?
4 **Say again that you're sorry. Say why you can't change your mind.**
– I'm ... . It's really kind of you ... . But I can't ... . I've ...

▸W 15–16, 4–6

3 MEDIATING

Jonas from Germany is in a British school during the time of the school prom. You look online with Jonas for information about hiring suits and limos.
Pick either A or B and tell him the most important information in German.

A

What you need for your prom:

- ☑ a smart dinner suit
- ☑ a white shirt
- ☑ a black or white bow tie
- ☑ black shoes, well polished

B

DINNER SUIT HIRE

- ☞ Hire your dinner suit from one of our 120 hire departments. There's probably one quite near your school.
- ☞ We will happily come to your school with a selection of dinner suits and accessories. Ask for our free fitting service.

LIMO HIRE – SPECIAL OFFER FOR SCHOOL PROMS

All our limos are equipped with TV/DVD units, CD players and overhead mirror – perfect for your prom night!

Prices from £70 per hour for a ten-seater limo + 20% deposit when you book the car.

▸ WB 4, p. 116

4 ROLE PLAY

PARTNER A: You're meeting some friends in a pizzeria at 7 p.m. on Monday July 5th. Invite Partner B to come too. Ask your partner to change his/her mind. Then Partner B invites you to a party, but you're going to the school prom on July 9th. Say that you're sorry.

PARTNER B: Look at your card on page 66.

Grange School

You are invited to the school prom
at 7.30 p.m. on Friday July 9th
at the Grand Hotel. Tickets: £25

5 AND YOU?

MORE HELP! p. 110

a) What do *you* think about school proms? Prepare a few sentences, then tell the class.

I like / I don't like the idea of school proms because ...
On the other hand ...

b) You have an invitation to a party, but you don't want to go. Who can write the funniest excuse?

Thank you for your invitation. Unfortunately I'm not able to come because I've already invited the Queen for table tennis on that day. I ...

▸ W 16, 7 ▸ W ⊙

STEREOTYPES

1 No hoodies

a) True or false? The sign tells people ...

1 what the shop sells and doesn't sell
2 what its customers mustn't wear
3 how many people are allowed in the shop
4 how many young people are allowed inside
5 how many things you can buy in the shop.

b) Which sentences do you agree with?

The shop owner ...
1 is biased against teenagers.
2 thinks teenagers who wear hoodies often steal.
3 is afraid that teenagers in groups are very loud.
4 is fair with all his/her customers.
5 has probably had teenagers in the shop who have stolen things.

2 A poster

a) Work with a partner. What do you think? Use your own ideas if you like.

1 This poster is for parents / children / ...
2 It links young people with fun / crime / ...
3 It wants adults to know / ask ... / ...
4 I / We think it's a good idea / provocative / ...

b) Find words or phrases which mean ...

1 this evening
2 driving too fast
3 drinking too much whisky, beer, ...
4 crimes
5 cannabis, ecstasy, ...

3 Opinions and facts

Look at the information below and tell the class about it.

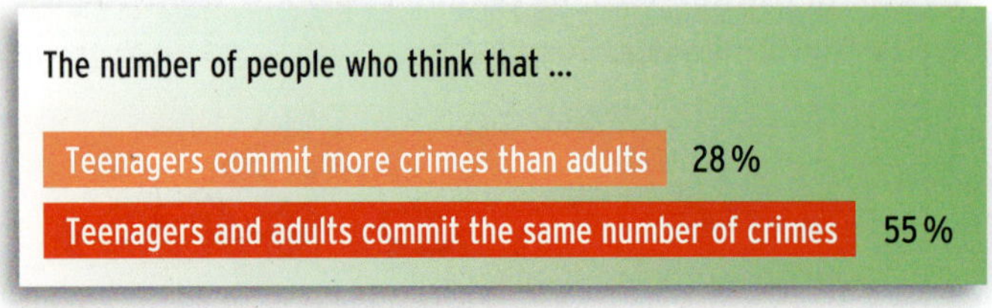

Only ... of teenagers commit ... But ... percent of the people think that ...
That's terrible / amazing. / That's what I expected.

4 A warning against stereotypes

a) Finish the sentences.

1 Some people will think that the man on the left could be dangerous because he's wearing ...
2 Some people will feel safe with the man on the right because he's wearing ...
3 The surprise when you look more carefully is that ...

b) Which phrase in the poster means:

"We're not different just because we wear different clothes".

TRAINING A discussion

5 A class discussion about the posters in exercises 1 and 2

a) Prepare what you're going to say.

- **Collect ideas, for example in networks.**

no hoodies: unfriendly shop; adults steal too!; biased against teenagers

fire poster: not everybody is dangerous; parents are worried

- **Then pick your two best ideas. Prepare at least two sentences for each idea.**
- **Think of arguments for and against the two posters.**

It's true that ... sometimes ... But in my opinion ...
People who work in shops often think that ... . I can understand them, but I think ...

b) If you're not the first speaker, be ready to react to what other people have said.

I agree with ...
I don't agree with ...
I think you're wrong. I think ...

I can understand ..., but ...
In my opinion you're biased against ... because ...
I can understand ..., but on the other hand I think ...

1 14
c) Listen to three short discussions. In which discussion do the speakers 1) give the fullest arguments and 2) react best to the other speakers?

d) Your discussion: Talk about the posters in small groups. Good luck!

Speaker 1: I'll start. I think the poster in exercise 1 ... . And I also think that ...
Speaker 2: Well, I agree with you when you say ..., but in my opinion ...

▸ W

A GREAT EXPERIENCE

1 *The Duke of Edinburgh's Award*

***The D of E Award* is for young people. There are four parts:**
- **voluntary work**
- **a sport**
- **a special interest**
- **a longer hike**

1 15 **a) Copy the table below on paper. Then listen to the radio report and write the missing information.**

1	Voluntary work	Michael helped ... people.
2	Sport	Kylie learned to ...
3	Special interest	Dan's activity was ...
4	The hike	Amina hiked for ... days.

1 15 **b) Listen again and pick the right answers.**

1 The number of young people who take part in the *Duke of Edinburgh's Award* each year is **a)** 275 **b)** 2750 **c)** 27 500 **d)** 275 000
2 Michael didn't know that old people were often so **a)** friendly **b)** difficult **c)** lonely **d)** interesting.
3 Kylie was able to practise her sport in **a)** a sports centre **b)** the school gym **c)** the mountains **d)** a friend's house.
4 Dan practised his special interest for **a)** a month **b)** six months **c)** a year **d)** two years.
5 Amina's hike was fun because the young people **a)** had lots of food **b)** got lost **c)** met nice people **d)** had good weather.

c) Work with a partner. Can you remember the missing words?

1 The young people who take part in the *Duke of Edinburgh's Award* have to be between fourteen and ...
2 Michael had never worked in a ... for old people before.
3 When she started climbing, Kylie felt ...
4 In your rucksack you have to carry your tent, your food, your sleeping bag and your ...
5 Three phrases which describe the *Award* are: hard work, working in a team and ...

1 15 **d) Now listen again and check your answers.**

2 AND YOU? Choose either a) or b).

MORE HELP! p. 111

a) Describe a hobby or activity which you do in your free time.
What? Where? How often? Alone? Fun/hard/...? Take part in competitions?

b) Describe a hike or a journey that went wrong.
When? Where? With ...? Equipment? What problem? In the end ...?

▸W 17, 8–9

A MACHINE AGAINST TEENAGERS

1 The machine is called a *Mosquito*.

a) Look at the advert and guess what the machine does.

1 It hurts you when you touch it.
2 It makes a horrible noise.
3 It phones your parents.

1◉16 **b) Now listen to the dialogue. Did you guess right?**

c) Listen again. Are the sentences true or false?

1 It's April 1st.
2 *Mosquitos* are used by some shops and supermarkets.
3 Young people can usually hear them, but most adults can't.
4 People who can hear the sound don't like it.
5 *Mosquitos* are only used in Britain.

2 An advert

1◉17 **Read the advert. Some information is wrong. Then listen to the radio advert and write the correct information on paper.**

3 You're going to hear five people talk about the *Mosquito*.

1◉18
- **First write the five names in your exercise book and read the statements below.**
- **Write the correct letter for each person while you're listening.**
- **There is one more statement than there are people.**

William	Alison	Natalie	Ben	Kirsty

Tip:
Read sentences A-F very carefully before you start listening.

A Most young people commit no crimes.
B Only teenagers are able to hear *Mosquitos*, adults can't.
C *Mosquitos* are safe and not very expensive.
D Not only teenagers but younger children hear *Mosquitos*.
E Groups of young men who hang around outside shops can be frightening.
F *Mosquitos* are used in Britain and other countries too.

4 AND YOU?

1◉19 **Listen to the sound from a *Mosquito*. Can you hear it? And is your teacher able to hear it too? What's it like? Tell the class.**

I think the sound is terrible / OK / not very nice / nothing special / ...

▸W 17, 10 ▸W ◉

A BLOG

1 Read the blog and look at the pictures. Why is Steve angry?

1⊙20

STEVE MY BLOG

"You must be joking!" I said when my friends at school told me that they had put up a *Mosquito* outside our supermarket here in Calne.

I often meet my friends outside the supermarket. Why? Because you can go into the shop to buy some chocolate or some crisps. And you don't get wet because you can stand under a roof.

Now it's true that some of us smoke. And yes, we sometimes leave empty cans or crisp bags on the ground. But we don't take drugs or anything like that. We're just ordinary kids. OK, some people are perhaps frightened of us because we're sometimes a bit loud, but lots of the older people aren't frightened of us. They often speak to us and tell us a joke, and we sometimes help them with their bags.

Well, after school we all went into town to see the *Mosquito* – and to find out if we could hear it. At first I didn't hear anything, but suddenly I heard this horrible, high-frequency noise. It was an awful sound! We couldn't stay there, so we ran to the park – that sound was just too horrible. So I suppose the people in the supermarket will say the *Mosquito* was successful.

A few of us tried to talk to the shop manager. I mean, we hadn't done anything illegal, had we? So why shouldn't we be allowed to meet on a pavement in town? But the manager didn't really listen to us. He said that some customers had complained about the conditions outside the shop. He said that they were frightened of the young people who were hanging around in front of the shop. We told some teachers about it, and they complained to the manager too, but they weren't successful. The machines aren't illegal, said the manager, so why should he take them down?

I think it's not fair that young people aren't able to meet in the street. Luckily there's a national campaign against *Mosquito*. It's called *Buzz Off* and I hope as many people as possible will support it. And there's a programme about *Mosquitos* on BBC2 tonight. I hope it's good!

Steve

Comments

Belgium has the right idea – I hear that *Mosquitos* are banned there. Sophie

It's a scandal that *Mosquitos* are allowed. If teenagers want to steal they'll only steal in another shop. The real answer is more youth clubs so that young people don't have to hang around in the rain. Good luck with your campaign! Kathryn

I don't like *Mosquitos*, but you must look at the argument from the other side. My parents have a shop and have a big problem with some young people who hang around in a gang that meets outside the shop. The customers are afraid of them. So what should my parents do? Dave

In my town they use pink lights in places where they don't want teenagers. Under the pink lights your face and hands look grey. Young people don't want to look horrible, so they move away. William

2 Read the blog and comments. Then pick the right answers.

1 Steve heard that there was a *Mosquito*
a) outside a shop
b) at the station
c) at the bus station.

2 Steve agrees that his friends sometimes
a) steal
b) leave litter in town
c) break things.

3 When he heard the *Mosquito*, Steve
a) put his hands in his ears
b) laughed
c) moved away.

4 Steve's teachers
a) were able to help
b) weren't able to help
c) didn't try to help.

5 Kathryn wants more
a) places where teens can meet indoors
b) shops
c) police officers.

6 William talks about a town which uses
a) sound **b)** colour **c)** water
against young people.

3 Opinions

a) Read the questions and say *yes* or *no*.

b) Answer *yes* or *no* and finish your answers with *because* ...

1 Does Steve often stand outside the supermarket in Calne?
2 Is it true that all adults are afraid of Steve and his friends?
3 Does Belgium have *Mosquitos*?
4 Does Kathryn think *Mosquitos* help against crime?
5 Can Dave understand people who use *Mosquitos*?

4 AND YOU?

a) Collect arguments for and against *Mosquitos*. Use ideas from pages 29–31 and your own ideas too. Write as many sentences as you can.

Mosquitos are a good / bad idea because ...
They're fair / not fair because ...

MORE HELP! p. 111

b) *Mosquitos* in your town or village: a good idea or not?

In my town / village young people often meet outside / in front of / ... They ...
Some people think ...

▸ W 18–19, 11

WRITING A STORY

1 The day when I lost my money

a) Later you're going to write this story with the help of the ideas in the green box:

Last weekend you went shopping. You had your money with you when you left your house, but when you wanted to pay it wasn't there.

- to town (Why?)
- travel (How?)
- arrive (When?)
- meet (Who?)
- go (Where?)
- look at (What?)
- pick (What? Why?)
- pay (no money!)
- What happened?

But before you start writing, do exercises 1b) and 1c). They will help you to write the story.

b) Read this example story. It's very boring and too short!

Last Saturday in town

I went to town. I wanted to buy a hoody.
I went by bus.
I arrived in town at two o'clock.
I met a friend.
We went to a clothes shop. We looked at the clothes.
I wanted to buy a hoody.
My money wasn't there.
Luckily my friend could pay for me.

c) Read the tips in red. They give you some ideas how you could write a better story.

- When? *On Saturday morning, last weekend, ...*
- Make one longer sentence: *I went to town because ...*
- More details! *The bus was very full. / The weather was ...*
- Use a different noun: *I arrived at the bus station / in front of the railway station, ...*
- More details! *I met Tom / a friend from school / from the football club.*
- Use *that* and give more details: *... that was next to the railway station.*
- Make one longer sentence: *... and we loooked at ...*
- Give examples: *T-shirts, caps, ...*
- Make one longer sentence: *But when I wanted to ... my money wasn't there.*
- How did you feel? *I felt angry/terrible/frightened/...*

d) Now write the story and make it better. Use the tips, but try to find different examples for the phrases in red.

Tip: If you write on a computer, you can make changes more easily.

● **e) What happened then? Write the end of the story.**

How did you get home?
Did you find your money? How/Where?

2 In town

a) Finish the story. Write at least 60 more words.

I had just bought myself a new laptop computer. I came out of the computer shop and I was happily thinking about what computer games I could play. Suddenly I realized that there was nobody in the street – only four young men with hoodies on. They were slowly walking towards me ...

b) OK, you've written your story. Can you now make it better?

Tip:

Perhaps you could ...
- use more time phrases like *at first, then, after, a few moments, when I came out of the shop, ...*
- use more adjectives (*expensive, fantastic, ...*) or adverbs (*loudly, quickly, ...*)
- start your sentences with adverbs like *unfortunately, luckily, suddenly, ...*
- describe how you felt, for example *I felt frightened, cold, afraid, ... / I wanted to shout, run, phone, ...*
- make longer sentences with *because, when, although, ...*

c) Now work with a partner. Can you make your partner's sentences better? And can your partner help you? Think of the tips above.

3 Your own story

a) Read the start of the story on the right and the tip below.

Tip:
- Describe your feelings.
- Use direct speech.
- Use time phrases: *when, while, then, ...*
- Use lots of different verbs: *left, thought, changed, ...*

When I left my house last Saturday morning, I felt really happy. "I have all day with my boyfriend," I thought.
The first thing that went wrong was that my bus was half an hour late. While I was in the bus, the weather changed and it started to rain. Then the bus stopped suddenly and I fell and hurt myself. So I wasn't happy when I got out of the bus.

b) Now choose either task 1 or 2:

1 **Finish the story above with at least 80 more words.**
2 **Write at least 100 words on one of these titles:**
   A **A big surprise**
   B **A day when I was very angry**
   C **A silly mistake**
   D **A fantastic afternoon**

Tip:
- You can think of something which really happened, but make up or change some details in your story.
- Look at all the tips on this page.
- Check your story when you've finished it!

► W 20, 12 ► W

1 Clare's diary

How is Clare feeling today? Why?

Tuesday 16th December

Why am I feeling nervous today? Easy: My driving test is tomorrow – and I hope I won't do anything stupid!

I had my first lesson the day after my 16th birthday. How did it go? Actually it was OK. I always enjoy my driving lessons. I have a good teacher, and he doesn't get angry with me very often. And I should feel confident, because I'll have another lesson tomorrow before the test.

But – well, you see, my best friend didn't pass his test last March. How many lessons had he had? Well, I know he started after he had left school, but perhaps he hadn't practised enough before he took his test.

I'm not looking forward to tomorrow ...

I don't have a car yet, of course. And car insurance is horribly expensive for young people – one of my friends is paying £2300 a year, and that's just for a small car. Who has so much money?!

Will I pass tomorrow? I hope so!

2 OVER TO YOU!

a) Match each sentence with a time phrase.

always • last March • today • tomorrow • before

1 Clare ... enjoys her driving lessons.
2 Why is she feeling nervous ...?
3 Well, her best friend didn't pass his test ...
4 But perhaps he hadn't practised enough ... he took his test.
5 Will Clare pass her test ...?

b) Copy the table and find one example from the diary for each box in it.

Tip: Forgotten the past perfect? See page 20.

CHECKPOINT

Tenses

	Positive	Negative	Question
Simple present	*I always enjoy*	*she doesn't get ...*	*Who has ...?*
Present progressive	?	*I'm not looking ...*	?
Simple past	*I had ...*	?	?
Will-future	*I'll have ...*	?	*Will I pass ...?*
Past perfect	?	*he hadn't practised*	?

► W 21–24 ► W ⊙ Weitere Übungen: www.new-highlight.de ► Extra Practice, pp. 76 ff. ► Summary p. 119–122

TEST YOURSELF Unit 2

Do these tests and check your answers on page 192. They'll show you what you've learned in this unit. Look again at the new words on pages 130–133. Look at the *Summary* on pages 119–121.

TEST 1 Odd word out – and why?

Example: bread, oranges, sausages, paper – *Paper, because it isn't food / you can't eat it.*

1 suits, hoodies, limos, dresses
2 awful, terrible, horrible, responsible
3 beautiful, pink, grey, yellow
4 brilliant, amazing, great, broken
5 car, train, limo, taxi
6 cupboard, rucksack, tent, sleeping bag

6 POINTS

TEST 2 Pick the right verb.

1 I ... voluntary work in a hospital.
a) work **b)** take **c)** do
2 I ... part in music competitions.
a) make **b)** take **c)** have
3 I don't ... any crimes.
a) complain **b)** make **c)** commit
4 I don't ... drugs.
a) take **b)** wear **c)** hire
5 And next week I want to ... my driving test.
a) make **b)** pass **c)** mind
6 Why don't the media ... young people like me?
a) realize **b)** carry **c)** support

6 POINTS

TEST 3 Finish the dialogue. You'll only need six words.

already • change • pity • joking • kind • sorry • unfortunately • waste

NATALIE Oh, hi Tim. Can you come to my party?
TIM Oh, I'm really (1), Natalie. I'd like to come, but (2) I'm going to a football match on Saturday.
NATALIE Oh, that's a (3)! Can't you (4) your mind?
TIM I'm sorry. It's really (5) of you to ask, but I've (6) bought my ticket for the match.

6 POINTS

TEST 4 Pick the right word.

1 My friend Amy hangs around / under in a gang.
2 Her gang often meets outside / above shops.
3 She smokes at / on least three cigarettes a day.
4 She often goes out at / in the evening.
5 She's often in trouble along / with her teachers.
6 But I think they're biased about / against her.

6 POINTS

● TEST 5 Put the verbs in the right form.

1 Usually I **(not enjoy)** parties.
2 But I **(go)** to our school prom last week.
3 I never **(hire)** clothes for a party before!
4 At the prom I **(meet)** a girl called Charlotte.
5 Charlotte and I **(meet)** again tomorrow.
6 I **(look)** forward to it!

6 POINTS

● TEST 6 Tell the story. (90 words)

6 POINTS

► W 25–30, Exam Training ► W 31–32, Portfolio

Unit 3
Colours of India

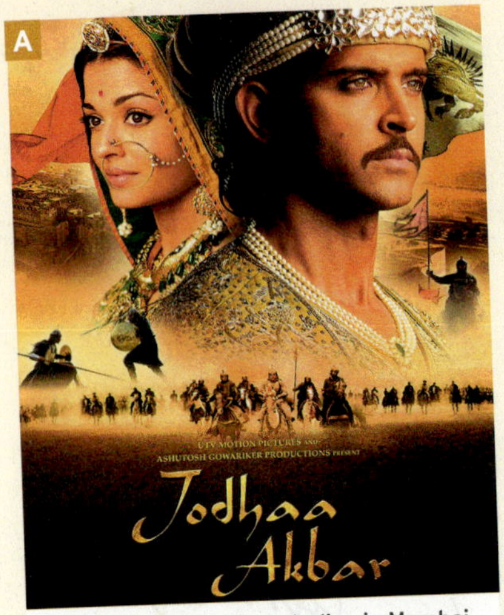

FILMS India's film studios in Mumbai (often called Bollywood) produce more films than Hollywood.

CITIES Mumbai and India's capital New Delhi are two of the world's largest cities.

MODERN INDUSTRY India's industries (call centres, cars, computers) are growing fast.

Money India uses rupees. On all notes you can see Mahatma Gandhi, who led India to independence from Britain in 1947.

1 Pictures of India

a) Work with a partner and talk about the pictures and information.

I'd really like to go to India and see ... – Me too. And I'd also like ...
Did you know that ... – No, I didn't. And I didn't know that ...
I'm not really interested in ... – No, but I'd like to know more about ...

b) Then compare some of your ideas in class.

SIGHTSEEING Lots of tourists come to see India's monuments, beaches and wild animals – 40% of all the tigers in the world live in India.

PEOPLE About 1.2 billion people live in India. Mumbai has more millionaires than Manhattan, but India has millions of very poor people too.

LANGUAGE India's official language is Hindi, but many states have their own language. And more people speak English in India than in Britain.

RELIGION Most Indians are Hindus, but India also has the second largest Muslim population in the world.

2 A factfile about India

a) Make a factfile with at least two of the topics A–H. The factfile on the right is only an example. Your factfile can be longer – and different!

b) A podcast of a radio interview
2⊙1 **You'll hear topics A–H. What's the right order?**
1 B, 2 …, 3 …

2⊙1 **c) Listen again. Make notes for your factfile on the topics that you picked in 2 a).**
● **Make notes on other topics too.**

● **d) Find more topics for your factfile. You can choose topics from these pages or think about your own interests (history, music, industries, Pakistan, …).**

Tip:
Use information from these pages and visit **www.new-highlight.de**
Webcode: **NHL-6-37**

Factfile: India

Cities	*India's capital city is …* *The largest city is …* *Other large cities are…* *The city of … is famous for …*
Money	*India uses rupees. 1 euro = … rupees* *On all notes there is a picture of …*

Factfile: Pakistan

History	*Before 1947 Pakistan was part of India. Today …*

► W 35, 1–3 ► WB 5, p.117

INDIA TODAY

1 Read texts A–F on page 39. Match each text with a phrase in the box.

wild animals • a special car • a holiday • a film star • two new jobs • a woman who wants to get married • Indian workers in Europe • children in awful conditions

2 *True* (*T*), *false* (*F*) or *not in the text* (*NIT*)?

A You don't have to bring your own tent for the hike.
B Katrina Kaif isn't very popular in Bollywood because she has a British accent.
C The *Tata Nano* is a car for only two people.
D Marriage adverts on the Internet are more successful than adverts in newspapers.
E Children under 14 are allowed to work in factories in India.
F The first job advert is for people who are good at using the phone.

3 The teenagers below are going to do a project about India. Decide which topic (A–F) on page 39 each person will be interested in.

Anna has just passed her driving test and is interested in cheap cars and cheap car insurance.

Brian's girlfriend was born in Britain, but her parents are Indian and have an Indian family life. So of course Brian wants to know what they think of topics like love and weddings!

Charlotte wants to earn some money when she leaves school and then go on an activity holiday. She doesn't like water sports very much, but loves mountains.

David's favourite film is *Slumdog Millionaire*, a British film about India. Now he wants to find out more about Indian cinema celebrities and the Indian film scene.

Emily thinks that it's terrible that young children work in factories in some countries. She prefers to buy clothes that are made by companies that pay their workers well.

4 MEDIATING

PARTNER A: Your partner likes hiking. Explain the main points in text A.
PARTNER B: Your partner is interested in small cars. Explain the main points in text C.

5 Your factfile

With information from page 39, write about one or two more topics in your factfile.

▸ Extra Reading, pp. 104–105

A

Hike in the Himalayas

- 9 day trip
- Climb to 4300 metres.
- Spend the night in the homes of Indian people.
- Guides speak English and have many years of experience.
- We provide all equipment.

Contact hikehimalays.com

B

Bollywood's new queen?

Katrina Kaif has a British mother and an Indian father. She came to *Bollywood* from Britain in 2003 and first she had to lose her British accent. Now she is one of the most downloaded film stars in India.

C

Your first car?

It has four seats, travels at 65 miles per hour (100 km/h) and costs less than the DVD player in some expensive cars: that's the Tata Nano. Made in India, it costs only 140 000 rupees (just over 2000 euros) and is one of cheapest cars in the world.

D

Marriage in India

Most Indian parents arrange marriages for their children. Partners are found in newspaper adverts or on the Internet.

Name: Hasina Bai
Height: 160 cm
First language: Hindi
Religion: Hindu
Vegetarian: yes
Work: computer worker
Age: 23 years
Living in: Bangalore
Education: school, college
Interests: dancing, computers.

E

Police save 17 children

The police closed a dangerous clothes factory in Mumbai yesterday. 17 children under the age of 14 were working in the sweatshop, some only eight years old.

The children were earning no more than their food. The United Nations thinks that 55 million children under 14 work in Indian factories, although it's illegal in India.

F

- Are you friendly and helpful?
- Can you speak English?

Then we have a job for you in one of our call centres. Our customers are large companies in Britain and Australia.
For more details, send your CV to gvi@allindiacallcentres.in

Large software company in Bangalore needs computer programmers

Job description: develop new computer programs for medical company. For application form phone +91.80.37530918-74

▸ W 36–37, 4–5

A DAY TRIP

1 **You're in New Delhi and you're going to go on a day trip. Look at pages 40 and 41. Where are you going to go?**

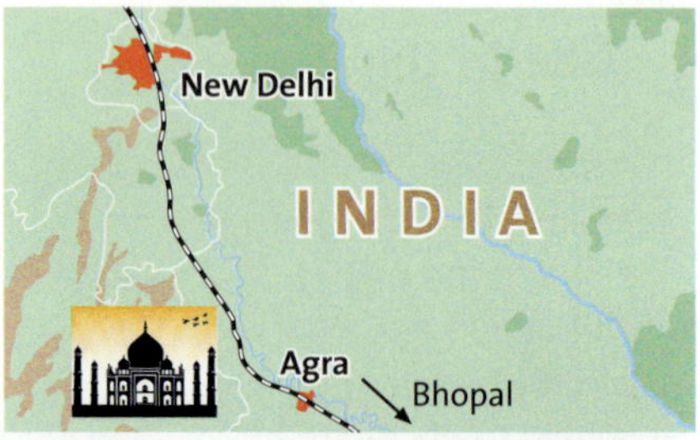

2 **On the metro to New Delhi station**

2 2 **a) Listen to the announcement. Are the sentences below true or false?**

1 You're travelling on Line 4.
2 There's a warning about people who steal things.
3 Get out of the train at the next station for New Delhi railway station.
4 Passengers will leave the train on the left.

b) Listen again. What do you hear? Pick the right words.

"For the kind attention of the (**1**): Please look after your (**2**) at all times."
"If all seats are taken, please give your (**3**) to older people and (**4**) with children."
"Please be (**5**) and stand clear of the (**6**)."

	A	B	C	D
1	customers	passengers	people	children
2	animals	children	things	bags
3	place	chair	seat	hand
4	parents	people	fathers	mothers
5	polite	relaxed	kind	careful
6	windows	doors	train	platform

3 **At New Delhi railway station**

2 3 **Copy the notes below. Then listen to the announcement and complete the notes.**

Bhopal Shatabdi Express

1) *Train number ...*
2) *Leaves from platform number ...*
3) *Leaves New Delhi at ...*
4) *Arrives at Agra Cantonment station at ...*
5) *... is included in the price of the ticket.*

► WB 6, p.117

4 At Agra Cantonment railway station

2 4 **a) Listen to the assistant at the tourist office. Match a *tonga* and *tuk-tuk* with the right picture.**

Tip:
Listen to phrases like *it's a sort of ...* or *it looks like a ...*

A

B

C

D

2 4 **b) Listen again.**
What does the assistant say?

1 "*Tongas* are
a) cheap b) quite expensive."
2 "A *tuk-tuk* is a sort of
a) bus b) taxi."
3 "A *tuk-tuk* isn't a
a) car b) tram."
4 "It looks like
a) a bus b) a motorbike."
5 "A *tuk-tuk* has
a) a roof b) an electric motor."
6 "The passengers sit
a) inside b) behind the driver."
7 "A *cycle rickshaw* has
a) three b) four wheels."
8 "It's a) more fun
b) slower than a *tuk-tuk*."

c) Work with a partner. Describe one of the photos (but don't say the name!).
It's quite ... and it looks like a ... / It has ... and passengers ...

Can your partner guess which photo you mean?

5 At the Taj Mahal

2 5 **a) Listen to the guide. What does she explain? Choose 1, 2, 3 or 4.**

1 how big the Taj Mahal is
2 how beautiful it is in the evening
3 who built it and why
4 how much it cost

● **b) Listen again and explain the numbers in German.**

1) 1592 2) 15 3) 14 4) 22 5) 3 to 4 million
1592 war das Jahr, in dem ...

6 AND YOU?

Would you like to visit the Taj Mahal?
Why / Why not? What other places would you like to see in India?
I'd like / I wouldn't like to see ... because ...

▸ W 38, 6–8 ▸ W

IS IT OK IF ...?

2⊙6 **1 Anna from Germany is staying in Mumbai with her friend Lalita.**
Read or listen to the dialogue. What does Lalita want to do? And Anna?

LALITA I know – let's go to a *dhaba* this evening.
ANNA A *dhaba*? What's that?
LALITA It's a cheap restaurant where you get good Indian food.
ANNA Oh, I'd like that. But I have to top up my mobile. I'm out of credit. Is it OK if we stop at a cash machine on the way?
LALITA A *cash machine*? What's that?
ANNA A machine where you can get money from your bank account, or ...
LALITA Oh, an ATM. Yes, no problem.
ANNA And it's so hot! Do you mind if I have a shower first?
LALITA Go ahead. While you have your shower, I'll make you a *lassi*.
ANNA A *lassi*? What's that?
LALITA Oh, sorry. It's a drink that you make from yogurt, and you can put in fruit, like mangoes, for example. It's very good when you're thirsty. What do you drink in Germany when it's hot?
ANNA Well, we drink water of course, or *Apfelschorle*.
LALITA *Ap... Appel...* Sorry, can you repeat that?
ANNA *Apfelschorle*. It's apple juice with fizzy water. It's good.

2 Asking politely

a) Read the dialogue. Then answer the questions.

1 What does Anna say when she **A** wants to go to a cash machine?
B wants to have a shower?
2 What does Lalita say when she wants Anna to say a word again?

b) Partner work. You're a guest – speak as politely as you can. Your partner reacts.

1 You see some fruit in the kitchen and want to eat a mango.
– *I'm hungry. Do you ... / Is it ... if ...*
– *Go ahead. / Yes, no problem.*
2 You need more credit for your mobile.
3 You're tired and want to sleep.
4 Your Indian friend said that the bus leaves at 9.45. You didn't understand.
5 You want to use the phone and phone home.
6 You're thirsty and need water.

MORE HELP! p. 112 **c) Work with a partner. Ask for at least six more things as politely as you can (for example TV / vegetarian food / cup of tea / change money). Your partner reacts. Then change roles.**

► W 39, 9

3 Explaining words

a) Look again at the dialogue. Explain ...

1 a dhaba **2** a cash machine **3** lassi **4** Apfelschorle

b) ROLE PLAY

PARTNER A: You can't think of the right English word or phrase. Explain it to your partner and he/she will give you the answer.

PARTNER B: Look at your card on page 66.

Tip: With the phrases on this page you can explain what you mean – even if you can't think of the right word!

1  It's a phone that you carry with you.

2  It means that you want to drink.

3  It's a fruit that is red, green or yellow outside and orange inside.

4  It's water with gas in it.

5 

It's the opposite of expensive.

6  It's where you stand under water in the bathroom.

MORE HELP! p. 112

c) Your partner has never heard of these things. Explain them to him/her in English. Use words and phrases from the dialogue and from exercise 3b).

A

B

C

D

E

F
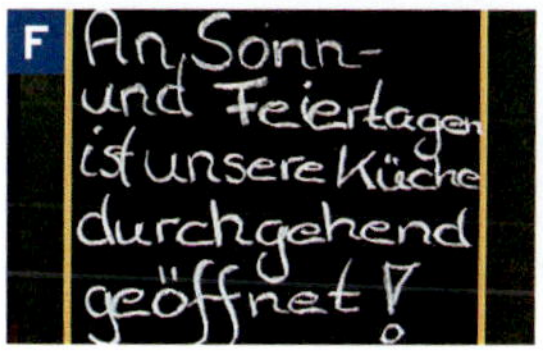

G

H

4 INTERPRETING

2⊙7

Saruga from Mumbai is staying with you. Interpret for your sister and Saruga.

SISTER Ich habe eine Idee. Wir könnten heute Abend in einem Restaurant essen.
YOU ...
SARUGA Good idea. But is it OK if I top up my mobile first?
YOU ...
SISTER Überhaupt kein Problem. Wir können unterwegs an einem Telefonladen halten.
YOU ...
SARUGA OK. And where are we going to eat? Can we eat something typically German?
YOU ...
SISTER OK, gehen wir in das Restaurant bei uns um die Ecke. Da kann man billig essen.
YOU ...
SARUGA Perhaps it's a bit like our *dhabas*.
YOU *(Du hast Saruga nicht verstanden. Bitte sie, zu wiederholen).*

▸ W 39–40, 10–13 ▸ W ⊙

PREPARING FOR THE WRITING EXAM

1 Writing full answers

a) Read the exam question and the tips.

A European survey wants to find out about how much young people travel.

- Answer the following questions in full sentences.
- Write at least 100 words.

1 How often do you travel by car? Where do you go? Who with?

A good answer could be:
I travel to school by car with my mum every day. For more points write more information, for example: *The traffic is always bad.*

2 Where did you spend your last summer holiday? If you went away: Did you fly? Why/Why not? If you stayed at home: What did you do? Did you go on day trips? How did you travel? Why?

Remember:
Use the simple past! Useful phrases: *We flew, we travelled by car, we took the train ...*

3 If you had lots of money, which country would you like to visit? Why?

If-clauses II:
*If **I had** lots of money, **I would** fly to ... and spend ...*

4 What do you think about the buses and trains in your town/area? What could be better?

Give your opinion:
In my opinion, the buses should ...
I think there should be more ...

5 How do you prefer to travel on long journeys? Why?

Describe your feelings:
I really like going by ...
Flying is great because ...

b) Now write your own answers to questions 1–5. Look at the tips and write full answers.

c) When you've finished, check your answers.

Checklist

- I've used time phrases: *last weekend / a year ago / in August / ...* ☐
- I've given reasons: *because I'd like to ... / wanted to ..., / because the buses are ...* ☐
- I've given more detail: *Usually I get up so late that I can't go by bike.* ☐
- I've described my feelings: *I'm often angry when ..., / I love ..., but sometimes ...* ☐
- I've given my opinion: *In my opinion ..., / I know some people say ..., but I think that ...* ☐
- I've written more information to get more points: *During the holiday I went ...* ☐

▸ W 41, 14

2 Writing a story (I)

a) First look at the exam question. Then read the tip and look at the plan.

Write a story. Your story has the title below.
Write about 100 words.

Disappointed!

Getting enough ideas for 100 words:
- It's easier to write if you first make a plan.
- Don't write sentences in your plan – use words or short phrases only.

What happened?	Details	My feelings
prepare for my barbecue	• invited ... • bought .... • phoned/texted...	• very excited • quite nervous • a bit afraid • relaxed
day of the barbecue	• everybody arrived – talked • then: rain!!!! • ran inside – and then...	• really happy • disappointed • angry • devastated • relieved

b) Now write the story from the plan above. Write at least 100 words.

3 Writing a story (II)

a) Think of the story with the title *Disappointed* that *you* want to write.

b) Make a plan for your story – like the plan above, but with different words in it.

c) Write your story in at least 120 words.

d) When you've finished, check your text. Use the checklists on pages 44 and 45.

Thinking of what story to write about:
- It's easier if you think of a time when *you* were really disappointed (a true story).
- You don't know the English for an important word in the story? Then change the details! Example: Your best friend didn't want to come with you to a concert in the *Stadthalle*. You don't know the English word for *Stadthalle*? Write that the concert was at school!

Checklist

- I've checked that my story is clear: I've read it to my partner, and he/she can understand it. ☐
- I've made some sentences more interesting: I've taken two short sentences and made one longer, more interesting sentence with *because, when, although, after, ...* ☐
- I've used adjectives *(amazing, awful, lazy)* and adverbs *(suddenly, unfortunately, luckily)*. ☐
- I've checked the spelling. If I wasn't sure, I found the right spelling in the dictionary. ☐
- Partner check: I've checked my partner's story, and my partner has checked my story. ☐

▸ W 41–42, 15–17

A BAD DREAM by Meenal Dave

1 Look at the title and pictures and photo.
Pick the right answers. You can pick more than one answer.

1 I think the story is about
a) a man who sells tea **b)** travelling by train **c)** a woman **d)** a marriage.
2 I think the story will be **a)** funny **b)** frightening **c)** strange **d)** provocative.
3 I think the story's ending will be **a)** happy **b)** sad **c)** awful **d)** a surprise.

Tip:
You can enjoy the story even if you don't understand every word in it.

I can't believe it! Why does my boss, Mrs Rao, give me more work at the last minute, just when it's time to leave the office? If I miss my train, I'll have to wait at the station for at least an hour, and then I'll be in the train for two hours – and probably in an empty compartment ...

Hurry up, please! Good God, does this traffic light have to be red now? All these people who are coming out of the station – please don't stand in the way of people who are running for a train! And why are the stairs at the wrong end of this long platform? My train is on Platform 4 and it's going to leave in a moment ... I must run ... just the last two steps and ... there! Damn. Missed it.

The man who sells tea says, "Now you'll have to wait for an hour." Why is he looking at me like that? And now there are almost no passengers on the platform ... It's a bit frightening. Even when the man who sells tea looks at me, I'm afraid. Maybe I should call home? I should also buy some water. And a magazine. My husband Vikram answers the phone. He's annoyed because I missed the first train. I buy two magazines and sit down.

Now the platform is completely empty. The boy who cleans shoes is sleeping peacefully. But the dog near me can't sleep. He stands, looks around: Is he listening for something? Two dogs are fighting on the platform opposite. Is he frightened of them? I notice that a woman is sitting next to me now. She's wearing a thick black burka, I can only see her hands. And she's carrying a large bag.

So many seats are free on the platform, why did she have to come and sit next to me? What is she thinking? Is she carrying a bomb in her bag? What if she leaves the bag here and walks away and the bomb explodes, what will happen to me? No, I mustn't think that will happen. Poor thing, she's just sitting quietly there. But does that mean she isn't dangerous? Should I go to another seat? Thank God the man who sells food arrives! "You're late," he says. "The first train has left. Why are you sitting here? You shouldn't be here when it's so late."

He's right. I should get up from here. You never know what she could do, this woman. She could have a knife in her bag and kill me and nobody would know. Look at her hands, how big and strong they are. Is there a criminal behind that burka? How do I get up? Why did I decide to travel at this time? If she tries something, I will tell her, listen woman, take what you want but don't kill me. I can't move my hands. The moment I see somebody, I'll get up. I look around the platform, without moving my head. There's nobody on the platform now. Where have all the people gone?

The train is late. I didn't even notice it when it arrived. OK, now I must go quickly to it and sit in the ladies' compartment. Oh no, the woman in the burka is coming in after me. Why must she follow me? The compartment is almost empty – we are only three women. A woman who sells fish is sleeping with her empty basket next to her. It's stinking, but I don't mind, at least there's another person here. And that woman in the burka is sitting opposite me.

It is dark outside just like the burka that she's wearing ... What should I do? I close my eyes, I hope the woman will go away. What is she doing now? People say that people like her are dangerous. You never know if they have a knife.

Oh God, somebody is shaking me. I open my eyes – it's the woman in the burka! Oh no, what will she do to me? Should I shout for help? The other woman is sleeping. So she won't know if I am killed. Should I jump off the train? Oh God, please, please help me! If you help me, I'll never travel on this train again. I'll even give up my job ... Better to be poor and hungry than to die like this!

"Sister," the burka woman is calling me, "I'm getting out here. But I want to thank you for being with me, imagine travelling alone when it's so late. I was so frightened ... you know ... so difficult ..." I can't believe it! She's frightened like me! I can't help laughing!

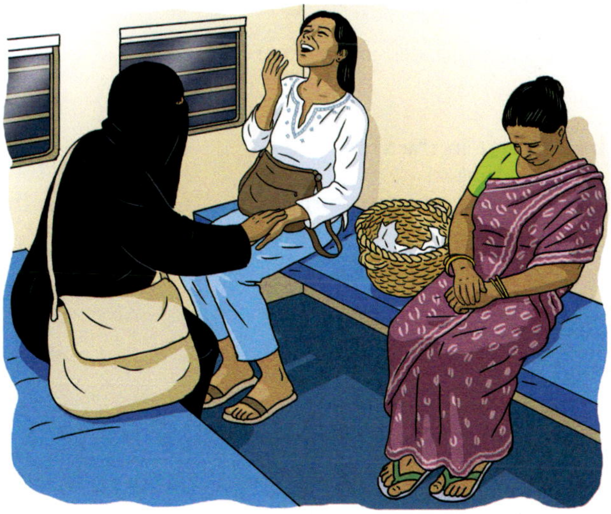

She holds my hand and says "God be with you". The train stops. I help her with her bag – it doesn't look dangerous now. Then she disappears in the railway station. The woman next to me wakes up. The stars shine again and show me the way home.

Adapted from: *Nightmare* by Meenal Dave

2 Understanding what happens in the story

a) Which paragraphs best match the titles below? (It can be more than one!)

A The woman who tells the story gets on the train.
B A woman in a burka sits next to her.
C The woman who tells the story misses her train.
D The woman who tells the story feels relieved.
E She's frightened of the woman in the burka.
F The woman who tells the story leaves the office.
G The woman in the burka touches her.
H The woman who tells the story closes her eyes.
I She buys two magazines and finds a seat.

b) Pick three adjectives and put them in the right order to describe how the woman felt in the story.

annoyed
sad
afraid
disappointed
relieved

TRAINING Understanding feelings in a text

3 Reading between the lines

Read the story again. Then work with a partner.

a) The woman's feelings

1 Find four times in the story when the woman who tells the story felt angry.
She felt angry when her boss gave her ...

2 Find six times in the story when she felt frightened.
She felt frightened when there were no passengers on ...

b) Language in the story

Why do you think the woman asks lots of questions?
... because she wants information?
... because she's frightened?

c) A symbol in the story

1 How does the woman describe the night:
A in paragraph 8?
B in paragraph 11?

2 Why do you think she sees more light in paragraph 11?

d) Why the writer wrote the story. Choose one answer.

The most important message in the story is that ...
1 you shouldn't travel at night,
2 you shouldn't leave work late,
3 you should be careful with stereotypes,
4 travelling by train is exciting.

4 AND YOU? Write either a) or b).

MORE HELP! p. 113

a) Imagine you are the person who told the story or the woman in the burka. Write an e-mail to a friend and tell him/her what happened to you at the station and on the train. Write about 100 words.

● **b) Write your own story with the title *A bad dream*. Write about 120 words.**

Tip:
Look again at the tips and checklist on page 45.

► W

Kirti Mandir, Porbandar

Welcome to Kirti Mandir!

Here in the centre of the city of Porbandar you'll find a museum and library next to the house where Mahatma Gandhi was born in 1869.

Gandhi's house has three floors. You can visit the rooms where Gandhi, his parents and his grandmother lived.

Visitor Information

- Daily flights from Mumbai.
- Trains leave Mumbai early in the morning and arrive in Porbandar early the next day.
- Luxury coaches from Surat and Ahmedabad.
- Kirti Mandir is open every day from 10 a.m. to 5 p.m. The entrance fee is only 5 rupees.

Mahatma Gandhi

Gandhi first used his ideas on non-violent protests when he worked in South Africa and helped the large Indian population there against unfair laws. He used the same ideas when he led India's non-violent campaign for independence from the British. He spent time in prison, but saw independence in 1947. His last successful protest was when he said that he wouldn't eat till violence between Hindus and Muslims stopped. Gandhi was killed in 1948.
Gandhi wore the clothes and ate the food of poor Indian people. The world calls him "Mahatma" (Great Soul) and Indians call him Bapu (father).

1 *True (T), false (F)* or *not in the text (NIT)?*

1 Kirti Mandir is where Gandhi died.
2 It's a bit outside the city of Porbandar.
3 Porbandar is 48 hours from Mumbai by train.
4 Visitors have to pay to visit the Kirti Mandir.
5 Gandhi never lived outside India.
6 He organized protests for Indian independence.
7 He died before Indian independence came.
8 He was killed by a Hindu extremist.

● **Correct the false sentences.**

● 2 Mahatma Gandhi

Find out about one of the topics below. Make notes, then tell your class.

- The Salt March 1930
- Non-violent protests against the British
- Peace between Muslims and Hindus
- How and why Gandhi was killed

3 Choose a writing activity

a) Write information about Gandhi in your factfile (see page 37).

● **b) Write your own brochure about a different place in India. (Mumbai, the Taj Mahal, a national park, ...)**

Tip:
Use ideas from the Kirti Mandir brochure.

LOOK AT LANGUAGE

1 Mistakes in a magazine

a) Read what Amisha said.

"My name is Amisha Patel. I want to be a computer programmer. I'm living in Delhi for three years – I go to college here. After college I'll get a job in Britain."

"I have an uncle who is a doctor in London, and a cousin who teaches in Brighton, and they like it there. And, well, the real reason ... you see, my boyfriend lives in Britain. He works for an Indian company that makes turbines for wind farms. The company has factories in Germany and Belgium and is building a big wind farm in Britain. Then I hope we'll get married, live in Europe for a few years, and then – who knows?"

b) Now read the magazine article about Amisha. There are six mistakes. Can you find them?

She said that she wanted to be a ~~nurse~~ computer programmer.

→ *Our guest this week ... Amisha Patel*

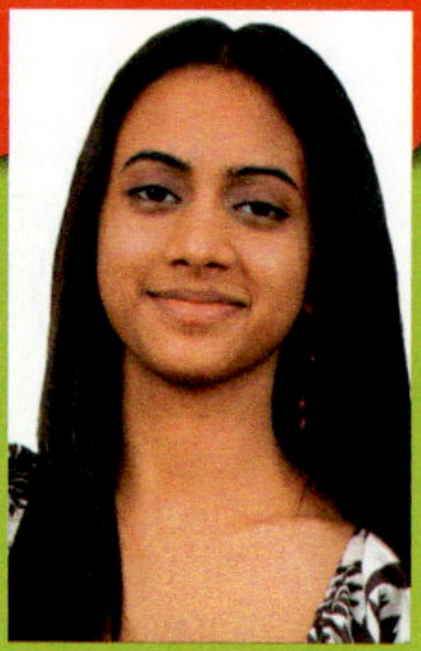

We met Amisha in Hari's Cafe and she told us about herself. She said that she wanted to be a nurse. She said that she was living in Delhi for five years. And after that? Amisha said that after college she would get a job in Britain.

"Why Britain?" we asked. Amisha said that she had an uncle who was a vet in London, and a cousin who taught in Birmingham. Then she smiled and told us the real reason. She said that her boyfriend lived in Britain and worked for a British company.

And what about the future? Amisha hoped that they would get married and come back to India.

2 OVER TO YOU!

a) Read the tip and the checkpoint.

Tip:
He/She said: " ... "
(mit Anführungszeichen)
→ direkte Rede
He/She said that ...
(ohne Anführungszeichen)
→ indirekte Rede

CHECKPOINT

Indirekte Rede *(Indirect Speech)*

Direct speech		*Indirect speech*
Simple present *"I want to be a nurse."*	→	Simple past *She said that she ... to be a nurse.*
Present progressive *"I'm living in Delhi."*	→	Past progressive *She said that she ... living in Delhi.*
Future *"I'll get a job."*	→	*would/'d* + verb *She said that she ... get a job.*

b) Copy and complete the checkpoint.
You can find all the sentences in the magazine article above.

▸ W 43–46 ▸ W ⊙ Weitere Übungen: www.new-highlight.de ▸ Extra Practice, pp. 84 ff. ▸ Summary p. 124

Do the tests and check your answers on page 192. They'll show you what you've learned in this unit. Look at the new words on pages 133–136. Look at the *Summary* on pages 119, 120 and 124.

TEST 1 Pick the right words for India's ...

1 film industry
2 capital city
3 largest city
4 official language
5 most famous building
6 population

→ Gandhi • Muslim • 200 million • New Delhi • Metro • 600 million • Taj Mahal • Bollywood • Mumbai • 1.2 billion • Hindi • rupees

6 POINTS

TEST 2 Pick the right definition.

1 a podcast
2 a wheel
3 A CV
4 a passenger
5 a knife
6 a guest

a) A paper that describes what you have done in your life.
b) You use it when you want to cut something.
c) A visitor who stays in a family.
d) A radio programme that you can download from the Internet.
e) Bikes have two of them, and cars have four.
f) Somebody who travels by train, bus, plane, ...

6 POINTS

TEST 3 Pick the right word.

1 I came to India out of / from Britain.
2 I'm interested in / for cars and bikes.
3 But I didn't know much around / about the Tata Nano.
4 It's one of the cheapest cars in / of the world.
5 You see them all over / above India.
6 They're cheaper than / then some expensive bikes in Germany.

6 POINTS

TEST 4 Jobs

Write the missing words.

→ call • cash • motor • wind • railway • passenger • programmer • industries

1 My daughter is a computer ...
2 She works in one of India's modern ...
3 Her company makes parts for large ... farms.
4 My husband works at Delhi ... station.
5 My best friend fixes ... machines or ATMs.
6 And I work in a ... centre.

6 POINTS

● TEST 5 My parents' visit to India

Put the verbs in the right form.

1 My parents (**not / like**) hot weather.
2 But they (**fly**) to India last year.
3 Mum (**not / be**) there before.
4 My dad (**find**) the weather very hot.
5 He said it (**be**) much too hot for him.
6 He said he (**stay**) in Britain next year!

6 POINTS

● TEST 6 Being polite

Dan is a guest in an Indian family. What does he ask? Write six polite questions.

6 POINTS

Unit **4**

What next?

1 A goodbye party

a) These students are soon going to leave school. What do you think they're talking about? Work with a partner and pick three topics. Now listen and check. Were you right?

planning a holiday • an interview • plans for the future • exams • applying for an apprenticeship • going to college • looking for a flat

2 13

b) What words did you hear in the dialogues?

1

Sarah Well, I've applied for an apprenticeship as a **a)** plumber **b)** computer programmer.
Livvy Sounds good. I'll keep my **a)** fingers **b)** legs crossed for you.

2

Emma I'd really like to do **a)** a course **b)** work experience in childcare.
Ben I'm hoping to do a **a)** full-time **b)** part-time course in web page design.

3

Amy I can't really decide, so first I want to get a job – probably **a)** here in Germany **b)** abroad.
Zack Well, it sounds great. I hope it **a)** works out **b)** is fun for you, Amy.

2 13

c) Compare your answers with a partner. Then listen again and check.

2 AND YOU?

a) **Complete the dialogue with a partner.**

b) **Write your own dialogue with a partner – how long can you make it?**

→ have an interview • earn some money • work abroad • do a course in … • do an apprenticeship as a … • get a job in an office/in a department store/at a hairdresser

A What are you planning to do when you leave school?
B Me? I'm not sure. / I'd like to… / I've applied for …
A I hope it works out for you.
B What about you?
A Well, I can't really decide / I'm hoping to … / Or perhaps I'll …
B Sounds good. I'll keep my fingers crossed for you.

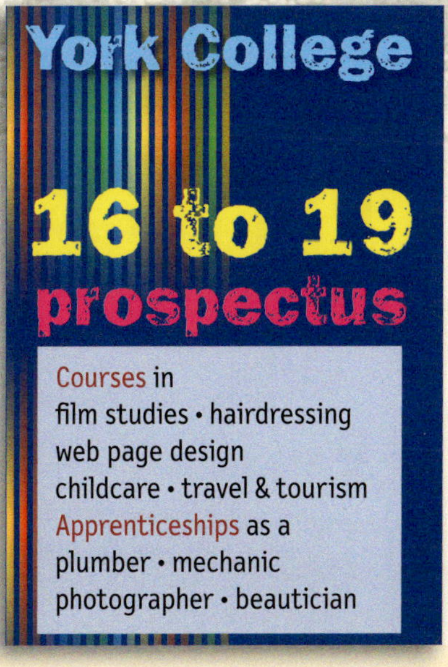

▸W 47, 1–3 ▸WB 7, p. 118

BETTER LUCK NEXT TIME

1 All's well that ends well

2 14 **What's the a) good news? b) bad news?**

SARAH Oh, hi Dan. Did you get that job in the call centre?
DAN No, I didn't. I thought I did well in my interview, but I still didn't get it.
SARAH Oh, I'm so sorry, Dan. I know you really wanted that job.
DAN Yes, I'm so fed up. You see, I want to have a holiday abroad with Ella next year. If I had got the job, I could have earned the money for my trip. Without it ... I don't know.
SARAH Poor you! I really hope that something comes up for you soon, Dan. Better luck next time!

Two weeks later ...

DAN Hey, Sarah, guess what! I applied for a job last week in a DIY store, and I got it!
SARAH Really? Oh, that's fantastic news, Dan. All's well that ends well, eh? Well done! I'm so happy for you. When do you start?
DAN Next Monday. I'm looking forward to it. The people who work there seem very nice. I met some of them when I had my interview. I'm so excited about it!
SARAH Ella must be happy! Perhaps you can have your holiday after all.
DAN Well, no. That's the other thing that I wanted to tell you ... Ella and I have broken up.
SARAH What? Are you serious? I ... I don't know what to say. I ...
DAN It's OK, Sarah. I know you never really liked Ella. I'll get over it.

2 Reacting to good and bad news

Read the four dialogues with a partner and fill in the gaps. You'll find all the missing words in the dialogues above.

1
A Did you ... a place on your course, Amy?
B No, I didn't. I ... well in my interview, but I still ... get it.
A Oh, I'm sorry, Amy. Better ... next time!

2
A Oh hi, Dave. How was your interview?
B I didn't get the job. I'm so ... up about it.
A Oh, I'm so ... Dave. I really hope something ... up for you soon.

3
A Oh, Alex. There's something I have to tell you: Steve and I have broken ...
B What? Are you ...? I'm really sorry.
A Thanks, Alex. But it's OK. I'll get ... it

4
A Hey, guess ...! I got that job at the Grand Hotel!
B Really? Oh, that's fantastic ..., Dan. Well done!
A I'm so excited ... it! The job looks great – I'm ... forward to it.

► W 48, 4–5 ► W

3 New contexts

a) Work with a partner. Read and complete the mini-dialogues.

1
A Great news: I passed my driving test yesterday!
B Really? Oh that's ...
Well ...!
I'm so ...

2
A What's wrong?
B My dad had an accident.
He's in hospital.
A Oh, I'm .... And I ...
he'll be OK soon.

3
A Hey, guess what!
I won a competition!
It's a holiday in Australia!
B What? ... serious?
I don't ...

MORE HELP! p. 114

b) Write your own mini-dialogues. Change the sentences in red – and you can also make the dialogues longer. Then practise them with your partner.

1

2

3
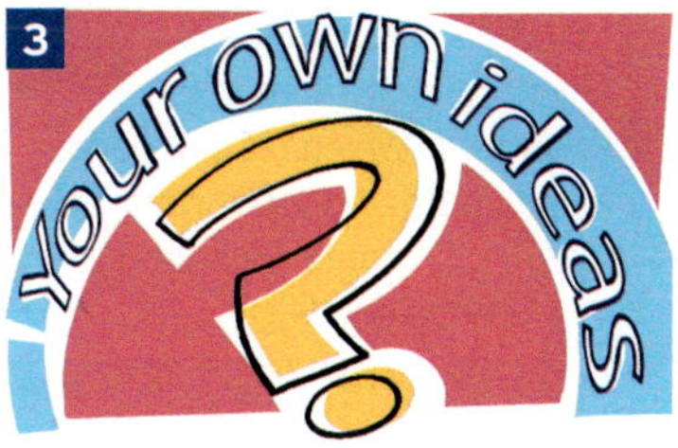

4 MEDIATING

a) You've told an English friend that you're interested in going to this college. Look at the website and tell your friend the most important information.

Berufskolleg Technik

- Mehr als 1700 Schüler/innen und werden in über 100 Klassen unterrichtet.
- Die Schule hat 40 Klassenräume und 12 Computerräume.
- Am 3. Feb. laden wir um 18.00 Uhr alle Schüler/innen und Eltern zu einem Informationsabend ein.

Useful phrases

There are more than ...
The college has ...
Twelve rooms ...
There's an information evening on ...

b) Now look at this website and tell your friends about *Girls' Day*.

Als „typisch Junge" gelten auch heute noch Berufe wie Elektriker oder Mechaniker. Sie haben einen Männeranteil von über 80 Prozent. Viele junge Frauen haben Angst, dass sie von ihren männlichen Arbeitskollegen nicht respektiert werden oder einen technischen Beruf nicht ausüben können.

Der Girls' Day, der einmal im Jahr für junge Schülerinnen veranstaltet wird, soll Mädchen einen Einblick gerade auch in untypische Berufe ermöglichen und so ihr Interesse wecken.

Useful phrases

Jobs like electricians and mechanics are still often ...
Women often don't choose these jobs because ...
On *Girls' Day* young women can ...

► W 49, 6–7 ► W ⊙

LIVING AWAY FROM HOME

1 Finding a room

You have a holiday job in Britain and you have to rent a room.

a) Look at the two online adverts.

A

First floor room, with bed, wardrobe and radiator.
Kitchen, bathroom and living/dining room are shared between three people.
Small garden good for barbecues.
£250 per month including electricity, gas, water, TV licence and Wi-Fi.

B

A one-bedroom apartment with entrance hall, living/dining room, kitchen with fridge/freezer, electric cooker, washing machine, very big bedroom, bathroom with shower and toilet. Deposit required.

b) Which advert is it: A or B?

1 The advert is for a flat.
2 You know that it's upstairs.
3 You can eat outside in summer.
4 There is equipment for washing clothes.
5 You have your own kitchen and bathroom.
6 You have to pay money which is paid back when you leave.
7 The price of electricity and water isn't extra.
8 The bedroom has a cupboard for your clothes.

▸ WB 8, p. 118

c) What do you think: Which place probably costs more? Why?
Which place would you prefer to live in? Why?

2 Fire instructions

***True (T), false (F)* or *not in the text (NIT)*?**

1 If you see a fire, the first thing that you must do is phone for help.
2 You mustn't go near a fire.
3 If you are upstairs, you should use the stairs when you go down.
4 Leave doors open so that other people can leave the building quickly.
5 No running!
6 When you leave your room, take the most important things like money and clothes with you.

IF YOU DISCOVER A FIRE

- First break the glass on the red box on the wall and sound the alarm.
- Attack the fire, but take no personal risks.
- Leave the building. DO NOT use a lift.
- Close the doors behind you.
- DO NOT collect personal belongings.
- Call 999 and ask for "Fire Brigade".
- DO NOT go back into the building.

3 Signs

a) Where would you see these signs? Give your ideas.

1

2

3

4

5

6

7

8

b) Compare your ideas with your partner and then in class. Who has the best ideas?

c) MEDIATING Tell your partner what the signs would be in German.

● 4 Sayings – tips for living your life

a) Read the sayings and pick the right answers.

A
What we learn with pleasure we never forget.
Alfred Mercier

1 You'll be successful if you work hard.
2 You never forget what a friend tells you.
3 If you enjoy learning something, you'll remember it.

B
Fall seven times, stand up eight.
Japanese proverb

1 Life has more bad times than good times.
2 Try a difficult job many times. You'll be successful in the end.
3 You can't do some things, even if you try many times.

C
Why? Why not? Why not you? Why not now?
Asian proverb

1 Don't ask many questions.
2 Be more relaxed. Too much activity is not always good.
3 If a job must be done, don't wait! Do it yourself.

D
The future belongs to those who believe in the beauty of their dreams.
Eleanor Roosevelt

1 Do in your life what you really want to do.
2 Too much dreaming leads to disaster in the future.
3 Dreams about the future don't help you with your life now.

b) Explain these sayings in German (or in English).

There's no place like home.

Better safe than sorry.

Don't cross your bridges before you come to them.

► Extra Reading, pp. 106–107 ► W 50–51, 8–10 ► W ⊙

DECISIONS, DECISIONS

1 Radio adverts

2◉15 **a) Listen to three adverts and pick one poster for each advert.**

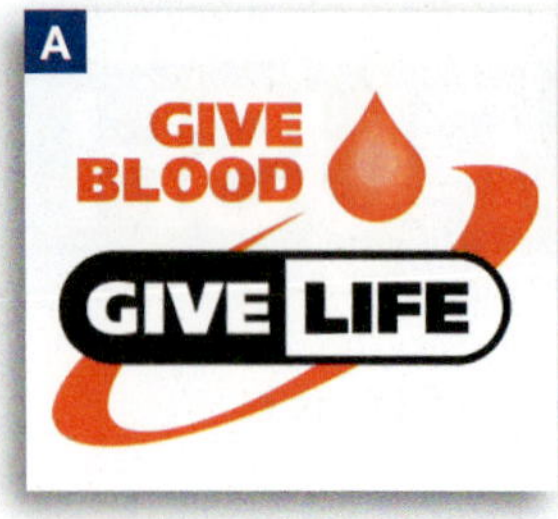

b) Read the sentences. Then listen again and pick one sentence for each radio advert.

Radio advert 1/2/3 ...

- **A** is an announcement about an event.
- **B** is a warning.
- **C** wants to sell you something.
- **D** tells you how to find a place.
- **E** wants you to do something that will help other people.

c) Listen again. What's the main point of each advert? You can say it in German.

2 A discussion about giving blood

2◉16

a) Listen to the four people and say who ...

1. has a brochure about giving blood.
2. has received blood in hospital.
3. has thought of giving blood, but never done it.
4. has given blood before.

b) Listen again and do A or B:

A What are the relationships between the four speakers?

1 Anna is in Connor's ...
2 Mr Watson is Connor's ...
3 Darren is Anna's ...

● **B Take notes. What do the four speakers say about giving blood? Tell the class.**

c) AND YOU?
Will you give blood when you're 18? Why / Why not?

3 Paul is reading from his diary.

2 17 **a) Listen and match Paul with the right brochure.**

1

2

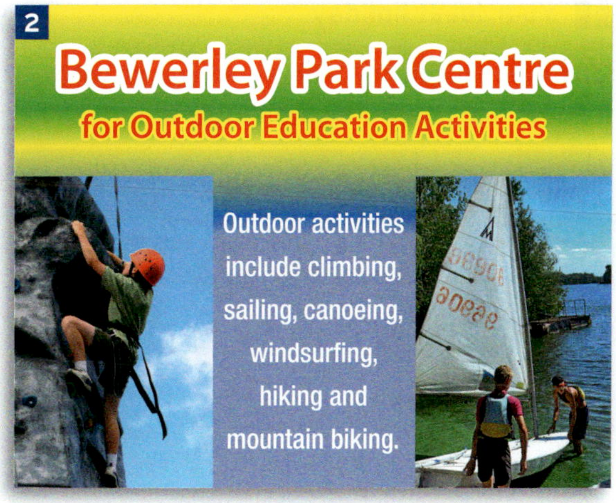

b) Listen again and pick the right answers.

1 Tomorrow Paul is going to travel by train and **a)** car **b)** plane **c)** bike **d)** bus.
2 He's going to work as a helper for **a)** a few weeks **b)** three months **c)** half a year **d)** a year.
3 He'll help **a)** young people **b)** disabled people **c)** children **d)** old people.
4 He'll work with people from **a)** London **b)** England (only) **c)** Germany (only) **d)** different countries.

MORE HELP! p. 114

c) Listen to Paul and then answer the questions.

1 Why is tomorrow a special day for Paul?
2 Why is he feeling nervous?
3 What sort of work is he going to do?
4 What is he looking forward to?

Tip:
When you've written your answers, compare them with your partner's. Then use some of your partner's ideas and make your answers fuller.

4 AND YOU?

Ask your partner two questions, then he/she asks you two questions. Give good, long answers. The tip will give you ideas.

1 What are your plans for next year?
2 When do you feel nervous? Give some examples.
3 Do you want to move away from home? Why / Why not?
4 Would you like to work with disabled adults? Why / Why not?
5 Would you like to work abroad? Why / Why not?
6 What sort of work would you like to do when you leave school?

Tip:
Say more than just one short sentence.
- "What are your plans for next year?" Give two or three examples: *Well, I'll ... and I hope that I can ... Perhaps I'll ... and I would also like to ...*
- "Would you like to work abroad?" Talk about the good and bad things. *Well, yes and no. I would like to work abroad because ... But it could be hard because ...*

▸W 52, 11–13 ▸W

YOUR FIRST HOLIDAY WITHOUT MUM AND DAD

2 18

1 Your ideal holiday

Where would you go? Who would you go with? What would you do? Talk to a partner.

I would like to ... / I wouldn't like to ...

You're 18, you can earn more money – and even save some. Then one day you can book your first holiday without your parents. What should you look out for? Three people who are just back from their first fun-packed holidays told us their experiences.

Four days in Istanbul

My girlfriend and I had a very small budget and we spent hours on the Internet and compared flights to different places before we chose Istanbul. It was a good choice, the only problem was that our plane left at 6.30 a.m., so we had to kip down and spend the night on the airport floor. It wasn't very comfortable!

In Istanbul we had a cheap hotel in the city centre. We had to share a bathroom with other hotel guests, but who cares? It was so central that we could walk to lots of places or take a tram. The trams are modern and they're cheap. The ferry from the European side of Istanbul to the Asian side is cheap too, and you get amazing views of the city.

Istanbul is a very beautiful city, and the people are great. They have a great sense of humour too. I can really recommend a holiday like this. It cost us about 100 pounds for four days (not including the flights) and it was fantastic. *Mike*

A week in Majorca

It was a last-minute decision, really. We didn't have time to compare different prices, so my friend and I found a special offer – a week in Majorca for £240, with flights and full board. We had a room with a balcony and our own bathroom in a hotel with three swimming pools, tennis courts, bars, etc. We just wanted to relax, so it was perfect.

My complaints? Well, there was a lot of noise from the street outside the hotel, and the beach was further away than the brochure said! Also, we had to pay £20 per person for the hotel bus from the airport to the hotel – that's a lot of money! Next time I'll make sure that the transfer is included in the price of the hotel. *Clare*

Tips for your first holiday abroad:

- Cheap flight?
  Be careful – if it's expensive to get to and from the airports, a more expensive flight from a different airport could be cheaper!
- Cheap hotel?
  If it's miles out of town, you could pay loads on buses or taxis. And waste your holiday time.
- Cheap transport from the airport?
  Don't pay through the nose for "cheap" taxis that people offer you at the airport. The local bus is usually much cheaper!

An away match in Rome

I've been an Arsenal fan for at least ten years. I had often supported the team in away matches, but this was the first time my parents didn't pay part of the trip, so I tried to cut some of the costs. I booked the match ticket online, I found my own flights and accommodation, and I paid a lot less than for a package deal. This was because I flew from Liverpool, but back to Birmingham – it can be cheaper if you don't mind using different airports. I also got a cheaper hotel in Rome and bought food for picnics, instead of eating in restaurants. It all worked out well – except that we lost the match! *Loren*

2 Who could have said ...

> **Tip:**
> It can be more than one person!

1 "I didn't want to organize anything."
2 "I don't mind an uncomfortable night."
3 "I'm interested in meeting people."
4 "I wanted to watch a special match."
5 "I just wanted to be lazy."
6 "I wanted to save money."

● **Give reasons for your answer.**

3 Finish the sentences.

1 Mike spent hours on the Internet because he wanted to ...
2 Clare was unhappy because ... and Loren was unhappy because ...
3 Loren was flexible with her plans, for example she ...
4 Cheap hotels can cost you more than you think because ...
5 The cheapest flights don't always mean the cheapest holiday because ...
6 Use local buses when you travel from the airport because ...

4 WORDPOWER

Find the expressions in the texts.

MIKE:
1 didn't have much money
2 say that other people should try it too

CLARE:
3 we only decided just before we travelled
4 with breakfast, lunch and evening meal

LOREN:
5 matches that aren't played in your home town
6 a holiday where flights, accommodation and food are included in one price

5 AND YOU?

a) Sum up how Mike, Clare and Loren spent their holidays: How did they travel? Where did they stay? What did they do? Write at least 60 words.

MORE HELP! p. 114

b) What do you like about Mike's, Clare's and Loren's holidays? What don't you like? Why? Which of their holidays would you like best? Write at least 80 words.

● **c) Imagine you've saved some money for a holiday. Where would you go? What would you do? Write at least 100 words.**

> **Tip:**
> Think of your answers in exercise 1.

▸ WB 6, p. 117

JOBS

1 Job alphabet

a) Work with a partner. Can you write a job for each letter of the alphabet?

Art teacher	E ...	I ...	M ...	Q ...	U ...	X-ray assistant
Bus driver	F ...	J ...	N ...	R ...	V ...	Youth club worker
C ...	G ...	K ...	O ...	S ...	W ...	Zoo manager.
D ...	H ...	L ...	P ...	T ...		

You get one point for each word, three points if no other student in class has the same!

b) Pick a job. What sort of activities do people do in the job? Write at least three phrases with different verbs.

Example:

Job: bus driver
- *drive a bus*
- *sell tickets*
- *open the doors*

Job: ...
- ...
- ...
- ...

c) Now write at least three qualities (adjectives) of a good worker.

- *friendly*
- ...
- ...
- ...

Tip:
You don't know the English word? Use a dictionary.

▸ WB 7, p. 118

d) Compare your answers in exercise 1c) with your partner, then in class. Which three qualities do you think are most important?

2 Two sentences that mean the same thing

a) For each sentence, pick a second sentence that means the same as the first.

1 I've been working in the shop for three months.
a) I'll stop working in the shop in three months.
b) I want to work in the shop for three months.
c) I started work in the shop three months ago.

2 I don't earn enough.
a) I have too much work.
b) I get too little money for the work that I do.
c) There isn't enough work.

3 My boss said, "I'll think about it."
a) She said that she had thought about it.
b) She said that she often thought about it.
c) She said that she would think about it.

b) For each sentence, complete the second sentence so that it means the same as the first. Use no more than three words.

1 I'll be unhappy if nothing changes.
➜ I ... happy if nothing changes.

2 If I don't get more money, I'll apply for another job.
➜ I told my boss that if I ... more money, I would apply for another job.

3 In the end my boss said that she would pay me more money.
➜ In the end my boss said, "... you more money."

3 Applying for a job

a) Read the parts of the letter of application and put them in the right order.

A I can start working from Saturday May 19th. I'm looking forward to hearing from you.

B 4 Blossom Street
Leamington Spa
CV31 6BD
Tel 0113 324869
Mob 07789902043
magkol@ukmail.com
May 3rd 20...

C Chief Librarian
Coventry City Library
Earl Street
Coventry
CV1 5RR

D My name is Magda Kolman and I am 17 years old. I was born in Poland and we speak English and Polish at home. I'm a student at Warwick Road School and I could work on either Saturday or Sunday until the end of June when I leave school. I could work full-time after that.

E I saw your advert for a job as library assistant and I would like to apply for the job.

F Yours faithfully,
Magdalena Kolman

G Dear Sir or Madam,

H I haven't worked in a library before, but I had a part-time job and served customers in a clothes shop last summer. Mr Sinclair, the manager, is happy to write a reference for me.

b) Imagine you're Magdalena Kolman. Copy and complete the application form with information from exercise 3a).

Title ______
First name ______
Family name ______
Gender ______
Date of birth *May 1993 2nd*
Address ______
Postcode ______

Phone ______
Mobile ______
Country of birth ______
Languages ______
Work experience ______
______
Reference from ______

4 Your letter of application

Write a letter of application for one of the jobs below. Use ideas and phrases from the letter in exercise 3a). Write at least 60 words.

● **Write more details (why you would like the job, why you're good for the job) and ask questions (money? travel? accommodation? ...?) Write at least 100 words.**

1
Work on a sheep farm in the Australian outback
Jobs for 3–6 months
Write a letter of application to
Jim Downey
Dowey Cattle Station
Central Arnhem Road
Katherine 0860
Northern Territory, Australia

2
Receptionist
in country hotel near Manchester
Work in a friendly team.
No experience required.
Accommodation provided.
Applicants must be UK/EU citizens or have a valid UK work permit.
Contact DoreenKing@theroyal.co.uk

3
Assistant
in international youth camp in Scotland
Help the camp managers with activities for young people. Evening and weekend work. German or French speakers preferred.
Apply to ABC Camp, Leanach, Strachur, Argyll PA27 8DB

▸W 53, 14 ▸W ⊙

1 The most embarrassing moment in my life!

a) Read Dan's letter to a youth magazine. Why was his job interview embarrassing?

OK, if I had stayed at home the night before my interview, I would have gone to bed before midnight. But I went out with my friends. So I was very, very tired in the morning. If I had been less tired, I would have heard the alarm clock. But I didn't hear it – so it was 9.20 when I woke up. And my job interview was at ten!

I jumped out of bed, dressed in ten seconds and ate my breakfast in five. I ran out of the house, but I was too late for the 9.20 bus. If I had caught the 9.20 bus, I would have arrived on time. But I got the 9.40 bus, and although I ran all the way to the office, I was five minutes late when I went into the manager's office. I felt hot, and tired, and very silly. Then I looked down at my feet ... and saw that I was still wearing my slippers. And that wasn't all. I also saw half my breakfast all over my jacket.

If I had woken up on time, I would have dressed more carefully. And if I had arrived on time for my interview, I would perhaps have got the job. *Dan Longmore*

b) Read the questions and answer *Yes* or *No*.

1 Did Dan go to bed before midnight on the evening before his interview?
2 Did he hear the alarm clock in the morning?
3 Did he dress carefully?
4 Did he eat his breakfast carefully?
5 Did he get the job?

● **c) Finish your answers with *because* ...**
Yes/No, because he had/hadn't ...

Tip:
You can find past participles in the *List of irregular verbs* on pages 190-191.

2 OVER TO YOU!

a) Choose a), b) or c) in the first sentence and complete the gaps in the example sentences. Then write the correct checkpoint in your exercise book.

Tip:
The examples are in the text.

CHECKPOINT

***If*-Sätze (Typ III)**

If-Sätze III verwendest du, wenn es
a) unwahrscheinlich **b)** möglich **c)** unmöglich
ist, dass die Situation noch vorkommt.

Beispiele:
If I had stayed at home, I would have gone to bed.
If I ... been less tired, I ... ... heard the clock.
If I ... ... the 9.20 bus, I ... ... on time.

b) Find two more *if*-clauses in Dan's letter.

▸ W 54–57 ▸ W ⦿ Weitere Übungen: www.new-highlight.de ▸ Extra Practice, pp. 92 ff. ▸ Summary p. 123

TEST YOURSELF

Do these tests and check your answers on page 192. They'll show you what you've learned in this unit. Look again at the new words on pages 136–139. Look at the *Summary* on page 120.

TEST 1 Find the right words. Pick a word from box 1 + a word from box 2.

alarm • away • call • dining • entrance • washing

\+

centre • clock • hall • machine • match • room

1 An office where people work on the phone.
2 The place in the house where meals are eaten.
3 Where you are when you go into a building.
4 A game that is not played in the team's home town.
5 Put your dirty clothes in: they'll come out clean!
6 It wakes you up in the morning.

6 POINTS

TEST 2 Application form

Give the correct information from the box.
Be careful: You won't need all the information.

Germany • male • John • CV23 7LU • Mr • Spanish • Smith • April 15th, 1993

1 Title: ...
2 Family name: ...
3 Date of birth: ...
4 Country of birth: ...
5 Gender: ...
6 Postcode: ...

6 POINTS

TEST 3 At home

Pick the right words from the box.

bathroom • cooker • freezer • fridge • lift • radiator • upstairs • wardrobe

1 My bedroom is ..., under the roof.
2 It's warm in my room when the ... is on.
3 I put my clothes in my ...
4 I make my meals on my electric ...
5 We put milk or cheese in the ...
6 We put ice-cream in the ...

6 POINTS

TEST 4 A holiday abroad

Put the verbs in the right form.

1 I **(spend)** ten days in Istanbul last May.
2 My girlfriend and I **(fly)** there from Glasgow.
3 We **(choose)** Istanbul because we had a small budget.
4 We **(find)** a cheap hotel in the centre.
5 We **(buy)** our own food.
6 So our holidays **(not cost)** too much.

6 POINTS

● TEST 5 A letter of application

Finish the text.

1 Dear ... or ...
2 I saw the advert ... a job in ... cafe.
3 I ... like to ... for the job.
4 I worked in a cafe ... year, and Ms Owen, the cafe manager, is happy to write a ...
5 I could ... from July ... the end of August.
6 ... ..., John Blake

6 POINTS

● TEST 6 Say it in English.

1 Hast du die Stelle im Laden gekriegt?
2 Nein. Das Interview ist gut gelaufen.
3 Aber ich habe die Stelle trotzdem nicht gekriegt. Und du?
4 Ich habe mich um eine Lehrstelle beworben.
5 Die Leute dort scheinen nett zu sein.
6 Ich hoffe, alles läuft gut!

6 POINTS

▸ W 58 ff., Exam Training ▸ W 33–34, Portfolio

Unit 1 (page 11)

Partner B

Your partner has tickets for a rugby match. Ask him/her:

- Who / playing?
- Where?
- Spell / name of stadium?
- What day / time?
- price?
- Which gate / use?

Unit 2 (page 25)

Partner B

Your partner wants to invite you to the pizzeria at 7 p.m. on July 5th. You can't go because you already have this ticket for the cinema. Apologise.

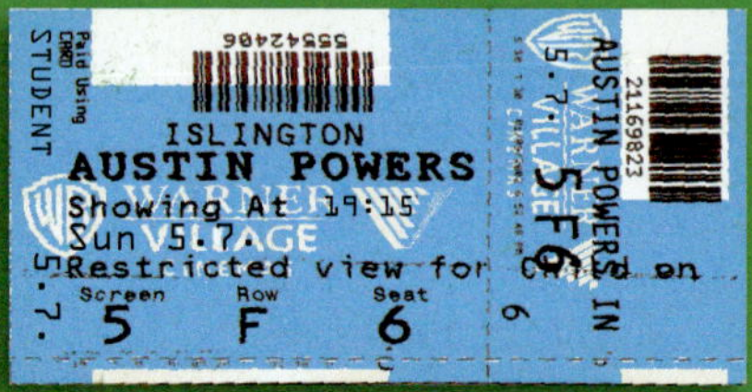

Now invite your friend to a party at your house at 8 p.m. on July 9th.

- *Can you make your partner change his/her mind?*

Unit 2 (page 80)

Partner B

Ask your partner about the club.

- spell / name of club?
- open Friday?
- What / main show?
- price?
- open at / time?
- OK / people under 18?
- documents?
- alcohol?

Unit 3 (page 43)

Partner B

Your partner can't think of the right English word or phrase. He/She will explain the words and phrases to you. Listen and look at the list of words below. Then tell him/her what the right words are.
You won't need all of the words.

shower	yoghurt
bank account	cheap
mango	tired
station	thirsty
mobile	fizzy water

Unit 3 (page 87)

Partner B

- *Your partner tells you how to go to the National Museum and Kendriya Bus Station. What are their letters on the map?*
- *Now tell your partner how to go to the India Gate and International Youth Centre.*
- *Compare your answers on your partner's map.*

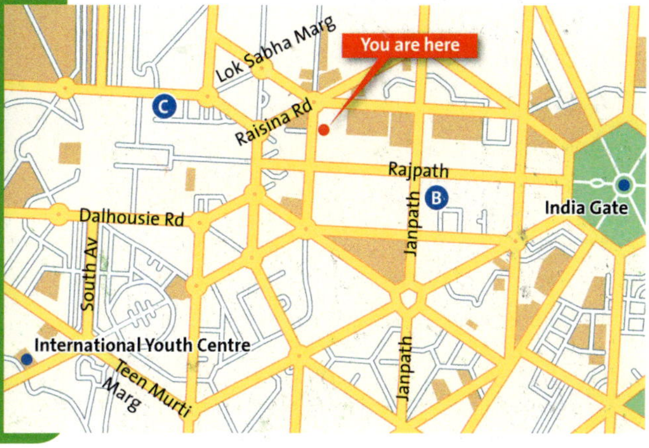

Unit 3 (page 90)

Partner B

You and your partner have planned to eat at the Mahib Indian Restaurant. Look at the map and tell your partner the way to the restaurant.

Start at ...
Go straight on (= *geradeaus*).
Go past ...
Cross over ... street/the river.
When you come to ..., turn left/right.
Take the first/second/third road on your left/right.
The restaurant is on your left/right.

Now your partner will repeat the directions. Listen and check that he/she has understood correctly.

→ EXTRA PRACTICE

REVISION Word order

→ Summary, p. 124

o 1 Blog messages about holidays

a) Match the messages with the pictures.

We never go away during the holidays.
I prefer to earn some money, so I often work in a shop during the day and I sometimes work in a restaurant in the evenings. **Jacob**

We always go to the sea in December.
We often have barbecues on the beach in the evenings. It's fun! **Mandisa**

We usually visit my grandparents in the north of the country. When we're there we often spend a few days in the Kruger Park. It's always great there. **Sarah**

1

2

3

b) Find the sentences in exercise 1a) and then write them with the extra information.

1 We go away during the holidays. ← *never*
2 I often work in a shop. ← *during the day*
3 I sometimes work in the evenings. ← *in a restaurant*
4 We often have barbecues in the evenings. ← *on the beach*
5 We visit my grandparents in the north of the country. ← *usually*

o 2 Your holidays **Write where and when you do these activities.**

1 I go swimming.
2 I meet my friends.
3 I go cycling.
4 I listen to music.
5 I play computer games.
6 I go inline-skating.

I go swimming in the pool in town once a week. Or Once a week I go …

● 3 A competition **Answer the questions. Write 2–3 full sentences for each question.**

Competition for a free flight to South Africa!
Just answer these two questions:

1 Do you usually go away in summer, and where do you stay?
2 What activities do you usually do during your summer holiday?

REVISION *Can, could, should, must* → Summary, p. 125

1 Paul's first visit to South Africa

Paul is asking his South African friend Piet for advice. Put the words in the right order.

PAUL What / should / I / in South Africa / visit / ?
PIET You / must / the Kruger National Park / visit. You / could / two or three days there / spend.
PAUL Should / I / some cities too / visit / ?
PIET Yes, you should. You mustn't / Cape Town / miss. If you're there in March, you / could / the world's largest bike race / see. And you / should / to Johannesburg / go / too. I have a good friend there. She / can / you / help.

2 MEDIATING

Read the brochure. Tell your partner what you can see or do in Johannesburg.

JOHANNESBURG FOR YOUNG PEOPLE

You could go down a gold mine that produced 1.4 million kilograms of gold. You could also visit Soweto, the township where many of the protests against apartheid took place. In Soweto you should visit the Apartheid Museum.

And if you love horses, you mustn't miss the South African Lipizzaner horse show – Johannesburg is the only city in the world with the famous Lipizzaner horses outside Austria.

3 MEDIATING

Now explain to a South African friend what you can see or do in Cologne (Köln).

Köln – *das* Reiseziel für junge Leute

Was kann man in Köln machen? Der Dom ist natürlich ein Muss! Auch ein Besuch in der Altstadt darf nicht fehlen. Ihr könntet zu einem Konzert ins Palladium oder E-Werk gehen. Fans vom FC Köln solltten auf alle Fälle zum RheinEnergie-Stadion fahren. Übernachten könnt ihr in günstigen Hotels oder auf Campingplätzen.

4 AND YOU? Your town

MORE HELP p. 109

Prepare a short talk about what you can see or do in your town or village. Use *can, could, must(n't)* or *should(n't)*.

PAST PERFECT

→ Summary, p. 121

1 Life story 1: Nelson Mandela **Read the information and finish the sentences.**

Fight against apartheid

1918 Born in Mvezo, a small village in South Africa.
1950 He helped black people who were in trouble with the police in Johannesburg.
1952 He organized peaceful protests against apartheid.
1961 He used violence against the apartheid government.
1962 He had military training.
In November he went to prison for sabotage and violence.
1990 He came out of prison.
1994 He became South Africa's first black president.

Mandela in prison on Robben Island.

1 Before he became South Africa's first black president, Mandela had come out of ...
2 Before he was sent to prison for sabotage and violence, he had had ...
3 Before he used violence, he had organized ... against ...
4 And before that, in 1950, he had helped ... who were ... with ...

2 Life story 2: Sandra's parents **Write the past participles.**

My parents got married in 1991. They had (**meet**) in a club where they had (**have**) dance lessons. My father hadn't (**be**) a very good dancer. They lived in Schwerte – my mother had (**come**) to Schwerte with her parents from East Germany.
When I started school, my parents had already (**get**) divorced. Dad had (**move**) to Mannheim where he had (**become**) ... a dance teacher!

3 Life story 3: Kahil's story
Pick the right verb and write the past participle.

→ come • live • lose • see • work

Before my parents came to Germany they had **(1)** in Turkey. In Germany they lived with friends who had **(2)** a few years before. My parents started a business in 1990. Before that, they had **(3)** in a pencil factory. When the factory closed in 2009, my parents gave work to ten people who had **(4)** their jobs. I first went to Turkey when I was five. I had never **(5)** my grandparents before.

Kahil

4 AND YOU?
Write a few sentences about your parents' or your life story.

My parents got married in ... . They had met ...
I was born in ... . My parents had moved there in ...

READING

1 Signs in South Africa **Pick the right sentence. You can use a dictionary.**

A A poster along the road

1 You can fall if you run.
2 Fireworks are dangerous.
3 Perhaps a car won't see you.

B A sign in a cafe

1 The room is very cold.
2 You can fall easily here.
3 No lights: you can't see.

C A sign on the beach

1 Rocks in the sea can hurt you.
2 A fish can hurt you.
3 A boat can hurt you.

2 In Cape Town

Sabine is visiting Cape Town. She phones Terry, a friend who lives there.

a) Read the dialogue and pick the right words from the box on the right.

	A	B	C	D
1	see	write	hear	listen
2	want	love	hate	leave
3	because	when	during	which
4	for	if	on	about
5	museum	boat	tour	island
6	meet	spend	visit	help

SABINE Hi, Terry. It's Sabine here.
TERRY Oh, hi Sabine! Great to **(1)** from you! Where are you?
SABINE I'm staying in the *Cape of Good Hope Hotel*.
TERRY Listen, we must meet. I'd **(2)** to see you. When do you have time?
SABINE Well, on Friday, for example.
TERRY Hmm, that's difficult **(3)**. I'm busy. What **(4)** tomorrow?
SABINE No, that won't work. I'm going to visit Robben Island, and I don't know when the **(5)** finishes. At the weekend perhaps?
TERRY Fine! Could we meet on Sunday morning? We could **(6)** the day together.
SABINE Sounds good. If you have time, that's great.
TERRY Of course I have time! I can come to your hotel at about 10 o'clock. OK?
SABINE Fine. Oh, err, Terry, I should tell you – my boyfriend Julian is here too. Is that OK?
TERRY !!!

b) Terry is disappointed because ...

1 he can't see Sabine.
2 she doesn't want to see him.
3 she isn't alone.

c) Imagine and write what Terry wants to say in the last line.

d) Write a title for the dialogue.

► You can find new words in the *Dictionary* (pages 142–168).

LISTENING

3 A week in Cape Town

1 9

Sabine and Julian's guide is explaining the programme for the week. Listen and write the missing information in your exercise books.

Tip: Read the information and guess what the missing words are before you listen!

WEEK IN CAPE TOWN – PROGRAMME	
This evening:	Tour of Cape Town by ... (1)
Wednesday:	Visit the ... (2)
Thursday:	Whale watching – don't forget your ... (3)!
Friday:	Trip to Robben Island. Boat leaves at ... (4).
Weekend:	Free for shopping and relaxing on the ... (5).
* If you get lost, have a problem, need help, phone: 0741 – ... (6).	

SPEAKING

4 ROLE PLAY

PARTNER A: You want to go to the top of the Table Mountain by cable car. Phone the tourist office and ask:

- **Trips by cable car**
  - how long?
  - trips in the morning?
  - last trip of the day?
  - how often?
  - price for two 17-year-old students?
  - cars work/in bad weather?
- **At the top of the mountain**
  - what see/do?
  - eat/drink?

PARTNER B: You work in the tourist office in Cape Town. Answer your partner's questions.

- Travel in Cape Town's fantastic cable cars to the top of the Table Mountain!
- Walk and see Cape Town, the sea, Robben Island or Mountain Gardens
- Relax and enjoy a meal in the cafe.
- First car up 8 a.m. Last car down 10 p.m.
- Cars every 15 minutes. Trip takes 5–6 minutes.
- Adults: 145 rand Children (under 18), students: 76 rand
- There are no trips if it's cloudy or the wind is too strong.

Phone 021 424-8181 for information.

READING

From Soweto to the Kruger Park
by **Dominique Mathebula**

A I was born in Soweto, a big township outside Johannesburg, and I was a child in the first few years after the end of apartheid. Life certainly wasn't easy there. Our house had electricity, but we only got running water when I was six. Before that, I often had to fetch water for my mother in a big heavy bucket. I didn't like that at all! When people think of Soweto, they always think of crime, violence, drugs and unemployment. Well, these problems certainly existed, but there were a lot of good things too. I had great friends when I was small, and we had good fun. We played outside and often got into trouble. Nothing serious, I mean. Just kids stuff. There were lots of bands in Soweto then – kwaito bands, rock bands, traditional bands – and when we grew older, some of my friends played in them. We often listened to music in the evenings – and in Soweto, listening meant dancing, singing and taking part! There was a special atmosphere in Soweto – people still felt proud of the role which they had played in the fight against *apartheid*. We felt that we belonged together.

B I left school as soon as possible. Then I had to find a job, which wasn't easy at all. After looking for a long time, I finally got a job in a fast food restaurant in Johannesburg. It was a pretty awful job and it wasn't well-paid, but I didn't think that I could do anything else. Then one day a teacher from my old school told me about a college in Johannesburg where young people could train for better jobs. I applied – and I got a place. I had to study in the evenings after work, but I really enjoyed it. The teachers were so positive, and I started to feel much more confident. I felt like a different person.

C One day I saw an advert for a job in a hotel – not just washing up and making the beds, but working in reception, really meeting the guests. It sounded good: I applied for it and was really excited about it. But I didn't get it, and I felt so disappointed! Luckily, my friends and family helped me through that awful time. And soon afterwards I saw an advert for a job in a hotel in the Kruger Park – and this time I was successful! So I packed my bags ...

D The Kruger Park was an amazing change from Soweto, but I enjoyed my work here from the first day. My first job was welcoming guests here in our hotel and looking after them. It was very different from my job in Johannesburg, where the customers never even looked at me; here the guests actually thanked me for my work. I often went with the guests when the rangers organized tours in the park, and then I wondered: Perhaps I could become a ranger too? Luckily, the park needed more rangers – so I did some training and now I'm a ranger myself. And if you ask me, it's the best job in the world!

▸ You can find new words in the *Dictionary* (pages 142–168).

E Our main job as rangers is looking after the animals. We have to check that they are safe and healthy and have enough to eat. The other part of our job is taking tourists into the park. Sometimes we get very close to lions, leopards, buffaloes, hippos, zebras and all our other animals, but it's not dangerous as long as tourists don't frighten the animals. My worst experience was when we had a male leopard near the outer fence: Crowds of tourists stopped in order to see him, but they came much too close and he became frightened. I tried to tell the tourists to go away, but I was too late – and I watched as the leopard tried to jump over the fence. The outer fence is electric – and it killed him. I saw it all, and it made me sick.

F Humans aren't usually in danger from the animals. The biggest danger for them is car accidents. One of the worst was when five Europeans were killed in the park a few months ago. They were driving too fast, and their car fell into a river.

1 Which is the best title for each paragraph (A–F) in the story?

Example: Paragraph A – Nr. 3. Paragraph B – Nr. ...

> **Tip:** There are eight titles – so you won't need all of them.

1 First experience of earning money
2 A good boss and more money
3 Life as a child: hard work and good fun
4 A new job, and then a new job again
5 What's most dangerous for visitors
6 Life in the park: exciting, sometimes sad
7 Bad news – and then good news after all
8 Leaving friends and family isn't easy

2 MEDIATING

You're telling Dominique's story to your uncle who works in Hamburg zoo. Explain in German what happened to the leopard and why Dominique was angry with the tourists.

3 An interview with Dominique for your school magazine.

a) Prepare eight questions for the interview.
Ask her about information in the article or about other things too (boyfriend, future, ...).

b) Work with a partner and play the interview.

PARTNER A: Ask the questions.
PARTNER B: Play Dominique. Answer with information from the text. You can invent information too.

WRITING

> **Tip:**
> Don't just copy sentences from the text. Use your own words.

4 Write a summary of Dominique's story (100–120 words).

Example:

Dominique wrote: "I was born in Soweto, a big township outside Johannesburg. Life certainly wasn't easy there. Our house had electricity, but we only got running water when I was six. Before that, I often had to fetch water for my mother in a big heavy bucket. I didn't like that at all! But not everything was bad, of course. We kids played outside when I was small and we often got into trouble. Nothing serious, I mean. Just kids stuff." (79 words)

You could write: When she was small, Dominique had a hard life in Soweto. But she still had time to play. (18 words)

5 A job advert

You've seen this advert and you're interested in this job. Write to the manager (90–100 words):

- say why you're interested
- ask when you can start / how long you can stay
- ask: age limit? (minimum 18?)
- ask: kind of work (cleaning, serving ...?)
- ask: pay? meals? your room? travel from Germany?

> **Work in July/August in the Kruger National Park**
>
> **OK, it's winter here in South Africa, but life in the park goes on. Come and join us!**
>
> - **work in hotels, campsites, restaurants**
> - **good pay**
> - **people from other countries**
> - **working language: English**
>
> Please write to the Manager, Berg-en-Dal Camp, Kruger National Park.

LISTENING

1 10

6 The day that Nelson Mandela came out of prison

Mrs Lungile Mfeka recorded her feelings on that day.

a) Listen to her radio diary and pick a), b) or c).

1 When Nelson Mandela came out of prison, Mrs Mfeka lived in **a)** Johannesburg **b)** Durban **c)** Pretoria.
2 She worked in **a)** a hospital **b)** a school **c)** a factory.
3 When Nelson Mandela came out of prison, she watched it on TV **a)** at home **b)** at work **c)** at a friend's house.
4 When Mr Mandela said "South Africans knew that apartheid had no future" he spoke for **a)** white people **b)** black people **c)** white and black people.

b) Now listen again and answer the questions.

1 On what date did Nelson Mandela come out of prison?
2 How many years had he spent in prison?
3 How old was Nelson Mandela when he came out of prison?
4 How long did Mr Mandela walk through the crowds before he arrived at the platform?

EXTRA PRACTICE

REVISION If-clauses (type I)

→ Summary, p. 123

1 Agony aunts

Agony aunts are people in magazines or websites who give advice about problems.

a) Read the two letters.

Hi Emma,

I have a boyfriend (he's called Dan), but my parents don't know about him.

They really love me – but if I tell them about Dan, they'll say that I'm too young (I'm 16).

But if I don't tell them, Dan and I will never be able to meet at my house.

What should I do? Please help me.

Charlotte

Ask Emma

Do you feel depressed or miserable about something? Tell Emma about it, and she'll help.

Hi Charlotte,

You'll never be happy if you don't tell your parents about Dan. And if you pick the right moment, perhaps your parents won't be as angry as you think. But you must talk to them, even if they're angry with you at first. It's your life – if you don't tell them now, it will only be more difficult later. Good luck!

Emma

b) Put the parts together and write five sentences.

1 If Charlotte tells her parents about Dan,
2 But if Charlotte doesn't tell them about Dan,
3 Emma says Charlotte won't be happy
4 She says if Charlotte picks the right moment,
5 She says Charlotte must talk to her parents

A even if they're angry with her at first.
B if she doesn't tell her parents about Dan.
C they'll say that she's too young.
D her parents won't be angry.
E she won't be able to meet Dan at her house.

2 Tom's friend

a) Complete Tom's agony aunt letter.

Tip: Verb in the simple present or future? Look at exercise 1.

Dear Emma,
My friend Jessica has taken cannabis for a few months. But I feel sure that if she (get) help, she (stop) taking the drug. The problem is that she doesn't know who she can talk to. If she (talk) to her parents, they (have) an awful argument. But if she (not talk) to them, she (not/stop) taking the cannabis.
I'd like to help her – what can I do?
Tom

b) Now write Emma's answer to Tom's letter. Use the sentences below or your own ideas.

Dear Tom,
Thank you for your letter. If people take drugs, …
If Jessica doesn't stop soon, …
On the other hand if she stops, …
If Jessica talks to her parents, perhaps …
And if you talk to one of Jessica's teachers, …
If you don't talk to anybody, …
Good luck!
Emma

REVISION If-clauses (type II)

→ Summary, p. 123

1 Charlotte isn't happy with Emma's advice.

a) Read what Charlotte says.

The agony aunt said that I should tell my parents about Dan. But she's wrong. I can't talk to my parents. Mum and dad would shout at me if I told them about Dan. If I invited him home, they wouldn't speak to me for a week. And it would be worse if he tried talking to them. The agony aunt wouldn't give answers like that if she was 16! It's not as easy as she thinks!

b) Copy the four *if*-sentences into the table.

Mum and dad ... shout at me	if I told them about Dan.
If I ... him home,	they ...
...	...

Tip: The *if*-clause doesn't always come first!

c) Now answer the questions about Charlotte. Start your answers with *if* ...

1 What does Charlotte think would happen if she told her parents about Dan? *If she told her parents about Dan, her parents ... at her.*
2 What would happen if she invited Dan home? *If she ..., they ...*
3 How would it be if Dan tried talking to Charlotte's parents? *If Dan ..., it ...*
4 What would be different if the agony aunt was 16? *If she ..., she ...*

2 Tom and Jessica

Tom has decided to talk to Jessica about her drugs problem. Pick the right forms of the verbs.

Tip: Look at exercise 1 for help.

You must talk to your parents about the cannabis, Jessica. OK, if you told them about the drugs, they (were / would be) angry. But if you (said / would say) that you wanted to stop taking the drug, they (helped / would help) you. They love you, don't they? I think that they would be disappointed if you (didn't tell / wouldn't tell) them. They can help you, Jessica. And you (were never / would never be) happy if you (didn't stop / wouldn't stop) taking these drugs!

3 AND YOU? Finish these sentences about yourself.

1 If our school had a school prom, I ...
2 If a shop in my town put up a *Mosquito*, I ...
3 If one of my friends took drugs, I ...
4 If a shop assistant told me to take off my hoody, I ...
5 I'd be disappointed if ...
6 I'd do the *D of E Award* if ...
7 My mum would be miserable if ...
8 People wouldn't be so biased against young people if ...

REVISION Tenses

→ Summary, p. 119–121

1 School stress

a) Read the dialogue. Why is Tim under pressure?

MUM What's wrong, Tim? You look angry!
TIM I can't find find my history book. I saw it on my table yesterday, but it isn't there now.
MUM Did you have it for your lesson last week?
TIM Yes, of course I did. And I had it two days ago when I did my homework.
MUM Did you put it in your bag last night?
TIM No, I didn't. I'll be in trouble tomorrow if I don't find it.
MUM Look, I'm busy now, but I'll help you look for it tonight.
TIM The silly thing is that we'll have a history test next week. Mr Jones told us last lesson. So I must find that book!

b) Copy the red time phrases in each sentence. Write if the time phrase is for the past or the future. Example: yesterday – past

c) Now pick the right form of these verbs.

(We'll have / We had) a maths test two days ago, (we'll have / we had) an English test yesterday and (we'll have / we had) a history test tomorrow. It's too much!

2 The driving test **Write the verbs in the simple past.**

DAN Oh, hi Amy. I **(try)** to phone you last week.
AMY Yes, well, I **(be)** very busy with driving lessons last week. I **(not/want)** to tell anybody because I **(had)** my test yesterday.
DAN Really? And **(it/go)** well?
AMY Yes, I **(pass)**! It **(go)** really well.
DAN Congratulations, Amy! And **(you/drive)** home after the test?
AMY No, but I **(drive)** to school yesterday. And I **(not/have)** an accident!

3 Saying sorry

a) Ella has invited Becca to her party, but Becca can't come. Find the correct verb forms in Becca's e-mail.

To: Ella From: Becca

Hi Ella,

I'm sorry I can't come to your party. I **(not/feel)** well last week and **(miss)** four days of school, so I **(spend)** a lot of time on school work this week. I **(work)** late last night, I **(get up)** at 6 a.m. this morning and I **(still write)** at the moment. But if you have time I **(see)** you at the weekend, OK?

b) Ella has invited you to her party too, but you don't want to go. Make up a good excuse, then send her an e-mail.

c) Now work with a partner. Write a phone dialogue with Ella. Practise it and then present it to the class.

LISTENING

1 Products for young people

1⊙21 **a) Listen and match each advert with a photo. You won't need two photos.**

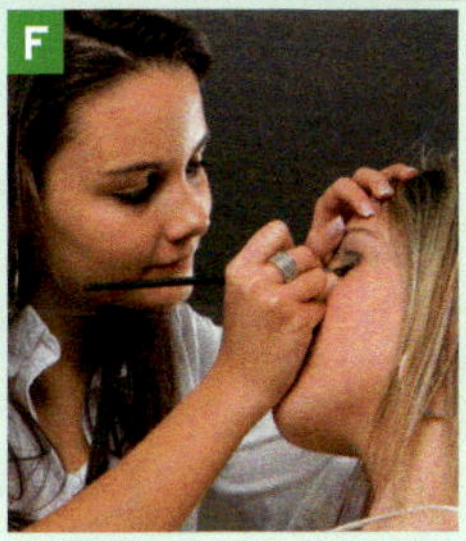

1⊙22 **b) Listen to the first advert again. Choose the right answer.**

1 The product costs **a)** £25 **b)** £45 **c)** £59.
2 You'll get **a)** a poster with your photo **b)** a cup with your picture **c)** three photos.
3 Girls under 18 **a)** aren't allowed **b)** pay less **c)** are only allowed with an adult.

1⊙23 **c) Listen again to the second advert. True or false? Correct the false information.**

1 The advert is for the Bonny BK99.
2 The product has a 1.3 megapixel camera.
3 For £15 a year you get 100 minutes of talk time.
4 You can also send as many texts as you like.

1⊙24 **d) Now listen again to the third advert. Copy the table and complete the information.**

	New Computer Game	
1	What's the game like?	Amazing and ...
2	What do you do in the game?	Fight against ... and fight for the ... of the world
3	Players have to	be clever and think ...
4	What does the game cost?	...

1⊙25 **e) Look at the words in the box. Then listen again to the fourth advert and complete the sentences with A, B, C or D.**

1 The magazine is for young men who want to feel ...
2 It's for young men who want to look ...
3 It gives information about ...
4 The magazine costs ...
5 You can buy it every ...

	A	B	C	D
1	healthy	amazing	good	different
2	cool	strong	great	happy
3	food	holidays	clothes	motorbikes
4	£4.20	£4.25	£4.50	£4.99
5	month	week	weekend	Tuesday

► You can find new words in the *Dictionary* (pages 142–168).

SPEAKING

2 Going out for an evening

a) MEDIATING

You're in York with Anna, a German friend. Tell her five things about the club – in German.

b) ROLE PLAY

Dave, an English friend, would also like to come to the club.

PARTNER A: Your partner is Dave. Answer his questions.

PARTNER B: You're Dave. Look at your card on page 66.

WRITING

3 A survey

An EU survey asks teenagers in Europe how they spend their free time.

- Answer the following questions in full sentences.
- Write at least two sentences to answer the questions.

1. How often do you go out in the evenings? Where do you prefer to go?
2. Do you often go to the cinema/the theatre/a club? Why/Why not?
3. Where do you prefer to meet friends: at your home/at their home/in town? Why?
4. How do you travel when you go out? Are there buses after 10 p.m.? Are they expensive?
5. Write about two places in your town or village where young people like to go in the evenings or at weekends. Write what's good or bad about the places.

4 Your own advert

As part of your work experience you have to write your own advert. Look again at photos A–F on page 79. Choose one product and make a magazine advert for it.

Your advert should have:

- a name
- a slogan
- some information
- the price (+ special offer?)

Tip:
Download a photo from the Internet or take one from a magazine and use it in your advert.

LISTENING AND SPEAKING

1 Life for teenagers today

What's good and what's difficult for teenagers today? Work with a partner and write a list.

→ family • money • school • work • boyfriend/girlfriend • clothes • media • pressure • ...

2 A UNICEF report on life for teenagers in different countries

a) Which countries in the box do you think

– have the best conditions for teenagers?
– are in the middle?
– have the worst conditions for teenagers?

→ Germany • Britain • Sweden • Poland • USA

1 26 **b) Now listen to part 1 of the radio interview. Did you guess right?**

1 27 **c) Now listen to part 2 of the interview. Which of the following topics are talked about?**

A having few books at home
B eating main meal with parents
C travelling abroad
D drinking too much alcohol
E feeling an outsider
F getting good marks in exams
G having experience of violence
H smoking
I being pregnant / having sex under 18

1 27 **d) Listen to part 2 again. In which categories A–I was Britain worst of all 21 countries in the survey? In which categories was Germany worst?**

3 AND YOU? What do *you* think?

a) Look again at the topics in exercise 2c). Rank them from A to I: A= most important I = least important
b) Compare and talk about your list with your partner, then in class.

I think ... is the most important thing / is less important than ...
If you ... then you can/can't ...
I think other things are even more important, for example if your parents are divorced/unemployed/...

4 A short talk

Give a short talk on what it's like to be a teenager in Germany today. Use ideas from this page and this unit and use your own ideas too.

Teenagers must / want to / can't / need / are ..., but ...
On the one hand ..., but on the other hand ...
I think the biggest problem is that ...
Adults / The media often say that ..., but I know / don't know many people who ...

▸ You can find new words in the *Dictionary* (pages 142–168).

READING AND WRITING

5 Look at the title, the photo and the text. What does Maryelen want to do?

The Teen Princess competition

The competition is for girls aged 13 to 15 (there is also a *Teen Queen* competition for girls between 13 and 19). The photos of fifty girls are shown on the competition's website and the public votes for them. The girls can win prizes like free clothes, make-up and international travel.

The organizers say that the competition is fun and popular with both the girls and the public. They say that the competition helps girls to feel confident. The experience, they say, is useful for the girls if they later want a career as a model. Critics think that beauty competitions are sexist because they are usually for women only. They want to ban beauty competitions because they put women under pressure and promote the idea that women are only important if they look good. But the organizers say that banning competitions would discriminate against the many girls who want to take part in them.

Teenager with one hand could become catwalk model

A teenager who was born with one hand and who needs a machine in order to digest food is on her way to winning a beauty competition.

Maryelen Loughran, 15, was born 12 weeks premature. Although she has had several important operations, she is not able to eat anything through her mouth and has special feeding equipment that she has to take with her everywhere she goes.

But Maryelen has never used her physical disabilities as an excuse for not doing things, and has even found the time and energy to earn her blue belt in karate. And now she is one of the last 50 girls in the *Teen Princess UK* competition. If she wins, she could be on Britain's catwalks in a few months.

How did this begin? Maryelen, who lives in Birmingham, said: "I'm a real girly girl and I love my clothes so I decided to go to the *Clothes Show* and have a look around."

The Clothes Show was at Birmingham's National Exhibition Centre, and that's where she was seen by a photographer from *Teen Princess*. He took some photos of Maryelen and sent them to her, and she then thought "Why not give it a go? It would be great to win!"

Maryelen's mother Angela knows that Maryelen is worried about her next operation, but she is confident about her daughter. "She is always so strong and is the first to try anything," she says. "Teachers at her school have said to me that sometimes they feel ashamed when they see her and they realize that they are worrying about something like a spot on their face." Compared with Maryelen's problems, their own seem so unimportant.

Maryelen is going to have another big operation on her stomach in May and hopes she will be well enough for the final round in the competition in August.

adapted from: *The Daily Mail*

6 *True (T), false (F) or not in the text (NIT)?*

1 Maryelen was born late.
2 A machine helps her to eat.
3 She would like to do karate, but unfortunately she can't.
4 Maryelen has won the *Teen Princess UK* competition.
5 When Maryelen went to the *Clothes Show*, she hadn't thought of the *Teen Princess* competition.
6 Maryelen's friends are happy that she's in the competition.
7 Maryelen will have to go into hospital before the final round of the competiton.
8 In the *Teen Queen* and *Teen Princess* competitions only family and friends can vote for the girls.

7 Explain these words/phrases in English. You can use a dictionary.

1 A *catwalk* (line 16) is a place where ...
2 A *real girly girl* (line 18) is a girl who ...
3 When I *give something a go* (line 26), I ...
4 When you're *worried* about something (line 28), you ...

8 MEDIATING

Write notes in German about Maryelen for an article in your school magazine.

9 Say it differently

For each sentence complete the second sentence so that it means the same as the first. Use no more than three words. Example:

A teenager *is on her way to winning* a beauty competition.
➜ A teenager could soon win a beauty competition.

1 Maryelen uses equipment and has to take this equipment with her.
➜ Maryelen uses equipment ... she has to take with her.
2 She has to take the equipment everywhere.
➜ She can't ... without the equipment.
3 That's where she was seen by a photographer.
➜ That's where a photographer ... her.
4 "It would be great to win."
➜ "It would be great if I ..."
5 Your own problems seem unimportant.
➜ Your own problems ... important.

Tip:
Find another way of saying the same thing, for example:
Jo is bigger than Dan = Dan isn't as big as Jo.
Ann isn't unhappy = Ann is happy.
Ben buys a cat. = A cat is bought by Ben.
You can use a word from the first sentence if you change its form, for example:
on her way to winning => could win

10 AND YOU?

What do *you* think about clothes shows or beauty competitions?

- **Write at least five arguments for these shows and five arguments against. Use ideas from the texts and your own ideas too.**
- **Then write *your* opinion about clothes shows or beauty competitions (100–120 words).**

REVISION Past tense

→ Summary, p. 120

1 Mahatma Gandhi

Copy and complete this text from a history book.

→ led • made • said • used • wanted • was

Gandhi and the British

When India was a British colony, many Indians **(1)** independence. Gandhi **(2)** the leader of the campaign for independence, but he never **(3)** violence against the British.
For example, in 1930 the British **(4)** that Indians should pay them more for salt. What did Gandhi do? He **(5)** thousands of people to the sea, where they all **(6)** salt from the sea, for free! So the British got no money at all.

2 Talking about Gandhi in class. **Write the verbs in the simple past.**

KEVIN What did the British do when Gandhi (**make**) salt?
TEACHER Well, they (**be**) angry, of course. And they (**put**) 60 000 Indians in prison.
ANNA And what (**Gandhi/do**) then?
TEACHER He (**wait**). And in the end the British (**talk**) to him and India (**become**) independent in 1947. The British (**leave**) on 1st January.
THEO I think it's great that Gandhi (**not/use**) violence. But does it always work?

3 Tenzing Norgay

MORE HELP! p. 113

Tenzing Norgay lived in Nepal and India. In 1953 he climbed Mount Everest, the highest mountain in the world. Tell his story, in at least 60 words, in the simple past.

... born in ... lived ... helped ... carried ... snow storm ... couldn't ... at the top of ...

1914–1930

1930–1940

1947

1953

REVISION Questions

→ Summary, p. 122

1 What have you learned about India?

Write the questions. Then write the right answers.

→ Where • What • Who • How • When • Why

1 ... can you travel cheaply in New Delhi? – You can take the Metro / ATM. (p. 41)
2 ... do tourists visit Agra? – They want to see the Taj Mahal / Gandhi museum. (p. 41)
3 ... is New Delhi? – It's in the north / south of India. (p. 36)
4 ... is Bollywood? – It's the name for India's film / car industry. (p. 36)
5 ... did India become independent? – India became independent in 1847 / 1947. (p. 36)
6 ... was Mahatma Gandhi? – He was the Indian leader who often / never used violence. (p. 49)

2 Six weeks in India

Read the dialogue and look at Dave's answers. Then write the cousin's questions.

COUSIN My mum told me that you've just come back from India. How long did you travel there?
DAVE I travelled for six weeks.
COUSIN Wow, that's a long trip! And when (**1**) your tour?
DAVE I started my tour in April.
COUSIN Where (**2**)?
DAVE I went to Delhi and Mumbai, and I also went north to the mountains.
COUSIN How (**3**)?
DAVE I travelled by train or by bus.
COUSIN And what (**4**) best in India, the cities or the mountains?
DAVE I liked the cities best. They're so full of life. They're great.
COUSIN And (**5**) the Taj Mahal?
DAVE Yes, I saw it during the day and at night.
COUSIN It sounds fantastic. But, tell me, Dave, why (**6**) there?
DAVE Well, I went there because I wanted to see a new country. It was a great experience!

3 Quiz questions about India

a) Write the questions. Then look on the Internet and write the answers.

1 where / factory disaster / kill 3000 people / 1984?
2 when / Indira Gandhi / India's first female prime minister?
3 for what sport / India / win / World Cup / 1983?

b) Write at least two more quiz questions about India. Write the answers too.

Slumdog Millionaire/ Oscars

Indirect speech → Summary, p. 124

A teen magazine asked young people: "What's life like for young people in India?"

1 What Kala said

"Life is good! I'm working in a shop in Kolkata this year – I'm earning money for college. I'm living with one of my aunts. I think lots of young people here in India have large families. And everywhere they find an uncle, aunt or cousin who helps them. Next year my brother will be in Britain, and he'll stay with a cousin."

These sentences are wrong. Correct the false information.

1 Kala said that she was living in Mumbai.
2 She said that she was earning money for a trip around the world.
3 She thought that not many young people in India had large families.
4 She explained that her brother would go to France next year.
5 She said that he would stay in a hotel.

2 What Dinkar said

"Thousands of young people here in India work in factories. Most of them make clothes, and many of them earn less than $1.25 a day. But my friends and I are luckier. We all have computers and mobile phones and listen to music on MP3 players."

Complete the sentences in indirect speech.

Tip: Remember to change the tense.

1 Dinkar said that thousands ... worked ...
2 He explained that most of them ...
3 And he said that many of them ...
4 But he said that he and his friends ...
5 He said that they all ...
6 And he said that they ...

3 What Lalit said

"Next year my family will move into a new house. We'll have running water and electricity, and I hope that every person in my family will have a room. Next year, too, I'll try to find work in a big city, but I won't find it easy."

Write what he said. Use indirect speech.

Lalit said that next year his family would move into a new house. He said that they ...

Tip: Write the right form of the verb. Choose the right pronoun.

LISTENING AND SPEAKING

1 Sightseeing in New Delhi

You're travelling in India and it's your first morning in New Delhi.

2 9 **a) You want to visit the Red Fort. Listen to your friend and look at the plan. Is the Red Fort at A, B, C or D?**

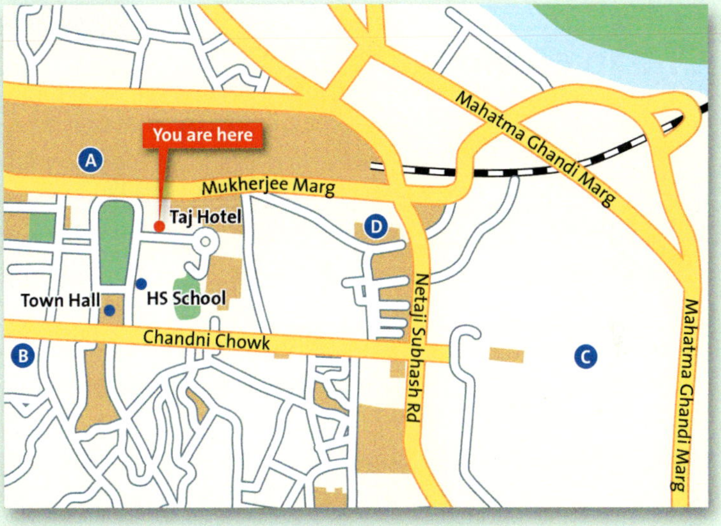

2 10 **b) When you leave the Red Fort, you want to visit the Akshardham Temple. An assistant at the fort tells you the way. Listen and pick the right answers.**

1 When you come out of the fort, **a)** turn left **b)** turn right **c)** go straight on.
2 Turn left again and take the **a)** first **b)** second **c)** third road on your right.
3 Walk straigt on. You go past a large **a)** monument **b)** park **c)** hotel on your left.
4 Turn left when you come to a big **a)** shop **b)** department store **c)** street called Vikas Marg.
5 You then cross over **a)** the railway **b)** the river **c)** a wide road.
6 Take the first road **a)** in front of you **b)** on the left **c)** on the right, and the Temple is in front of you.

2 ROLE PLAY

PARTNER A:

- **Tell your partner the way to the National Museum and Kendriya Bus Station.**
- **Your partner tells you how to go to the India Gate and the International Youth Centre. What are their letters on the map?**
- **Now compare your answers on your partner's map.**

PARTNER B: Go to page 67.

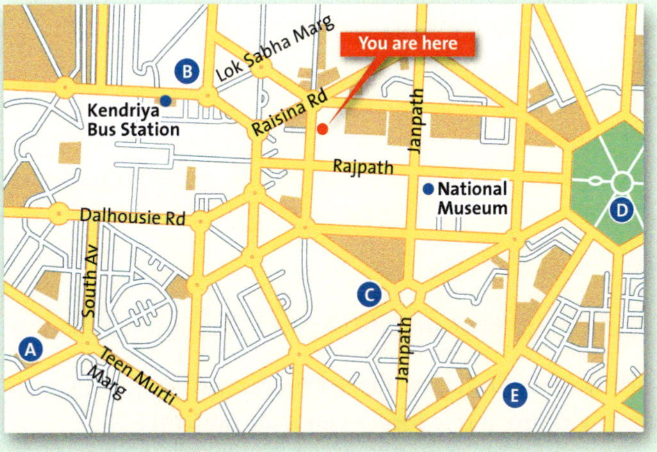

▸ You can find new words in the *Dictionary* (pages 142–168).

READING AND WRITING

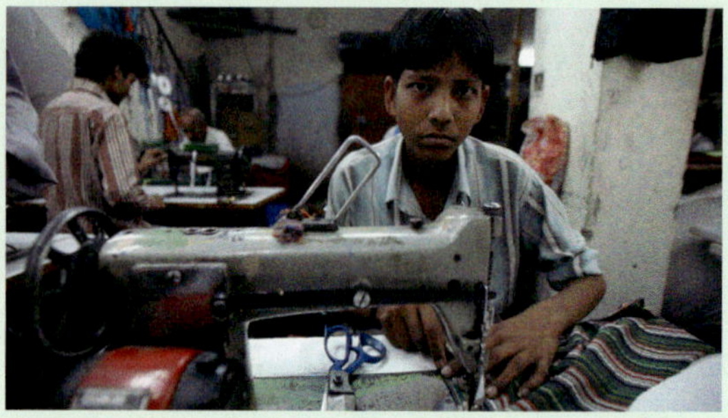

3 Look at the photo. What's often a problem with cheap clothes?

Cheap clothes

Many people like shopping for clothes and enjoy finding clothes with the right style, colour and price. Should they also consider the lives of the people who make the clothes?

Kirsty Elliott (17) laughs a bit nervously when she talks about how she shops for clothes. "I love it," she says. "I love going into shops. I enjoy it even when I don't buy anything." And what does Kirsty look for when she shops for clothes? "The main thing is that it should be something a bit different," she says. "But of course, the price is important too."

Is shopping for clothes a female thing? Not any more. True, Kirsty's boyfriend Josh doesn't shop for clothes as often as Kirsty, but he buys all his clothes himself. "I certainly don't want my mum to buy my clothes for me," he says. "Looks are important. The girls notice what you wear." And the guys too? "Yes, the guys too."

Kirsty and Josh have to be careful with their money, so how can they buy clothes that look good? "If you look in different shops," says Josh, "you'll usually find clothes that look good and that don't cost too much. They're usually made in China or India." And this isn't surprising – 30% of all Indian exports are clothes. Millions of people in India need people like Josh and Kirsty for their jobs – European shoppers get cheap clothes, and Indian workers earn money for their families. It sounds perfect – but is it?

Millions of Indian clothes workers work many hours a day for 15 cents an hour in factories that are dark, dirty and dangerous. And although the law says that children under 14 aren't allowed to work in factories in India, many of the workers in Indian factories are young children – 55 million of them, says the United Nations. Is it fair, say the critics, that people in poor countries have to work in such awful places just so that people in richer countries can have cheap clothes?

The problem is that if you close the factories, people have to find other jobs, where they often have to work even harder and earn even less. Or there's no work at all. In Nepal, where clothes factories closed after campaigns by European critics, the workers became unemployed, or earned money as sex workers. The problem is, say the factory managers, that you can't compare what people earn in India and in Europe. Prices are lower in India, so if people earn a lot less than in Europe, that doesn't mean it's unfair.

Do Kirsty and Josh think about the Indian factories? "Yes, I do," says Josh, "but I don't know what I can do about it. I need cheap clothes." And what about cheap clothes in second-hand shops, or at parties where people exchange clothes? "They're a good idea," says Josh. "But some of my clothes must be new."

4 Are the following sentences *true (T)*, *false (F)* or is the information *not in the text (NIT)*?

1 Kirsty and Josh both buy their own clothes.
2 They often wear clothes that are made outside Europe.
3 More Indians work in car factories than in clothes factories.
4 The text says that people in Europe should not buy clothes that are made in India.
5 Josh says he'll stop buying clothes that are made in poor countries.

5 Pick the right answer.

1 When Kirsty shops for clothes
a) she always buys something.
b) she doesn't always buy something.
c) she's only happy if she buys something.
d) she often finds that the price isn't right.

2 In Josh's opinion
a) clothes are cool for girls, not for boys.
b) it's great if your parents buy your clothes.
c) he should buy clothes as often as Kirsty.
d) other boys notice what he wears.

3 The United Nations says that 55 million
a) children work in Indian factories.
b) people work in Indian factories.
c) factories in India make clothes.
d) children in India are under 14.

6 Finish the sentences.

1 Millions of people in India need people like Josh and Kirsty for their jobs because ...
2 Workers in many clothes factories in India have a hard life because ...
3 But closing factories doesn't always help the workers because ...

7 Definitions

Match the words or phrases from the text (1–5) with the correct definitions (A–H). There are more definitions than words.

1 main
2 female
3 dark
4 awful
5 unemployed

A terrible
B wet
C typical
D without a job
E with no light
F for girls and women
G most important
H stupid

8 A survey for *Fairtrade*

Fairtrade **pays people in poor countries more money for their work. It wants to find out what young people think about clothes. Answer the questions in full sentences. Write at least two sentences for each question.**

FAIRTRADE

1 What sort of clothes do you wear? Why?
2 How often do you buy clothes?
Where do you buy them?
3 What are the most important things for you when you buy clothes? Why?
4 *Fairtrade* clothes are often more expensive.
Would you buy *Fairtrade* clothes?
Why / Why not?

TEST PRACTICE

LISTENING AND SPEAKING

Indian food is very popular in Britain. You can buy it in supermarkets, in restaurants or as take-away food. There are over 8000 Indian restaurants in Britain. One Indian meal, chicken tikka masala, is now more popular than fish and chips.

1 ROLE PLAY

PARTNER A: You and your partner have planned to eat in at the Mahib Indian restaurant. Now he/she tells you how to find it.

- **Listen and make notes so that you can find the restaurant.**
- **Now check that you've understood: Look at your notes and tell your partner the way to the restaurant.**

PARTNER B: Look at your card on page 67.

2 At the Mahib Indian restaurant **Listen and match each food with a picture.**

2 11

A

B

1 Dahi
2 Gosht
3 Kofta
4 Aloo
5 Sabzi
6 Mithai
7 Kulfi
8 Lassi

C

D

E

F

G

H

3 Indian restaurants

2 12 **a) Listen to John. Ask your partner these questions.**

1 Why does John like Indian restaurants?
2 Have you ever tried food from another country? What was it?
3 Do you sometimes eat in restaurants? Why / Why not?

b) Listen again. Your partner asks you these questions.

1 Why does John like to order take-away meals?
2 What's your favourite food? When do you eat it?
3 Can you tell me about a special meal that you once had?

Tip:
Give your partner more details – even if he/she doesn't ask for them.
For example:
- Give more than one reason.
- Don't just say *Yes* or *No*. Say: *Yes, for example ...* Or: *No, but ...*

▸ You can find new words in the *Dictionary* (pages 142–168).

READING AND WRITING

4 Travel experiences

Read the text, then pick the right words for the gaps from the box below.

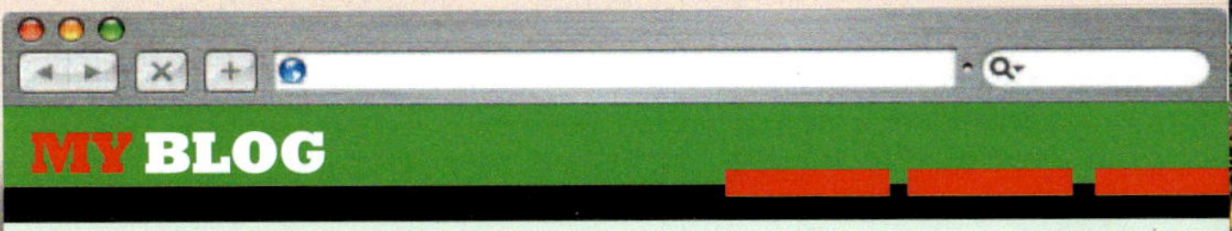

My first day in India
I'm in Chennai ... and wow! Where do I start? I've (1) seen friendlier people, busier and dirtier streets or so much traffic. And it's the first time that I've (2) how rich I am compared with the people around me.

I walked for five hours (3) the city centre today. It was fascinating and very tiring. When I came back to my friend's flat, I (4) a shower and long rest. I can still hear the traffic in the wide street below, the (5) of hundreds of people on their way home from work. The sun has gone down and the lights are on.

It was a good thing that my friend had (6) me that Indian streets are very different from streets back home. So I was prepared for the smells and for people using the street as a toilet. I was also prepared for the colours, the beautiful people and the colourful clothes. Many people wanted money from me, but many more just said *Hello* to me with a big (7) and were happy to see me. It was an awesome experience – full of surprises, a bit frightening, fascinating and very, very wonderful. I'm so (8) that I've come here!

	A	B	C	D
1	usually	always	never	again
2	realized	answered	chosen	received
3	above	through	about	on
4	felt	asked	needed	found
5	voices	faces	clothes	food
6	said	explained	thought	told
7	hand	smile	sign	tooth
8	nervous	afraid	sad	glad

5 AND YOU?

Write about 100–120 words on one of the following topics:

a) Imagine you went to India last year and kept a diary.
Look at the notes and write your diary for two days.
Day 1: arrive at airport • bus to hotel • arrive at hotel • hot – shower • good evening meal
Day 2: wake up • sun • get money • buy suncream • beach • meet nice boy ...

b) "A day of travelling teaches you more than a day at school." Do you agree?

c) When I met an interesting person

REVISION Who, that / Passive

→ Summary, p. 122, 125

1 Inken's youth camp in Wales

Write a better text and make one sentence instead of two.

1 I picked a camp. It was in the west of Wales.
The camp (that) I picked was …
2 I met other assistants. They were very friendly.
The other assistants (who) I …
3 We looked after children. They were 6–9 years old.
4 We did activities there. They were exciting.
5 I saw beaches. They were fantastic.
6 We organized a party on the last evening. It was fun.

- More information about people: ***who***
  The girl who I met was Spanish.
- More information about things: ***that***
  The flat that I saw last week wasn't cheap.
- You can sometimes write the sentences without *who* and *that*:
  The girl I met was Spanish.
  The flat I saw last week wasn't cheap.

2 MEDIATING

Now tell your friend Inken about Dave's experience in a youth camp in Scotland.

"I was in a camp in Scotland for three months and I was quite well paid. All my meals were provided and I had free accommodation. Activities were organized for the children and they were sometimes taken on trips. I went with them and made sure that they were safe. The worst moment was when a child had an accident. A doctor was called and I was asked lots of questions about what had happened. Luckily it was nothing serious and the child was happy again the next day.
This holiday job was a great experience. I can recommend it."

Tip:
was/were can be simple past:
was in a camp = war in einem Ferienlager
was/were can be passive:
was paid = wurde bezahlt

3 An apprenticeship in a motorbike shop

Put the verbs in the passive.

CITY of BRISTOL COLLEGE

Apprenticeships in a motorbike shop

Students **(teach)** *for a few months in college. Then each student* **(train)** *in the shop by an expert who has worked as a motorbike mechanic for many years. All students* **(show)** *how to service and repair motorbikes.*

- *You* **(pay)** *from the first day of your apprenticeship.*
- *An exam* **(take)** *at the end of each year.*

How do you find out more? Visit www.cityofbristol.ac.uk/apprenticeship, call 0117 312 5000 or send an e-mail to apprentice@cityofbristol.ac.uk

REVISION Tenses

→ Summary, pp. 119–122

1 A postcard from the Lake District

a) Choose the right form of the verbs.

Hi!

We're in the Lake District.
Every day we (climb / are climbing) a mountain. Yesterday we (climb / climbed) the highest mountain, Scafell Pike.
But today it (rains / is raining) so we (stay / are staying) at home. We ('ll drive / drove) back home tomorrow.

Hope you're well and good luck in your exams!

Daniel

To
Gr
Lo
12

Simple present (was du öfters machst)
We visit my grandparents every weekend.
Present progressive (was du gerade machst)
I'm staying at home today.
Simple past (was in der Vergangenheit geschah)
I phoned Sue last night.
Future (was noch passieren wird)
I'll leave next week.

2 An e-mail from your cousin Andy

Find the right form of the verbs. Look at the red box above if you need help with the tenses.

Hi!

I hope you're OK.
Today I **(revise)** for my exams. I **(have)** four exams last week and I **(have)** five exams next week! **(you / have)** a lot of school work too? And **(you / have)** exams before you leave school?

Luckily one of my friends **(invite)** me to his birthday last week. We all **(go)** to a pizzeria and after the meal we **(watch)** a horror film. Usually I **(not like)** horror films, but this film was OK. Tell me, what **(you / usually / do)** when you go out with your friends?

I usually **(have)** a Saturday job in a shop, but I **(not work)** there at the moment. When my exams are finished, I **(work)** there full-time and earn some money. Then in September I **(start)** college. What are your plans for autumn and next year? Good luck for your last few weeks at school!

Andy

3 Your answer

Write back to Andy and answer his questions.
Write at least 80 words.
Look at the red box in exercise 1 if you need help with the tenses.

Tip:
- Describe your feelings:
  School will be over on … and I'll be so happy!
  I can't imagine it!
- Give examples:
  I have a lot of school work every evening.
  Last night I worked until … and …

EXTRA PRACTICE

If-clauses (type III)

→ Summary, p. 123

1 Not a good weekend

Match the sentences on the left with the correct ends on the right.

1. If Dad had cooked one of my favourite meals, I would have enjoyed my dinner ...,
2. If my mobile had worked, I would have phoned one of my friends ...,
3. If my homework had been easy, I would have done it in half and hour ...,
4. If it had been sunny, I would have met my friends in the park ...,
5. If there had been a good film on TV, I would have watched it ...,

a. ..., but it was hard, so I had to work until quarter past ten.
b. ..., but he didn't: he cooked some awful vegetables I didn't like!
c. ..., but it didn't, because I was out of credit and I hadn't topped it up.
d. ..., but there wasn't, so I played a boring computer game.
e. ..., but it rained, so I stayed inside.

2 Last summer holiday

a) **Write five sentences:** If I had spent my holiday in India, I would have seen the Taj Mahal.

1 India

(see) the Taj Mahal

But I didn't!

2 South Africa

(visit) a national park

But I didn't!

3 Italy

(enjoy) days on the beach

But I didn't!

4 London

(see) the London Eye

But I didn't!

5 Paris

(climb) the Eiffel Tower

But I didn't!

And who cares? I spent my holiday at home and had lots of fun!

b) **Now write more sentences about different places you could have visited.**

Turkey • Berlin • Ireland • Australia • ... **Who can write most sentences?**

LISTENING

2 19

1 Five short conversations **Listen and choose a), b) or c).**

1 What course does the woman want to do at college?

2 What sort of work is the man going to do in the next few months?

3 Why is the woman a bit nervous?

4 What does the woman want to buy?

5 What job did the man apply for?

2 20

2 Your first day at work in a large office

First read the statements below. Then listen to the people and give the missing information.

1 Work in the office starts at ... a.m. Your lunch break lasts ... minutes.
2 The manager wants to see you in ... minutes in her ...
3 In the next hour you'll hear a ... . You should then go ... the building.
4 Your colleague has a problem with his ... . Please take some packets to the first ...
5 Your train is now about ... minutes late. It will arrive in London only ... minutes late.

▸ You can find new words in the *Dictionary* (pages 142–168).

READING AND WRITING

3 Living at home

a) Read the text, then pick the right words for the gaps from the box below.

More men in their 20s living at home

A new generation of young British men are not leaving their family home until they're well over 24 years old, new statistics show today. Money **(1)** mean that more and more young adults are living **(2)** their parents, with 57% of men and 38% of women between the ages of 20–24 living at home. When they are in their late 20s, more than 20% of men still live with their parents, but less than 10% of women.

What are the reasons **(3)** this trend? One reason **(4)** be that more young people are going to college. Or perhaps young adults can't find any cheap houses or **(5)**.

But Mary MacLeod, chief executive of the *National Family and Parenting Institute*, that has studied the problem, is sure that money is the **(6)** problem. "It's harder to get a job and it's harder to pay for everything," she said. She also said that women often **(7)** away from home because they like to be more independent than men. "Men enjoy the comfortable **(8)** at the hotel of mum and dad, where the washing and cooking is done for them," she said.

	A	B	C	D
1	talks	bags	problems	pains
2	to	with	out	in
3	for	at	from	to
4	should	could	won't	shouldn't
5	flats	cars	clothes	food
6	one	hard	easy	main
7	travel	work	drive	move
8	chair	life	help	money

b) Read the text again and answer the questions.

1 Do *more than half* or *less than half* of all men between the ages of 20 and 24 live with their parents?
2 Give three reasons why young men live with their parents.
3 Do you agree with the opinion in the last sentence of the text? Why? / Why not?

4 Four opinions

a) Read the texts.

Miriam, Brighton

I'm 20 and I'm in my second year at college in Brighton. I live at home in London during the holidays, but my parents want me to pay £15 a week rent for my room, so I have to take a job to earn the money. I think that's unfair, but they say I should learn to pay for things.

Thomas, Newcastle

OK, I know it's not cool to live at home once you're over 20, but why? I'm 23 years old and I have a job. I have a girlfriend, but we're not ready to live together in our own flat. And I enjoy living in my parents' house. So what's the problem?

Lizzy, Sheffield

I'm 22 and still living at home. It's cheaper than renting a room or flat, but I would like more independence. I get annoyed when at the age of 22 my parents still phone me in the evening and want to know when I'll be home. I'm not a kid any more!

Carl, Wolverhampton

When I got married, I lived with my wife for three years in our own flat. But we got divorced this year, and now I'm living with my parents again. A flat just for me would be too expensive – and anyway, I like my mum's Sunday dinner and she washes my clothes too!

b) Answer the questions.

Who ...

1 thinks it's great to live with his/her parents?
2 pays mum and dad for living at home?
3 says that a flat for one person costs too much?
4 once spent a few years away from home?
5 doesn't really feel free?
6 spends part of the year away from home?

c) Finish the sentences.

1 Lizzy is still living at home because ...
2 Thomas is happy at home with his parents because ...
3 Miriam has to work during her college holidays because ...
4 Carl has an easy life at his parents' because his mother ...

5 AND YOU?

Answer the questions in full sentences. Write at least two sentences for each question.

1 Do you want to live at home when you start earning money? Why / Why not?
2 What will you miss most when you move away from home?
3 Some parents want their children to pay them rent if they live at home when they're over 18. Do you think this is fair? Why / Why not?

READING

Woman of the year

Jane Walker, who has just won a *Woman of the Year* award at the age of 45, left school when she was 16 without taking any exams. She had had a difficult time as a child, and at the age of 15 she was earning all the money she needed in order to live. When she left school, she was afraid that other people would look down on her because she had so little qualifications. She thought that she had no future.

Jane first worked for a local newspaper. Then, when she was 32, she went on a holiday to Manila, in the Philippines. It was her first visit there and she went in order to have a relaxing time on the beach, but one day a taxi took her past one of Manila's shanty towns – the areas where very poor people live in primitive houses made of old pieces of wood and metal. She got out of the taxi and followed two children, and they led her to an enormous rubbish tip. Here she saw hundreds of children, some as small as two years old, looking for food in the rubbish. She saw that many of them had their houses in the tip – if you could call them houses. And when the children looked at her, she saw in their eyes a question she knew from when she had been a child: Why isn't anybody helping me?

The visit changed Jane's life. She collected money in Britain and came back to Manila where she opened a day centre where the children could be safe. Then she opened three schools, where the children receive a good education. They can also learn ballet, football, guitar, swimming and singing. She's now building a fourth school, away from the enormous rubbish tip, out of 72 old metal ship containers. Not bad for the girl who thought that she had no future!

1 *True, false* or *not in the text*?

1 Jane Walker did well in her exams at 16.
2 She felt confident when she left school.
3 She first went to Manila in order to help poor children.
4 The taxi driver showed Jane the shanty town because he thought she could help.
5 Many of the children Jane saw lived in the rubbish tip.
6 When Jane saw the poor children in Manila, she remembered her own problems as a child.
7 Jane now lives in Manila.
8 The fourth school is not finished yet.

2 Answer the questions.

1 Why has Jane Walker won a *Woman of the Year* award?
2 Did she have a successful education?
3 What's the best alternative title for the whole article?
a) An unusual holiday
b) Four new schools
c) A hard start shouldn't hold you back.
d) Living in rubbish

3 MEDIATING

Explain the main points of the text for a German friend who is interested in helping poorer countries. Write about 80 words.

▸ You can find new words in the *Dictionary* (pages 142–168).

LISTENING AND WRITING

4 An inspiration

2 21 **a) Listen to the radio show about a person who is an inspiration. Write the missing information.**

Kylie has chosen this person:

Name: Trevor **(1)**

Lives in **(2)**

His radios can be used in places with no **(3)**

They're made in **(4)**

They're good for **(5)**

Trevor left school at the age of **(6)**

radio with handle

b) Listen again. Choose the right options.

1 The person Kylie has chosen **a)** is a doctor **b)** was a swimmer **c)** is ill **d)** comes from Nottingham.
2 Trevor had his idea for the radio when he was **a)** travelling in Africa **b)** watching TV **c)** talking to a friend **d)** listening to the radio.
3 He heard that people in Africa needed radios for information about **a)** health **b)** schools **c)** the weather **d)** food.
4 They couldn't use batteries because they **a)** are bad for the environment **b)** didn't have any **c)** didn't work **d)** cost too much.
5 With Trevor's radio people could **a)** use cheaper batteries **b)** use the sun's energy **c)** make their own electricity **d)** listen only by day.
6 The radios are made by **a)** people who live in villages **b)** disabled people **c)** young people **d)** old people.
7 When Trevor left school he **a)** was unemployed **b)** travelled **c)** worked in his father's factory **d)** worked and went to college.
8 Kylie likes him because he shows that you can make the world a better place even if you **a)** like watching TV **b)** don't travel **c)** don't have a lot money **d)** leave school at 16.

5 AND YOU? **Choose one of the following topics. Write about 100 words.**

- **A great invention**
- **A person who is an inspiration for me**
- **"Qualifications aren't important. Everybody can be successful in life." Do you agree?**

NELSON MANDELA South Africa's famous President

2⊙22

1

Nelson Mandela was born in a small village in 1918. He was the first person in his family who went to school. His African name was Rolihlahla. A teacher gave him the English name Nelson.

2

When Mandela was a boy, white South Africans had all the best houses, schools and hospitals. Black people had to live in different areas where conditions were worse (for example no running water).

3

After university Nelson Mandela worked in Johannesburg. He was a lawyer and he often helped poor black people – even if they were so poor that they couldn't pay him.

4

In 1943 Mandela joined the African National Congress (ANC) that fought for rights for black people. Although the police often shot and killed black people, the ANC didn't use violence.

5

In 1961 Mandela changed tactics. He decided that the white government would only listen if the black people used violence, so he organized attacks against offices, police stations, etc.

6

In 1962 the white government banned the ANC. Mandela and other ANC leaders were sent to a prison on Robben Island – a rock which is seven kilometres away from Cape Town.

► You can find new words in the *Dictionary* (pages 142–168).

2 23

7

On Robben Island black prisoners had to break rocks into small pieces. They had numbers, not names and got less food than white prisoners. But Mandela became a symbol of resistance to the government.

8

In many countries people organized campaigns that supported Mandela. And back in South Africa there was violence and killing in the streets. People said "The future for South Africa is chaos."

9

The pressure was too great for the white government. In 1990 – after 27 years in prison – Nelson Mandela was allowed to come out. For black South Africans a dream had come true.

10

But black South Africans were still poor and very angry about the past and the white people were very frightened. Mandela tried to keep peace between them. For this he won the Nobel Peace Prize in 1993.

11

South Africa had its first free elections in 1994, and Nelson Mandela was elected president. Although the country had enormous problems with crime and unemployment, Mandela was soon popular with black and white South Africans. Mandela was president until 1999.

READING LOG 1

WHEN?	WHAT HAPPENED?
In 1918 ...	Mandela was born ...
When he was a boy ...	...
After university ...	...
...	...

READING LOG 2

What you have learned about Mandela.

I didn't know that ...
I think Mandela got the Nobel Peace Prize because ...
I would / wouldn't have given him the prize because ...

FRIENDS

2 24

Give me a house

Give me a house, said Polly.
Give me land, said Hugh.
Give me the moon, said Sadie.
Give me the sun, said Sue.

Give me a horse, said Rollo.
Give me a hound, said Joe.
Give me fine linen, said Sarah.
Give me silk, said Flo.

Give me a mountain, said Kirsty.
Give me a valley, said Jim.
Give me a river, said Dodo.
Give me the sky, said Tim.

Give me the ocean, said Adam.
Give me a ship, said Hal.
Give me a kingdom, said Rory.
Give me a crown, said Sal.

Give me gold, said Peter.
Give me silver, said Paul.
Give me love, said Jenny,
Or nothing at all.

Charles Causley

2 25

Secret love

Chalked on a wall in the playground
These words inside a heart:
"David loves Susan for ever,
And we shall never part."

But nobody knew, and nobody guessed,
The secret behind what it said:
That Dave was the History teacher,
And Sue was the Deputy Head.

Mike Jubb

READING LOG 1
Write about the text that you like best.

I like ... because it's
funny / amazing / brilliant / different / sad / ...
I like ... because it took me by surprise.
I like ... because it made me think about ...

READING LOG 2
Write your own version of *Give me a house*.

Give me a *computer*, said Freddie.
Give me ..., said Hugh.
Give me ..., said ...
Give me ..., said Sue.

▸ You can find new words in the *Dictionary* (pages 142–168).

2⊙26

SONG You've got a friend

When you're down and troubled,
And you need some loving care,
And nothing, nothing is going right,
Close your eyes and think of me
And soon I will be there
To brighten up even your darkest night.

You just call out my name,
And you know wherever I am
I'll come running to see you again.
Winter, spring, summer or fall,
All you have to do is call,
And I'll be there, yeah, yeah.
You've got a friend.

If the sky above you
Grows dark and full of clouds,
And that old north wind begins to blow,
Keep your head together
And call my name out loud,
Soon you'll hear me knocking at your door.

Now, ain't it good to know that you've got a friend
When people can be so cold?
They'll hurt you, yes and desert you
And take your soul if you let them.
Oh, but don't you let them.

You've got a friend.
Ain't it good to know you've got a friend.
Ain't it good to know you've got a friend.
You've got a friend.

Carole King

SAYINGS

Don't walk in front of me, I may not follow.
Don't walk behind me, I may not lead.
Just walk beside me, and be my friend.

Albert Camus

A true friend is somebody who can make us do what we can.

Ralph Waldo Emerson

READING LOG 3
What's a friend for?

SLUMDOG MILLIONAIRE A film set in Mumbai

2◎27

READING LOG 1
Make notes on Jamal, Salim and Latika when they're children and when they're adults. Write:

- where they live
- what happens to them
- how they feel

What a sensation! Jamal Malik, a young man from the poorest part of Mumbai, has answered all the questions on *Who Wants to Be a Millionaire?* If he can answer tomorrow's question, he'll win an amazing 20 million rupees. Everybody in India is so excited … But the host of the TV show is sure that Jamal has cheated. He contacts the police, who take Jamal to a police station.

The police are sure that a poor boy with no education can't answer quiz questions correctly. They beat Jamal and hurt him, because they want him to say that he cheated. But Jamal insists that he didn't cheat. He says that he has been lucky, he knew the answers because of things that happened in his life. "What things?" ask the police. So Jamal tells them the story of his life …

And this is the story that Jamal tells the police: Jamal's mother was killed when he was a little boy. Jamal now lives with his older brother Salim in a very poor part of Mumbai. They have a very hard life because they have no money, but they agree that they will always help each other.

One day, they find a girl who has no home. She's called Latika. They help her and she joins them.

Then a man called Maman takes the three children to his house and gives them food. But Maman is a criminal. He blinds children and sends them into Mumbai where they have to beg for money in the streets.

Salim, Jamal and Latika run away. The two boys jump on a train, but Latika can't run fast enough and she is left behind. The two boys lose their best friend.

▸ You can find new words in the *Dictionary* (pages 142–168).

2 28

Salim and Jamal travel around India. They steal and cheat to get money, at the Taj Mahal, for example. But Jamal can't forget Latika, and the two brothers go back to Mumbai to find her. They find Latika with Maman, who wants to sell her as a prostitute. They try to save her, but Maman comes home and finds the two boys in his house! They fight and during the fight, Salim takes a gun and kills Maman.

Jamal and Salim live together in Mumbai. Frightened of Maman's gang, Salim starts to work for another criminal, Javed. He becomes violent – and jealous of Jamal's beautiful love for Latika. He throws Jamal out of their home so that he can have sex with her. Jamal is shocked and fights his brother, but Salim has a gun. Latika shouts, "Leave, Jamal – or Salim will kill you." So Jamal leaves, and Salim takes Latika to a different place so that Jamal can't find them.

Again and again Jamal wants to find Latika. One day he finds Salim's new address and the brothers meet. Jamal learns that Latika is now living with the criminal boss, Javed. Jamal gets a job in Javed's house. He finds Latika when she's watching *Who Wants to Be a Millionaire?* He tells her that he loves her and will wait for her at the station every day at 5 o'clock. Latika comes to the station one day, but Javed's men see her. They cut her face and take her away. How can Jamal see her again? He has a mad idea: Latika will see him if he answers questions on the show.

That's Jamal's story. The police officers believe him and Jamal is allowed to answer the 20 million rupee question. Salim and Latika see Jamal on the TV show.
Can Jamal win 20 million rupees? Will Latika leave Javed's house? Can Jamal and Latika be together at last? Watch the film and find out! (Tip: the photo below is the final scene!)

READING LOG 2

Write your reader's diary.

How long did it take you to read this text?
Did you read alone, with a partner or in class?
Was it easy / difficult to read?
Were there many new words?
Did you use a dictionary?
What new phrases / words did you learn?
What parts of the story did you (not) like?
Would you like to see the film? Why / Why not?
What do you think will happen at the end?

2 ◉ 29

HOME | NEWS | MUSIC | SPORT | SCIENCE | BUSINESS

Teenager Power

September 2009

She hasn't got a rich family. She hasn't won the lotto. But at 17, Ashley Qualls, a computer geek from Detroit, has bought a house for $250,000. So where did she get all that money? Well, this amazing American teenager has her own business and she is already a millionaire. Ashley's idea was very simple. Her website, whateverlife.com, offers free designs that teenagers can use for their websites.

Ashley, who is known as "AshBo" to her friends, started to work with websites when she was about nine years old. While other children were watching TV or playing outside, she was teaching herself HTML (a programming language that is used for websites). She loved working with colours and web designs.

In 2004, she borrowed $8 from her mother and bought the web address: whateverlife.com. She didn't want to start a business. She just wanted a website to show her designs to her friends.

But more and more people started to visit the website and download Ashley's designs. After a few weeks, she had 100 visitors. Then 5,000. Now her website has over 3,000 designs and gets between 120,000 and 360,000 visitors a day.

"When I started, I was excited when there were two people on the site and one was me!" says Ashley.

Of course, other companies soon wanted to have adverts on her site and in September 2005 Ashley got her first cheque from a big advertising company, Value Click Media. It was for $2,700. "It was more than I earned in a month," her mother says. That was just the start. The next cheque was for $5,000, the third was for $10,000.

When the first money arrived, her mother couldn't believe it. She wasn't sure if people really could make money from a website. But Ashley was confident from the start. She told her mother, "I'm really sure about this. I think it's really going to happen."

READING LOG 1

What can you say about Ashley?

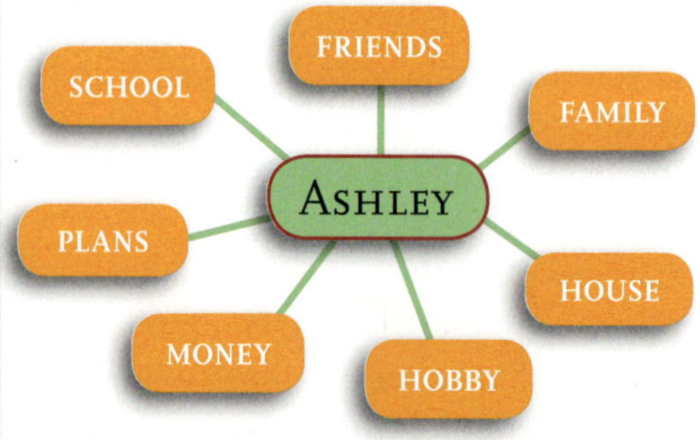

▸ You can find new words in the *Dictionary* (pages 142–168).

2 30

Ashley was an excellent student at school, but when the business got bigger, it was difficult to find time for the business and school. In January 2006, six months before her 16th birthday, she left school. She decided to study from home. "Everybody was shocked," she says. "They asked, 'Are you sure you know what you're doing?' But I had this one chance to do something different."

Most websites for teenagers are designed by adults. When you go to Ashley's site, you see that it was designed by a teenager. Ashley understands what teenagers want. "They look at me and think, 'She's my age, she must know what I like.' "

The business now earns about $70,000 a month. (The designs are still free. The money comes from the adverts.) Ashley is learning how to be the 'big boss'. Her mother now works as her manager and Ashley has a business adviser who helps her too. She also pays some of her friends who work for her after school and at weekends.

It's not easy to be somebody's boss and their friend. Last year one of Ashley's friends was helping her, but Ashley thought she wasn't working hard enough. Ashley says that things were difficult between them for a few days, but now they are friends again. Ashley has strict rules for everybody who works for her. "I tell them I need at least 25 layouts a week," Ashley says. "It's just business."

Ashley had the right idea at the right time, and some people say that she was just lucky.

But she works hard too. "You have to believe in yourself and believe in what you're doing," says Ashley. "These have been the best few years of my life, and also the most stressful … . If people think running a business like *WhateverLife* is easy, they're completely wrong."

Sometimes Ashley misses the normal life of a teenager. More than once she has returned to her old school, Lincoln Park High School, just for the day. Her friends will finish school soon. "I miss school sometimes, and it's a pity that I won't leave school with my friends. They're all excited about the end of school and I won't have that experience."

What about the future? Ashley has lots of plans. "I love doing what I do," she says, and she wants to try some new ideas in her business. She also wants to go to college – perhaps to design school in New York, which she calls her "dream city". But she doesn't want to sell her business. One company offered her one and half million dollars and a car. Ashley likes saying "Yes" to new ideas, but she said "No" to that.

READING LOG 2

Say what you feel about this story. Give reasons for your answers.

Is it interesting?
Is it an inspiration for you?
Do you want to be like Ashley?
Do you have advice for people like Ashley?

Unit 1

→ p. 9

5 AND YOU?

b) Imagine you're Makhaya Ntini as a boy. Read the article and pick the right words.

I live in a small town / village with my parents, brothers and sisters.
We don't have much money and I have some / don't have any shoes.
Every day I go out to the fields / town and look after our village's horses / cows.
It's often very cold early / late in the morning, and when I want to keep my hands / feet warm I stand in fresh, warm / cold cow dung.
Last week something special / boring happened. Some people from England / town came to our village in a big black car. They were looking for children who could throw / work well. I knew that I could do that because I often threw balls / stones and hit the cows' horns.

Well, the people from town were sad / surprised when they saw how I could throw a ball. "You must go to college / an office," they said. "You must / mustn't play cricket every day and one day you will be a terrible / fantastic cricket player. Perhaps you'll even play in the national / village team."

And that's my dream: One day I want to be the first black / white player in our national cricket team.

→ p. 10

2 Starting and finishing conversations

c) Imagine you meet a boy or girl at the cinema. Find the missing words and write the dialogues.

TOM	Do you ... if I sit here?
KAREN	No, it's ...
TOM	Thanks. – Do you often ... to the cinema?
KAREN	No, I'm ... Pretoria. I've come to Cape Town ... the rugby match. My ...'s Karen, by the way.
TOM	And I'm Tom. – Well, let's ... it's a good film!

KAREN	What a great film! I'm so happy that I ... to see it!
TOM	Yes, ... too. But I've ... to go now. It has ... nice talking to you, Karen. Enjoy your ... in Cape Town!
KAREN	Thanks, Tom. See you again some time ...?
TOM	I hope ... You can text me ... 079 274 6087.
KAREN	Take ..., Tom. Let's keep in ...!

→ p. 12

1 Before 1994, life for black people was hard.

e) What do *you* think about apartheid and the life for black people before 1994? Look on page 12 and the green box. Find examples of:

- **what many white people had and most black people didn't have**
- **what white people were allowed to do and black people weren't allowed to do.**

→ taxis • jobs • townships • pass • violence • land • government • sex violence • school • houses • kitchens • running water

Black people couldn't use the same taxis as ...
The police used violence against black people, but not against ...

→ p. 19

6 A terrible holiday

On a holiday in South Africa you stayed in the *Magic Campsite*. It was terrible. Write a letter to the manager, Mrs Petra von Wyk, and complain about these things:

- loud people next to us
- shower dirty and broken
- pool closed in the afternoon
- no fruit or bread in the shop
- unfriendly receptionist

You can use the phrases on the right.

Dear Mrs ...

I want to ...

The people next to us ...

The shower ...

The brochure says that the pool is open all day, but ...

Also, the shop ...

When we complained to the receptionist she was ...

She said that ...

Yours ...

→ p. 69

4 AND YOU? Your town

Prepare a short talk about what you can see or do in your town or village. Use *can, could, must(n't)* and *should(n't)*. The Johannisburg brochure on page 69 can help you.

My town / village

You could go / walk to ...
It's famous / a great experience / ...

You could also visit ... where ...

In ... you should visit ...

You can also see / have a meal in ...

If you love ..., you mustn't miss ...

And you shouldn't miss ...

Unit 2

→ p. 23 **3 AND YOU?**

Do you think adults are often biased against teenagers? Write at least five or six sentences.

a) Before you write, get some ideas:

- **Look again at the exercises on pages 22 and 23 and collect useful phrases.**
- **Complete sentences 1–6 with the words in the green box.**

→ biased • commit • driving • hang around • look • voluntary

1 In the media you often read that young people are loud and ... in gangs.
2 And some people think that teenagers often ... aggressive.
3 But many young people do ... work and help people in hospitals, for example.
4 Some have a weekend job and others have ... lessons.
5 Most young people don't ... crimes.
6 I think that adults are quite often ... against young people.

b) Use ideas from a) and finish the sentences about the police.

I think that the police are quite often biased against teenagers.
The police often think that teenagers look ... and commit ...
But many police officers try to ...
Teenagers are often in trouble with the police if they ...
OK, some young people are loud and aggressive, but many of them ...
On the one hand ..., but on the other hand ...
I think that most teenagers ...
And I also think that ...

c) Now pick another group: the media, teachers, parents, ...
Do you think they're often biased against teenagers? Why? When?
Write at least five or six sentences. Lots of words and phrases in a) and b) will help you!

→ p. 25 **5 AND YOU?**

What do you think about school proms? Prepare a few sentences, then tell the class.
Before you write, get some ideas: Do you like parties? Why / Why not?

I like the music / the food / ...
I don't like wearing special clothes / talking to people / dancing / ...

What's special about school proms?

– Many girls buy beautiful / special / expensive / ... dresses.
– Many boys hire black ...
– The prom is often in a special / big / ... room in a hotel.
– Some people hire a limo and travel to the prom in it.
– It's the last time many students in a year meet.
– Unfortunately the tickets are usually quite / very expensive.

Use phrases for giving your opinion:

I think / In my opinion ...
– that's stupid / a waste of money / ...
– that's great / fantastic / ...
– that's a pity.

Use some of the ideas on page 110 in your answer:

I like the idea of school proms because I like dancing and I also like ...
At a prom the girls often wear ... and the boys ...
The prom is often in ...
Unfortunately the tickets are ...
I think it's a pity that ...
And / But I also think that ...

→ p. 28 **2 AND YOU?**

a) Describe a hobby or activity which you do in your free time.
First read the two model answers. Look at
- **how you can start sentences**
- **how you can give the information**
- **how you can give your opinion.**

My hobby is swimming. I go swimming at a swimming pool near my house.
I go there about once a month, sometimes more often. I usually go alone, but sometimes my brother or a friend comes too – it's more fun with other people!
I enjoy swimming and I always feel much better when I come out of the pool. I can now swim much faster than before, and my friends say that I should take part in competitions. But I don't want to – I prefer doing this activity for fun.

I really enjoy judo. I do judo once a week on Thursday evenings, in a judo club that meets in the gym of a school in town.
I'm the only student in my class who does judo.
Judo isn't easy when you start and you have to practise a lot. But it's good fun and I now have some good friends at the judo club.
Last year I took part in a judo competition. I was quite nervous, but it was very exciting and our team came third out of ten teams. Not bad!

Now describe your own hobby or activity in at least five or six sentences.
Take ideas from the texts above.

→ p. 31 **4 AND YOU?**

b) *Mosquitos* in your town or village: a good idea or not?
Use and finish some of the sentences below. Use your own ideas too. When you've finished your text, give it to a partner – perhaps he or she can give you more ideas.

In my town / village young people often meet outside the cinema / in front of the station / ...
They sometimes talk very loudly / smoke / ...
Some people think that they look aggressive / dangerous / ..., but on the other hand they often help older people / ...
If we had *Mosquitos*, the young people would ... and they would ... . They wouldn't ...
I think it would / wouldn't be fair because ...

Unit 3

→ p. 42 **2 Asking politely**

c) Imagine you're a guest. Ask for the six things in the pictures. Be polite and write a question for each picture.

Is it OK if ...? ... mind if ...?

→ p. 43 **3 Explaining words**

c) Your partner has never heard of these things. Explain them to him/her in English.

A It means that you aren't allowed to ...
B It's what you say before ...
C You ... this when you go out. It tells people like ... who you are.
D You can't go ... Only people who live ...
E It's where you go down if you ...
F On Sundays you can get hot ...
G It's a sort of machine which makes you ... if you ...
H It means that the shop will be ... and that the things are ... here than usually.

→ p. 48

4 AND YOU?

a) Imagine your are the person who told the story. Write an e-mail to a good friend and tell him/her what happened to you at the station and on the train. Before you start, ask yourself:

- **What's the name of the person I am writing to?**
- **How can I start my e-mail?**
- **What were the main parts of the story?**
- **What details can I leave out of my story?**
- **How can I finish my e-mail?**

Hi ... ,

Something really nice/strange/amazing/beautiful/... happened to me yesterday evening when I travelled home from ...

I left the office late because ... and I missed my ...
I had to ... for the next train.
The platform was ... and I ...
And I felt really ... when a woman ...

When my train came, I got into a compartment, and the woman in the burka ...
I closed my eyes because I was so ...
But I woke up when ...
I thought that she wanted to ...
But she said ...

And then I felt ...
And I felt so stupid because I had been afraid of her!
Isn't that a great story?

→ p. 84

3 Tenzing Norgay

Tenzing Norgay lived in Nepal and India. In 1953 he climbed Mount Everest, the highest mountain in the world. Tell his story, in at least 60 words, in the simple past.

1914–1930: Tenzing – was born in 1914 – boy – lived – village – mountains – helped his parents – carried water – when mother cooked.

1930–1940: Tenzing – young man – carried bags – for people – climbed mountains – hard work – enjoyed it.

1947: Tenzing – climbed – Mount Everest – terrible snow storm – cold – couldn't go on – almost died – turned back.

1953: Tenzing – tried again – this time – at the top of – great moment – felt very happy.

Unit 4

→ p. 55

3 New contexts

b) Write your own mini-dialogues. Use these ideas and your own ideas too.

A Great news: We/win/football match/last ...
B Really? Oh that's ... Well ...! I'm so ...

A What's wrong?
B I/go town/by bike. I/have/accident. I/fall/hurt/arm.
A Oh, I'm .... And I ... you'll be OK soon.

A Hey, guess what! I/win/prize. It's a ...
B What? ... you serious? I don't ...

c) Can you make the dialogues longer? Use your own ideas! Then practise them with your partner.

→ p. 59

3 Paul is reading from his diary.

c) Listen to Paul and then answer the questions.

1 Why is tomorrow a special day for Paul? He's going to
a) travel by train for the first time.
b) visit York for the first time.
c) start work that he has been looking forward to for a long time.
d) start a job that he doesn't want to do.

2 Why is he feeling nervous? Because he's thinking of problems like
a) travelling by train.
b) not having a lot of money.
c) being away from his girlfriend.
d) living away from home.

3 What sort of work is he going to do? He's going to
a) look after disabled children.
b) look after disabled adults.
c) work only in the kitchen.
d) work only on a farm.

4 What is he looking forward to? Meeting
a) young British helpers.
b) young people in the nearest town.
c) disabled adults from different countries.
d) young helpers from lots of countries.

→ p. 61

5 AND YOU?

b) What do you like about Mike's, Clare's and Loren's holidays? What don't you like? Why? Which of their holidays would you like best? Write at least 80 words.

1 **First write about one good thing that each person did and add your opinion:**

Mike visited an interesting large city – and I like big cities too. Clare ... Loren ...

2 **Then write about one thing that each person did that you don't like and add your opinion:**

Mike slept on the floor at the airport. I wouldn't like to do that. Clare ... Loren ...

3 **Now say which holiday you like best:**

I like Mike's / Clare's / Loren's holiday best because he/she ...
I'd really like to do that too.
I think that's a good idea.
I'd also like to ... in my holidays.
I've never done that before, but it sounds good and I'd like to try it.
...

Wordbank 1 — Unit 1

African animals

antelope (Antilope)

buffalo (Büffel)

eagle (Adler)

giraffe (Giraffe)

gorilla (Gorilla)

hippo (Nilpferd)

hyena (Hyäne)

jackal (Schakal)

leopard (Leopard)

rhino (Nashorn)

vulture (Geier)

zebra (Zebra)

Wordbank 2 — Unit 1

A holiday in South Africa

WHAT YOU DID

- I made a trip into the country.
- I visited Johannesburg.
- I went to a streetmarket.
- I tried sandboarding.
- I explored a national park.
- I went to a football match.
- I took lots of photos on a safari.
- I went to the desert.

WHAT YOU SAW

- fantastic countryside
- high mountains
- wild animals
- a street entertainer
- sandy beaches
- great sandboarders
- exotic fruit and vegetables
- boys playing cricket
- excited fans

countryside *Landschaft;* desert *Wüste;* exotic *exotisch;* explore *erkunden;* sandy *sandig;* streetmarket *Straßenmarkt;* street entertainer *Straßenkünstler*

Wordbank 3 — Unit 2

Who's where in the picture?

Nate is behind Sam.

Olivia is in the middle.

Olivia is between Joseph and Zara.

Zara and Anna are on the left.

Sam and Nate are in the background.

Joseph is next to Olivia.

Laura, Keira and Joseph are on the right.

Keira is in front of Laura.

Anna, Laura and Keira are in the foreground.

Wordbank 4 — Unit 2

Clothes and accessories

bag, cap, dress, helmet, jacket, jeans, shorts, shoes, sneakers, suit, T-shirt, trainers, umbrella, uniform

put sth. on (etw. anziehen)
take sth. off (etw. ausziehen)
change (sich umziehen)
wear (tragen)
try sth. on (etw. anprobieren)
fit (passen)

Which size do you take?
(Welche Größe haben Sie?)
It fits tightly/loosely.
(Es sitzt eng/weit.)
It suits you well.
(Es steht Ihnen gut.)

Wordbank 5 Unit 3

Working with maps

near / close to ... (bei/in der Nähe von ...)
in the north / south / east / west / northeast / ... (im Norden / Süden / Osten / Westen / Nordosten / ...)
neighbouring countries (Nachbarländer)
... lies to the north / ... of India (... liegt nördlich / ... von Indien)
the river flows from east to west (der Fluss fließt von Osten nach Westen)
the northern / southern / ... border (die nördliche / südliche / ... Grenze)
in the centre (im Zentrum)
... is about 80 km from ... (liegt ungefähr 80 km von ... entfernt)
plain (Ebene)
desert (Wüste)
on the coast (an der Küste)
high mountains (Hochgebirge)
rainforest (Regenwald)
peninsula (Halbinsel)
densely populated (dicht besiedelt)

Wordbank 6 Unit 3

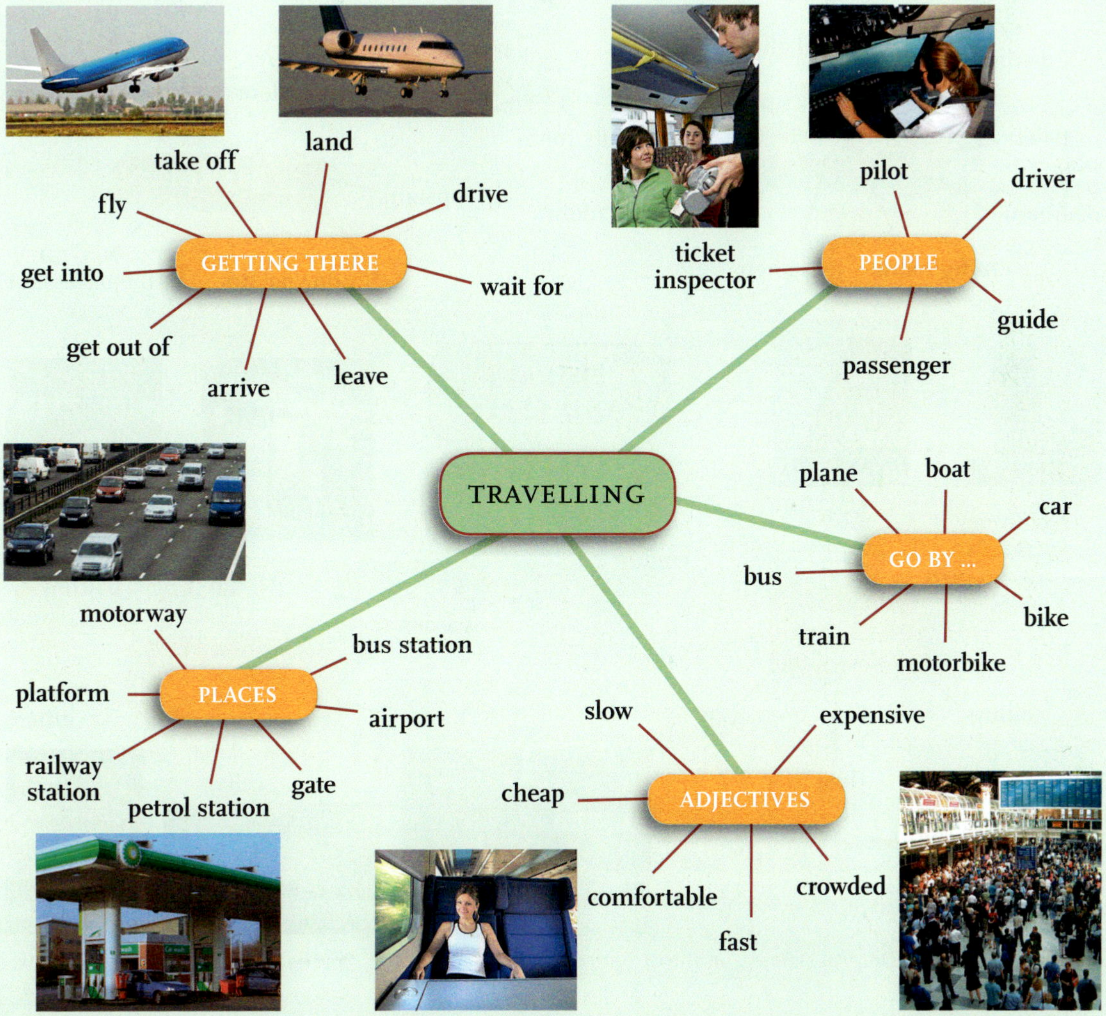

Wordbank 7

Unit 4

The world of work

People at work
colleague (Kollege, Kollegin)
boss (Chef/in)
employee (Angestellte/r)
employer (Arbeitgeber/in)
staff (Personal)
instructor (Ausbilder/in)
trainee (Auszubildende/r)
commuter (Pendler/in)

A good worker should be ...
flexible (flexibel)
hard-working (fleiβig)
punctual (pünktlich)
reliable (zuverlässig)
skilled (qualifiziert)
thorough (gründlich)
able to deal with stress (belastbar)
a teamworker (teamfähig)

Other expressions
work overtime (Überstunden machen)
shift (Schicht)
hire (anstellen)
transfer (versetzen)
give notice (kündigen)
salary (Gehalt)
career (Karriere, Laufbahn)

Wordbank 8

Unit 4

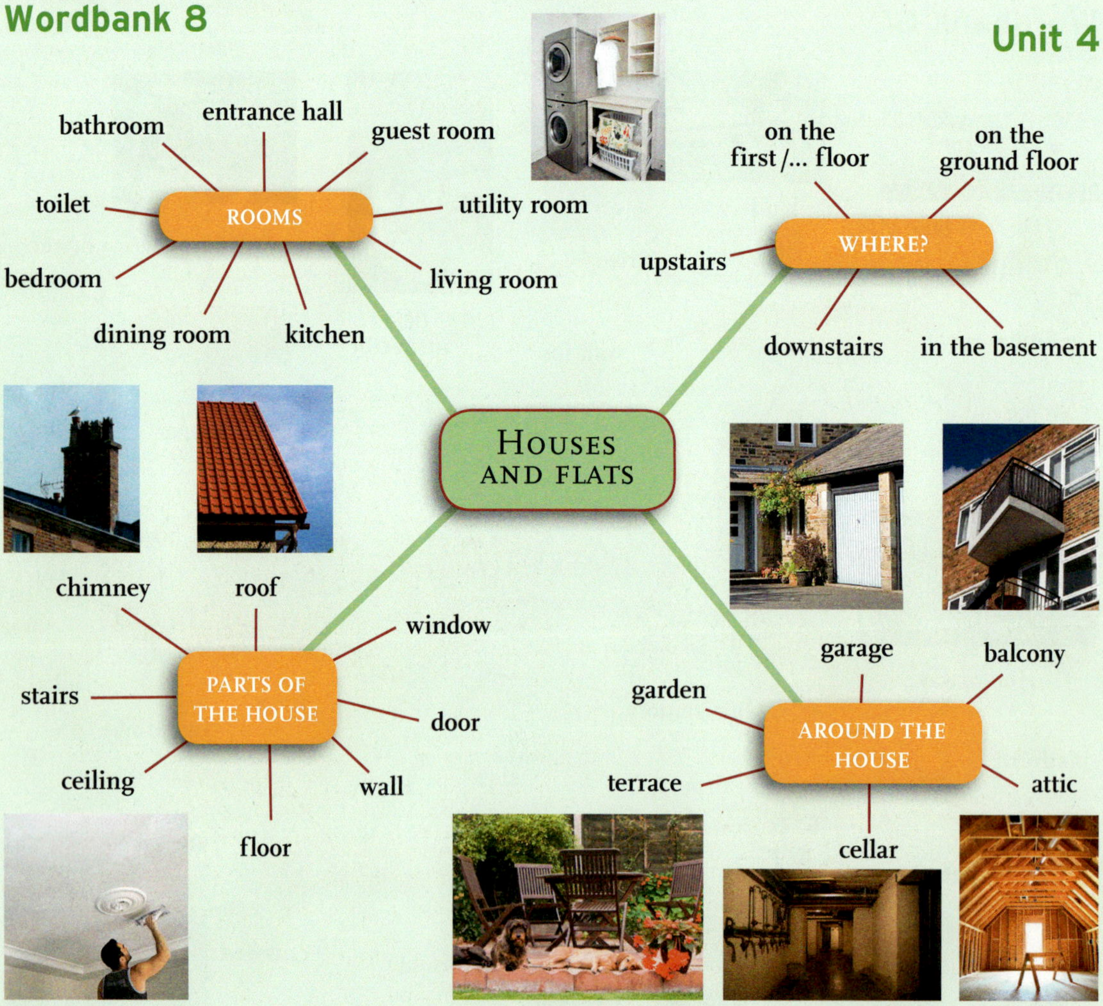

in the basement *im Untergeschoss;* on the ground floor *im Erdgeschoss;* on the first floor *im ersten Stock;* downstairs *unten*

SUMMARY

SIMPLE PRESENT Revision

→ Extra Practice, p. 78, p. 93

Mit der einfachen Gegenwart (*simple present*) sagst du, was jemand immer wieder oder regelmäßig tut.

Bejahte Aussagesätze

I We You	work.
He She	works.

Verneinte Aussagesätze

I We You	don't	work.
He She	doesn't	work.

Fragen

Do	I we you	work?
Does	he she	work?

! Diese Zeitangaben findest du oft in Sätzen im *simple present*:

every day • every Monday • every week • every month • every year • on Mondays • always • usually • often • sometimes • never

PRESENT PROGRESSIVE Revision

→ Extra Practice, p. 78, p. 93

Mit der Verlaufsform der Gegenwart (*present progressive*) sagst du, was gerade passiert.

Bejahte Aussagesätze

I'm You're He's She's We're They're	learning	English now.

Verneinte Aussagesätze

I'm not You aren't He isn't She isn't We aren't They aren't	learning	French now.

Fragen

Is	he she	leaving now?
Are	we you they	leaving now?

! Diese Zeitangaben findest du oft in Sätzen im *present progessive*:

now • at the moment • today

Mit dieser Form kannst du auch sagen, was du planst:

I'm travelling to Australia next week.

SUMMARY

SIMPLE PAST Revision

→ Extra Practice, p. 78, p. 84

Mit der einfachen Vergangenheit (*simple past*) sagst du, was in der Vergangenheit geschah.

Bejahte Aussagesätze

I You He She We They	watched a film yesterday.

Verneinte Aussagesätze

I You He She We They	didn't watch a film yesterday.

Fragen

Did	I you he she we they	watch a film yesterday?

! Regelmäßige Verben haben die Endung *-ed*:

answered, arrived, danced, finished, happened, invited, jumped, missed, needed, organized, visited, worked

! Unregelmäßige Verben haben besondere Vergangenheitsformen:

bring – brought
do – did
drink – drank
eat – ate
forget – forgot
put – put

! Diese Zeitangaben findest du oft in Sätzen im *simple past*:

last year/month/week/Friday
in July/2009
on February 14th
at 3 o'clock

PAST PROGRESSIVE Revision

→ Extra Practice, p. 78

Mit der Verlaufsform der Vergangenheit (*past progressive*) sagst du, was in der Vergangenheit gerade im Gange war.

Bejahte Aussagesätze

I He She	was	reading.
You We they	were	reading.

Verneinte Aussagesätze

I He She	wasn't	reading.
You We they	weren't	reading.

Fragen

Was	I he she	reading?
Were	you we they	reading?

! Ein stummes e am Ende des Verbs fällt bei der *ing*-Form weg:
arrive – arriving come – coming

! Bei manchen Verben wird der letzte Buchstabe verdoppelt:
stop – stopping run – running

PAST PERFECT → Extra Practice, p. 70

Wenn zwei Handlungen in der Vergangenheit passieren, steht die frühere Handlung im *past perfect*.

The class laughed	because the teacher had said something funny.
When we arrived at the cinema	the film had already started.

Das *past perfect* wird mit *had* und dem Partizip Perfekt des Verbs gebildet.

Das Partizip Perfekt von regelmäßigen Verben endet auf *-ed:*
answer – answered
talk – talked
mix – mixed

! Das Partizip Perfekt von unregelmäßigen Verben musst du auswendig lernen. Du brauchst diese Form auch für das *present perfect* und kannst sie in der *List of irregular verbs* (dritte Spalte) auf den Seiten 190–191 finden.
leave – left – left
drink – drank – drunk

WILL-FUTURE Revision → Extra Practice, p. 78, p. 81

Wenn du voraussagen willst, was in der Zukunft geschehen wird, benutzt du *will* oder die Kurzform *'ll*.

Bejahte Aussagesätze

I You He/She We They	'll	go.

Verneinte Aussagesätze

I You He/She We They	won't	go.

Fragen

Will	I you he/she we they	go?

! Will benutzt du auch, um spontan Hilfe anzubieten: Wait, I'll help you.

GOING TO-FUTURE Revision

Mit *going to* sagst du, was in der Zukunft wahrscheinlich geschehen wird.
Es kann um Pläne und Vorhaben gehen oder um etwas, das bald geschehen wird.

I'm going to fall!
Are you going to join the sports club?
He/She's going to do an apprenticeship.
We're going to buy a new car.
They're going to get divorced.

QUESTIONS Revision

→ Extra Practice, p. 85

Für Fragen in der einfachen Gegenwart benutzt du ***do/does*** + Grundform des Verbs.

Do	I we you they	agree?

Does	he she	agree?

Für Fragen in der einfachen Vergangenwart benutzt man ***did*** + Grundform des Verbs.

Did	I he she we you they	agree?

! Das Verb steht in der Grundform, nicht in der Vergangenheitsform:

Did you ~~agreed~~?

Manche Fragen beginnen mit Fragewörtern:

What do you think of bullying?
Why does she do it?
When did it happen?
How did you feel?

Manche Fragen beginnen mit ***can, will, would, should*** oder ***must***:

Can Murat speak Turkish?
Will Merve arrive tomorrow?
Would you like a cola?
Should I take the job?
Must Alina go to the doctor?

RELATIVE CLAUSES Revision

→ Extra Practice, p. 92

Mit Relativsätzen kannst du zusätzliche Informationen über eine Person oder eine Sache geben. Bei Personen verwendest du ***who***, ansonsten benutzt du ***that***.

The people who work there seem very nice.
The job that I applied for is in a call centre.
The flat that I'm looking for should be cheap.

Manchmal kann man im Englischen ***who / that*** auch weglassen.
Im Deutschen geht das nicht.

The job I applied for is in a call centre.
The flat I'm looking for should be cheap.

IF-CLAUSES (Type I) Revision

→ Extra Practice, p. 76

Mit *if*-Sätzen (Typ I) sagst du, was unter bestimmten Bedingungen geschehen wird. Es ist durchaus möglich, dass die Bedingungen noch erfüllt werden.

If I miss the bus, If you talk to your parents,	I'll walk to school. they can help you.
Im Nebensatz (mit *if) steht das Verb im simple present.*	Im Hauptsatz steht *will, 'll, can, should* + Grundform des Verbs.

IF-CLAUSES (Type II) Revision

→ Extra Practice, p. 77

Mit *if*-Sätzen (Typ II) sagst du, was unter bestimmten Bedingungen geschehen würde. Es ist aber ziemlich unwahrscheinlich, dass die Bedingungen noch erfüllt werden.

If I found my dream job, If I had enough money,	I'd be very happy. I'd start my own business.
Im Nebensatz (mit *if) steht das Verb* im *simple past.*	Im Hauptsatz steht *would* (oder *'d)* + Grundform des Verbs

IF-CLAUSES (Type III)

→ Extra Practice, p. 94

Mit *if*-Sätzen (Typ II) sagst du, was unter bestimmten Bedingungen geschehen wäre. Die Bedingung kann nicht mehr erfüllt werden.

If I had known your phone number, If the team had played better,	I'd have sent you a short message. they would have won the match.
Im Nebensatz (mit *if*) steht *had + past participle.*	Im Hauptsatz steht *would/'d + have + past participle.*

Der if-Satz kann auch hinter dem Hauptsatz stehen:

We would have come to the station if you had phoned us.

DIRECT AND INDIRECT SPEECH

→ Extra Practice, p. 86

Sowohl mit der direkten als auch der indirekten Rede kannst du wiedergeben, was jemand gesagt hat.

Hi, everybody! Delta Goodrem is my favourite star. She's a great singer. I often listen to her music. I went to her concert last month. I'll surely buy her new CD.

Direct speech	Indirect speech
Was gesagt wird steht zwischen Anführungsstrichen.	Jemand berichtet, was gesagt wurde.
"Hi, everybody!" said Alex.	Alex said hallo to everybody.
Die Pronomen bleiben unverändert.	Die Pronomen werden oft verändert.
"Delta Goodrem is my favourite star," said Alex.	He said that Delta Goodrem was his favourite star.
Die Verbformen bleiben unverändert.	Die Verbformen werden oft verändert, wenn das einleitende Verb (z. B. *say*, *tell*) im *simple past* steht.
"She's a great singer," he told us.	He told us that she was a great singer.
"I often listen to her music."	He said that he often listened to her music.
"I went to her concert last month."	He said that he had gone to her concert last month.
"I'll surely buy her new CD."	He said that he would surely buy her new CD.

Verschiedene Verben können die indirekte Rede einleiten, zum Beispiel:

say • tell • add • complain

WORD ORDER Revision

→ Extra Practice, p. 68

Häufigkeitsangaben stehen meist vor dem Verb.

We never go away during the holidays.
I usually play football on Mondays.
Dad sometimes works in the evenings.

Bei Orts- und Zeitangaben gilt in der Regel: Ort vor Zeit.

I often work in a restaurant in the evenings.
I play football at the school stadium once a week.
We often visit my grandparents in Turkey in the summer.

CAN/CAN'T/COULD Revision → Extra Practice, p. 69

Mit *can/can't* sagst du, was jemand (nicht) tun kann oder darf.

I You He/She We They	can can't	play football.

Mit *could* sagst du, was jemand tun könnte.

We could go swimming this afternoon.
Could you help me, please?

SHOULD/SHOULDN'T Revision → Extra Practice, p. 92

Mit *should/shouldn't* rätst du jemandem, etwas zu tun oder nicht zu tun.

I You He/She We They	should shouldn't	help him.

MUST/MUSTN'T Revision → Extra Practice, p. 69

Mit *must* sagst du, was jemand tun muss.

I You He/She We They	must	go home.

Mit *mustn't* verbietest du jemandem, etwas zu tun.

I You He/She We They	mustn't	go into the water.

! you mustn't = du darfst nicht

PASSIVE Revision → Extra Practice, p. 92

Mit dem Passiv *(passive)* sagst du, dass etwas mit einem Gegenstand oder einer Person gemacht wird oder wurde. Wichtig ist, **was** passiert ist, nicht wer es gemacht hat.

English is spoken in India.
Helpers are wanted on a sheep farm.
A doctor was called.

Das Passiv wird mit einer Form von *be* und dem Partizip Perfekt des Verbs gebildet.

VOCABULARY

Dieses Wörterverzeichnis enthält neue Wörter des Buches in der Reihenfolge, in der sie im Buch zum ersten Mal vorkommen.

In der eckigen Klammer steht, wie die Wörter ausgesprochen werden.

Ein blauer/roter Pfeil heißt: Schau dir den blauen/roten Kasten rechts an.

Der graue Pfeil heißt: Schau in die rechte Spalte.

In den roten Kästen stehen wichtige Hinweise.

Fette Wörter sind besonders wichtig.

Diese Zahl gibt die Seite an, auf der die Wörter zum ersten Mal vorkommen.

Die blauen Kästen fassen Wörter in Gruppen zusammen. So lernst du sie besser.

perfect ['pɜːfɪkt]	vollkommen, perfekt	far – further – furthest
further ['fɜːðə]	weiter	
make sure (that) ... [ʃʊə]	dafür sorgen, dass ...	→ I'll *make sure* nobody finds out about this.
local ['ləʊkl]	örtlich, einheimisch	
61 **away match** [ə'weɪmætʃ]	Auswärtsspiel	
accommodation [əkɒmə'deɪʃn]	Unterkunft; Unterbringung	
uncomfortable [ʌn'kʌmftəbl]	unbequem, ungemütlich	→ This chair is so *uncomfortable*!
flexible ['fleksəbl]	flexibel	
expression [ɪk'spreʃn]	Ausdruck	→ He used *expressions* that I've never heard
sum up [sʌm'ʌp]	zusammenfassen	sum up – summary

Writing

Das **rote** Sternchen kennzeichnet neue unregelmäßige Verben (vgl. unten).

Dieses Zeichen bedeutet: Aufgepasst!

39 **provide** [prə'vaɪd]	zur Verfügung stellen	→ The car is *provided* by the company.
***cost** [kɒst]	(Geld) kosten	→ I hope he likes it. It *cost* a lot of money.
vegetarian [vedʒə'teəriən]	Vegetarier/in, vegetarisch	→ There's no *vegetarian* restaurant in this town
CV (curriculum vitae) [siː'viː, kə'rɪkjələm'viːtaɪ]	Lebenslauf	→ I have to send a full *CV* with my job applica...
computer programmer [kəmpjuːtə'prəʊgræmə]	Computerprogrammierer/in	
computer program [kəm'pjuːtəprəʊgræm]	Computerprogramm	! *program* = Computerprogramm; *programme* = (Radio-/Fernseh-)Sendung

Schräg gestellte Wörter gehören nicht zum Pflichtwortschatz.

a last-minute decision	*eine Entsc... letzter Mi...*
perfect ['pɜːfɪkt]	vollkomm...
further ['fɜːðə]	weiter
make sure (that) ... [ʃʊə]	dafür sorg...
local ['ləʊkl]	örtlich, ei...

Am Ende jeder Unit ...

... siehst du, wie die drei Formen der neuen unregelmäßigen Verben aus der Unit lauten.

***Irregular verbs**

Infinitive form	Simple past form	Present perfect fo...
hang around [hæŋ]	I hung around [hʌŋ]	I've hung around [...

... kannst du überprüfen, wie gut du die neuen Wörter schon beherrschst – und wie gut du dich an bekannte Wörter erinnerst.

Test yourself

1 Use all the letters and make words. The first and last letters are always right. Write the words in your exercise book.

a) agsevirgse **b)** untneuralftoy **c)** seetyoretp **d)** jenoruy **e)** aufwl **f)** liculky

Do you remember?

Odd word out: One word isn't OK. Write it in your exercise book.

1 voice • ground • rhythm • sound
2 hire • rent • expect • borrow
3 suit • survey • per cent • opinion
4 worried • wet • bored • lonely
5 crime • gym • drugs • litter
6 safe • true • illegal • confident

Unit 1

Lerntipp 1: Mistakes are important

Fehler sollen wichtig sein? Wozu? Um daraus zu lernen!

Schreibe immer, wenn du einen Fehler gemacht hast, den falschen Satz oder das falsch geschriebene Wort auf eine Karte deiner Vokabelkartei (oder auf eine Seite deines Vokabelheftes). Oben drüber schreibst du das Wort **Wrong** und auf die Rückseite (**Right**) den richtigen Satz/das richtige Wort. Nun versuchst du beim Lernen immer zuerst, selbst den Fehler zu finden, bevor du das Kärtchen umdrehst. Viel Erfolg!

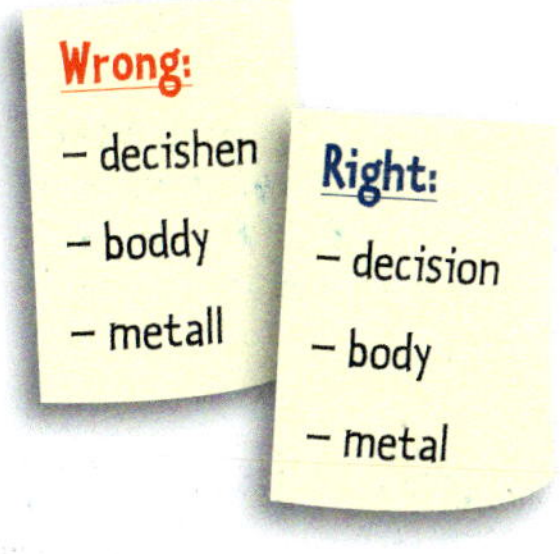

→ nation
national park
nationality

6	**rainbow** ['reɪnbəʊ]	Regenbogen	→
	nation ['neɪʃn]	Nation →	
	South Africa [saʊθ'æfrɪkə]	Südafrika	
	correct [kə'rekt]	richtig, korrekt	→ What's the *correct* pronunciation of 'Cape Town'?
	Cape Town ['keɪptaʊn]	Kapstadt	
	cricket ['krɪkɪt]	Kricket	
	culture ['kʌltʃə]	Kultur	→ Our children learn to respect different *cultures*.
	lion ['laɪən]	Löwe	
	elephant ['elɪfənt]	Elefant	
	tiger ['taɪgə]	Tiger	→ Two *tigers*. 
7	***choose** [tʃu:z]	(aus)wählen, aussuchen	→ We were allowed *to choose* our favourite singer.

Reading

8	**simple** ['sɪmpl]	einfach	→ There's only one rule, but it's *simple*: No alcohol.
	although [ɔ:l'ðəʊ]	obwohl	→ *Although* it was raining, I went to school by bike.
	fight **for** something	um etwas kämpfen	
	during ['djʊərɪŋ]	während	
	***stand: I stood** [stʊd]	sich stellen: ich stellte mich	→ Nobody opened, so I *stood* in front of the door and waited.
	talent ['tælənt]	Talent	
	stone [stəʊn]	Stein	→ Some *stones*.
	***hit** [hɪt]	treffen	→ The player threw the ball and *hit* the goal.
	brilliant ['brɪliənt]	toll, glänzend, großartig	
	give somebody a hug [hʌg]	jemanden umarmen	→ She *gave me a hug* before she left.
	queue [kju:]	(Warte-)Schlange →	
9	**a lot** [ə'lɒt]	viel; sehr	→ Some babies cry *a lot*.
	once [wʌns]	früher	→ My father *once* lived in Ireland.
	organization [ɔ:gənaɪ'zeɪʃn]	Organisation	
	be afraid (of) [ə'freɪd]	Angst haben (vor)	→ I'*m* not *afraid of* spiders. They aren't dangerous.
	already [ɔ:l'redi]	schon	→ We're going on holiday soon. I've packed *already*.
	complete [kəm'pli:t]	vervollständigen	
	full [fʊl]	ganz; voll; vollständig	

→ queue
queue (up)

Speaking

10	**chat** [tʃæt]	sich unterhalten, plaudern	→ We didn't go out. We just *chatted* all evening.
	stadium ['steɪdiəm]	Stadion	
	by the way [baɪðə'weɪ]	übrigens	→ What time is it, *by the way*?
	amazing [ə'meɪzɪŋ]	unglaublich, erstaunlich	→ The meal was really good – and *amazingly* cheap.
	I've got to ... [gɒt]	ich muss ...	
	It has been nice talking to you.	Es war nett, mit dir zu sprechen.	

stay [steɪ]	Aufenthalt, Besuch	→ I ate a lot of chips during my *stay* in England.
See you again some time?	Sieht man sich mal wieder?	
I hope so.	Das hoffe ich.	→ Can you come to Mick's party? – *I hope so.*
text me **on** 071...	schick mir eine SMS unter 071...	
Take care. [teɪ'keə]	Mach's gut.	
Let's keep in touch. [ki:pɪn'tʌtʃ]	Wir hören voneinander. *(Lass uns in Verbindung bleiben.)*	
seat [si:t]	Sitz, Platz →	→ Excuse me, is that *seat* free?
11 **allow** [ə'laʊ]	erlauben, gestatten, zulassen	→ The people here don't *allow* dogs in their restaurant.

→ sit
seat

Listening

12 **grandchildren** ['græntʃɪldrən]	Enkelkinder	
running water	fließendes Wasser	
pass [pɑ:s]	Ausweis	
13 **kwaito** ['kwaɪtəʊ]	Kwaito *(südafrikanische Musikrichtung)*	
choir ['kwaɪə]	Chor	→ I'm singing in the church *choir*.
virus ['vaɪrəs]	Virus	
accent ['æksənt]	Akzent	
sick [sɪk]	krank →	→ The *sick* boy was taken to hospital.
clinic ['klɪnɪk]	Klinik	
have a test	einen Test machen lassen	
be HIV positive ['pɒzətɪv]	HIV-positiv sein	→ The little boy is very ill. He*'s HIV positive.*

→ ill
sick
healthy

Project

14 *Blacks/Whites*	Schwarze/Weiße	
massacre ['mæsəkə]	Massaker	
riot ['raɪət]	Aufstand	
World Cup [wɜ:ld'kʌp]	(Fußball-)Weltmeisterschaft	
president ['prezɪdənt]	Präsident/in	
coloured ['kʌləd]	Farbige/r *(Südafrikaner/in mit schwarzen und weißen Vorfahren)*	
Table Mountain ['teɪblmaʊntən]	Tafelberg	→ The *Table Mountain* near Cape Town.
wildlife ['waɪldlaɪf]	Wildtiere und -pflanzen	
poverty ['pɒvəti]	Armut	
15 *give a talk*	einen Vortrag halten	
do research [rɪ'sɜ:tʃ]	Forschung betreiben, forschen	
necessary ['nesəsəri]	notwendig, nötig	
extra ['ekstrə]	extra, zusätzlich	
sandboard ['sændbɔ:d]	sandboarden	
national anthem [næʃnəl'ænθəm]	Nationalhymne	
keyword ['ki:wɜ:d]	Stichwort	

Training

16	**warning (against)** ['wɔːnɪŋ]	Warnung (vor)	
	zoo [zuː]	Zoo	
	***lie** [laɪ]	liegen	
	keyword ['kiːwɜːd]	Schlüsselwort; Stichwort	

Writing

18	**order** ['ɔːdə]	bestellen	→ We'd like *to order* two cups of coffee, please.
	informal [ɪn'fɔːml]	formlos, informell, „locker"	
	a few [ə'fjuː]	ein paar	→ I've invited *a few* people.
	broken ['brəʊkən]	kaputt, zerbrochen	→ My favourite cup is *broken*. Can you fix it?
	screen [skriːn]	Bildschirm	
	damaged ['dæmɪdʒd]	beschädigt	
	power cable ['paʊəkeɪbl]	Stromkabel	
	replacement [rɪ'pleɪsmənt]	Ersatz	→ They'll send a *replacement* for the damaged camera.
	memory card ['memərikɑːd]	Speicherkarte	
	receive [rɪ'siːv]	erhalten, bekommen	
	let me know	geben Sie mir Bescheid	→ Please *let me know* when you're arriving.
	asap (= **a**s **s**oon **a**s **p**ossible) [eɪeseɪ'piː]	so bald wie möglich	→ The plumber said he'd come *asap*.
	shower ['ʃaʊə]	Dusche	
	Also, ... ['ɔːlsəʊ]	Außerdem ...	
19	**keyboard** ['kiːbɔːd]	Tastatur	→
	mouse [maʊs]	(Computer-)Maus	→
	visit ['vɪzɪt]	Besuch	
	campsite ['kæmpsaɪt]	Campingplatz, Zeltplatz	
	unfriendly [ʌn'frendli]	unfreundlich →	

→ friendly – **un**friendly
happy – **un**happy
healthy – **un**healthy

Look at language

20	**force** [fɔːs]	zwingen	
	artist ['ɑːtɪst]	Künstler/in →	→ My friend is an *artist*. He's a singer.
	act [ækt]	(in einem Film/Theaterstück) spielen →	
	foreign language ['fɒrən]	fremdsprachig; Fremdsprache	→ I never watch *foreign language* films. I don't speak any *foreign languages*.
	action ['ækʃn]	Handlung	
	past perfect [pɑːst'pɜːfɪkt]	vollendete Vergangenheit	

→ art
artist

→ act
actor
role

Test yourself

21	**president** ['prezɪdənt]	Präsident/in	→ Katie is *president* of an international students' organization.

* Irregular verbs

Infinitive form	Simple past form	Present perfect form
choose [tʃuːz]	I chose [tʃəʊz]	I've chosen ['tʃəʊzn]
hit [hɪt]	I hit [hɪt]	I've hit [hɪt]
lie [laɪ]	I lay [leɪ]	I've lain [leɪn]
stand [stænd]	I stood [stʊd]	I've stood [stʊd]

Test yourself

1 That's wrong! The orange letters show you a mistake in the spelling of the words. Write all words in their correct spelling in your exercise book.
a) chooze b) simpel c) alredy d) stadiom e) chior f) informall g) recieve

2 Which word rhymes with ... ? Find the rhyme word and write it in your exercise book.
1 queue: a) sure b) zoo c) toy
2 seat: a) campsite b) quiet c) complete
3 accent: a) brilliant b) island c) understand
4 allow: a) rainbow b) cow c) although

3 Odd word out: One word isn't OK. Write it in your exercise book.
1 state • country • map • nation
2 hit • meet • throw • miss
3 speak • talk • chat • choose
4 artist • actor • action • singer

Do you remember?
Write two lists in your exercise book: a) Descriptions; b) Sports words.
brave • competition • dirty • frightened • hit • match • player • poor • self-confident • soccer • stressed • surprised • team • throw • unemployed • win

Are your answers right? Check on page 193.

Tipp:
Schau dir die vorangegangenen Wortlisten gut an.

Unit 2

Lerntipp 2: Einsprachige Wörterbücher

Keine Angst vor einsprachigen Wörterbüchern! Sie geben dir wertvolle Hinweise für den Umgang mit unbekannten (oder bekannten) Wörtern – wenn du weißt, wie du sie „lesen" musst. Schau dir diese Erläuterungen an:

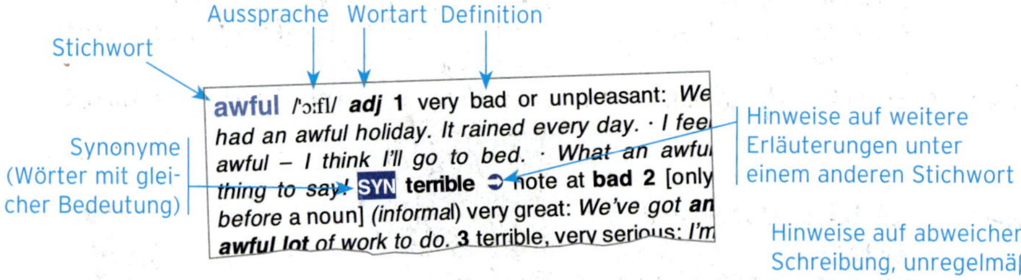

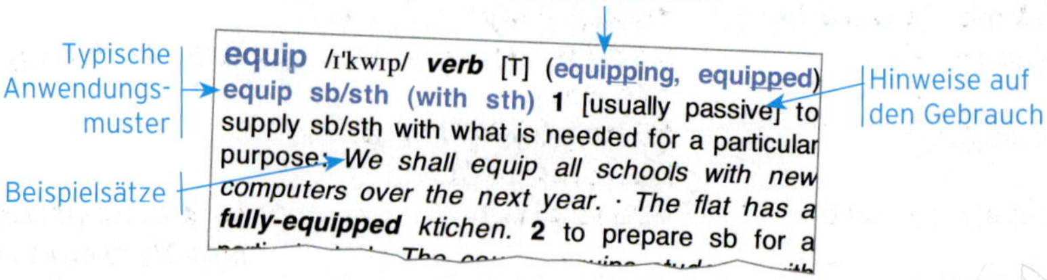

adj = adjective
T = transitive verb
sb = somebody
sth = something

Jetzt weißt du, ob folgende Aussagen richtig oder falsch sind:
(1) The word *awful* is an adjective. (2) It means "very nice". (3) Its synonym is "informal".
(4) The simple past of *equip* is "equiped". (5) You often use *equip* in the passive.
(Lösungen S.193)

22	**teenage ...** ['ti:neɪdʒ]	Teenager-	→ My friend works as a *teenage* model.
	kick [kɪk]	Kick, Hochgefühl	→ Some people get a *kick* from driving fast cars.
	question ['kwestʃən]	verhören; befragen	→ The police *questioned* the shoplifter.
	be biased against somebody ['baɪəst]	gegen jemanden voreingenommen sein	→ Doctors shouldn't *be biased against* obese people.
	quite [kwaɪt]	ziemlich, recht	→ Your brother sings *quite* well.
	relaxed [rɪ'lækst]	entspannt	
	aggressive [ə'gresɪv]	aggressiv, angriffslustig	
	provocative [prə'vɒkətɪv]	provozierend, herausfordernd	→ When the team got out of the bus, the fans shouted *provocative* things.
	***hang around** [hæŋə'raʊnd]	herumhängen	
	driving lesson ['draɪvɪŋlesn]	Fahrstunde	
	voluntary ['vɒləntri]	freiwillig; ehrenamtlich →	
23	**main ...** [meɪn]	Haupt-	→ Don't ride your bike on *main* roads.
	commit a crime [kə'mɪt]	ein Verbrechen begehen	→ The boy *had* never *committed* a crime before.

→ voluntary
volunteer

Speaking

24	**I'd love to ...**	ich würde sehr gern ...	→ *I'd love to* travel to Scotland one day.
	unfortunately [ʌn'fɔ:tʃənətli]	leider; unglücklicherweise	→ We had a great weekend. *Unfortunately*, the weather wasn't very good.
	That's a pity. ['pɪti]	Das ist schade.	
	I change my mind [maɪnd]	ich ändere meine Meinung	→ Good news! My mum *changed her mind*. I'm allowed to go to the concert.
	You must be joking. ['dʒəʊkɪŋ]	Du machst wohl Witze.	
	dress [dres]	Kleid	
	Come on!	Komm schon!	
	kind [kaɪnd]	nett, freundlich	
	anyway ['eniweɪ]	sowieso, ohnehin	→ I could take your letter if you like. I'm going to the post office *anyway*.
	barbecue ['bɑ:bɪkju:]	Grill; Grillfest	
	react (to) [ri'ækt]	reagieren (auf)	
25	**limo** ['lɪməʊ]	Luxuslimousine	→
	either ... or ['aɪðə]	entweder ... oder	→ *Either* we'll walk *or* we'll call a taxi.
	excuse [ɪk'skju:s]	Entschuldigung, Ausrede, Vorwand	→ I'm sorry I'm late. I had to phone my friend. – That's *no excuse*!
	I'm not **able to** come ['eɪbl]	ich kann nicht kommen	→ I *was able to* read when I was five years old.

Reading

26	**stereotype** ['steriətaɪp]	Stereotyp, Klischee(vorstellung)	
	hoody ['hʊdi]	Kapuzensweatshirt/-jacke	→ Two *hoodies*.
	customer ['kʌstəmə]	Kunde/Kundin	
	inside [ɪn'saɪd]	(nach) drinnen; in; innerhalb (von)	→ There are two keys *inside* the box.
	owner ['əʊnə]	Besitzer/in, Eigentümer/Eigentümerin →	
	probably ['prɒbəbli]	wahrscheinlich	→ Look at the clouds. You'll *probably* need an umbrella.
	link (to/with) [lɪŋk]	in Verbindung bringen (mit); verbinden (mit)	→ The video cameras *are linked to* a computer.
	cannabis ['kænəbɪs]	Haschisch	
	below [bɪ'ləʊ]	unter, unterhalb (von); unten	→ Don't write *below* the red line on the form.

→ owner
manager
shop assistant
customer

27	**carefully** ['keəfli]	sorgfältig, aufmerksam	→ Always listen *carefully* to the announcements.
	argument ['ɑːgjumənt]	Argument	→ ! *argument* = (1) Argument; (2) Streit

Listening

28	**hike** [haɪk]	Wanderung	
	take part (in) [teɪk'pɑːt]	teilnehmen (an), mitmachen (bei)	→ How many countries *took part in* the last Olympics?
	rucksack ['rʌksæk]	Rucksack	
	carry ['kæri]	tragen	→ I *carried* the baby in my arms.
	sleeping bag ['sliːpɪŋbæg]	Schlafsack	
	journey ['dʒɜːni]	Fahrt, Reise	
29	**mosquito** [məs'kiːtəʊ]	Stechmücke, Moskito	→ 
	horrible ['hɒrəbl]	scheußlich →	
	statement ['steɪtmənt]	Aussage	
	while [waɪl]	während	→ You could lay the table *while* I'm cooking.
	outside [aʊt'saɪd]	außerhalb (von), vor	→ Let's meet *outside* the cafe.

→ **-ble**
cable
horrible
miserable
responsible
terrible
trouble

Reading

30	**roof** [ruːf]	Dach	→ I have to work on *roofs* in my job.
	can [kæn]	Dose, Büchse	→ Let's buy two *cans* of cola.
	ordinary ['ɔːdnri]	normal, gewöhnlich	
	awful ['ɔːfl]	furchtbar, schrecklich	→ ! *awful* = furchtbar; *awesome* (AE) = toll
	suppose [sə'pəʊz]	annehmen, vermuten	→ A new laptop is quite expensive, I *supppose*.
	conditions [kən'dɪʃnz]	Verhältnisse, Zustände	
	luckily ['lʌkɪli]	glücklicherweise	→ We were a bit late. *Luckily*, the train was late too.
	national ['næʃnəl]	national, landesweit	→ I took part in a *national* music competition.
	it's called ... [kɔːld]	er/sie/es heißt ...	→ The band's new song *is called* "Love".
	support [sə'pɔːt]	unterstützen	→ The organization *supports* sick African children.
	tonight [tə'naɪt]	heute Nacht, heute Abend	→ Are you going out *tonight*?
31	**ban** [bæn]	verbieten	→ The government *banned* smoking in city centres.
	scandal ['skændl]	Skandal	
	real ['riːəl]	wahr, echt, richtig	→ I'm blonde now, but my *real* hair colour is red.
	answer (to a problem)	Lösung (eines Problems)	→ There's no easy *answer to* this problem.
	grey [greɪ]	grau	

Writing

32	**detail** ['diːteɪl]	Detail, Einzelheit	
	railway station ['reɪlweɪsteɪʃn]	Bahnhof	
33	**realize** ['riːəlaɪz]	erkennen, feststellen	→ I woke up and *realized* it had all been a dream.
	direct speech [də'rekt'spiːtʃ]	direkte Rede	
	half an hour [hɑːfən'aʊə]	eine halbe Stunde	→ The programme starts *half an hour* later today.
	task [tɑːsk]	Aufgabe	
	on	über	→ I wrote a report *on* "Students and their pets".
	make up [meɪk'ʌp]	erfinden, sich ausdenken	→ The story isn't really true. I *made* it *up*.

→ driving lessons
driving test

Look at language

34	**driving test** ['draɪvɪŋtest]	Führerscheinprüfung →	
	actually ['æktʃuəli]	eigentlich	→ The food at the party was *actually* quite nice.
	pass [pɑːs]	bestehen	
	enough [ɪ'nʌf]	genug	→ Is there *enough* room for two in the little tent?
	insurance [ɪn'ʃʊərəns]	Versicherung	
	positive ['pɒzətɪv]	positiv	
	negative ['negətɪv]	negativ	→ Some teenagers react very *negatively* to stress.

*Irregular verbs

Infinitive form	Simple past form	Present perfect form
hang around [hæŋ]	I hung around [hʌŋ]	I've hung around [hʌŋ]

Test yourself

1 Use all the letters and make words. The first and last letters are always right. Write the words in your exercise book.
a) agsevirgse **b)** untneuralftoy **c)** seetyoretp **d)** jenoruy **e)** aufwl **f)** liculky

2 Opposites: Find the opposites and write them in your exercise book.

1 nervous – ...
2 luckily – ...
3 ... – unkind
4 above – ...
5 inside – ...
6 ... – negative

3 What's right, a) or b)? Write the answers in your exercise book.

1 If you do 'voluntary' work, you **a)** *receive* or **b)** *don't receive* money for it.
2 If you say 'That's a pity', you think something is **a)** *fun* or **b)** *sad*.
3 If you say you'll 'probably' come, you mean you might **a)** *come* or **b)** *not come*.
4 If something is 'awful', it's **a)** *great* or **b)** *horrible*.
5 If you 'support' people, you **a)** *help* them or you **b)** *think about* them.

Do you remember?

Odd word out: One word isn't OK. Write it in your exercise book.

1 voice • ground • rhythm • sound
2 hire • rent • expect • borrow
3 suit • survey • per cent • opinion
4 worried • wet • bored • lonely
5 crime • gym • drugs • litter
6 safe • true • illegal • confident

Are your answers right? Check on page 193.

Tipp:
Schau dir die vorangegangenen Wortlisten gut an.

Unit 3

Lerntipp 3: Nachschlagespiele

Am meisten Spaß machen diese Spiele, wenn man daraus einen Wettbewerb macht, aber natürlich kann man sie auch allein spielen. Je öfter ihr spielt, desto schneller könnt ihr schließlich Wörter nachschlagen!

1 Bringt 10 Wörter in die richtige alphabetische Reihenfolge, z.B. *mouse, roof, positive, biased, mosquito, young, space, while, enough, stadium.*

2 Entscheidet schnell, welches von 2 Wörtern in einer alphabetischen Liste zuerst kommt, z.B. *national or nation? warning or virus? soldier or slow? tonight or touch? unfriendly or unfortunately? spring or spread?*

3 Nummeriert 10 Wörter, die mit dem gleichen Anfangsbuchstaben beginnen, von 1–10 nach ihrer alphabetischen Abfolge, z.B. *although, artist, action, accent, aggressive, argument, amazing, actually, act, already.*

(Lösungen s. S. 193.)

Tipp:
Schreibe dir das Alphabet auf und lege den Zettel daneben.

ABC DEFGH
IJKLMN
OPQRST
UVW
XYZ

36	**India** [ˈɪndiə]	Indien	
	New Delhi [njuːˈdeli]	Neu-Delhi	
	large [lɑːdʒ]	groß	→ There's a *large* number of people outside.
	industry [ˈɪndəstri]	Industrie	
	rupee [ruːˈpiː]	Rupie →	
	note [nəʊt]	Geldschein	→ Sorry, I only have a £20 *note*.
	independence [ɪndɪˈpendəns]	Unabhängigkeit	
37	**monument** [ˈmɒnjumənt]	Denkmal	
	billion [ˈbɪljən]	Milliarde	→ A *billion* is 1,000,000,000.
	millionaire [mɪljəˈneə]	Millionär/in	
	official language [əfɪʃlˈlæŋgwɪdʒ]	Amtssprache	→ Mexico's *official language* is Spanish.
	religion [rɪˈlɪdʒən]	Religion, Glaube	
	Indian [ˈɪndiən]	indisch; Inder/in	→ Did you know that Paul's girlfriend is *Indian*?
	the second largest/...	der/die/das zweitgrößte/...	→ I think this is *the second* best CD by this singer.
	factfile [ˈfæktfaɪl]	Faktensammlung	

→ **Money**
dollar
euro
pound
rand
rupee

Reading

38	**get married** [getˈmærɪd]	heiraten →	→ Tom and Sue *got married* in May.
	marriage [ˈmærɪdʒ]	Ehe →	
	(very) much [mʌtʃ]	sehr	
39	**provide** [prəˈvaɪd]	zur Verfügung stellen	→ The car *is provided* by the company.
	***cost** [kɒst]	(Geld) kosten	→ I hope he likes it. It *cost* a lot of money.
	vegetarian [vedʒəˈteəriən]	Vegetarier/in, vegetarisch	→ There's no *vegetarian* restaurant in this town.
	CV (curriculum vitae) [siːˈviː, kəˈrɪkjələmˈviːtaɪ]	Lebenslauf	→ I have to send a full *CV* with my job application.
	computer programmer [kəmpjuːtəˈprəʊgræmə]	Computerprogrammierer/in	
	computer program [kəmˈpjuːtəprəʊgræm]	Computerprogramm	→ ! *program* = Computerprogramm; *programme* = (Radio-/Fernseh-)Sendung

→ be married
get married
marriage
wedding

Listening

40	**passenger** [ˈpæsɪndʒə]	Fahrgast, Passagier/in	
	attention [əˈtenʃn]	Beachtung	→ I didn't give the problem enough *attention*.
	at all times	jederzeit, immer	
	taken [ˈteɪkən]	besetzt, belegt	→ Excuse me, is this seat *taken*? – No, it's free.
	stand clear (of ...) [klɪə]	zurücktreten (von ...)	
	included (in the price) [ɪnˈkluːdɪd]	(im Preis) enthalten	
41	**a sort of ...** [sɔːt]	eine Art ...	
	motor [ˈməʊtə]	Motor	
	wheel [wiːl]	Rad	
	***build: I built** [bɪld, bɪlt]	bauen: ich baute	→ This tower *was built* in 1889.

Speaking

42	**top up a mobile** [tɒpˈʌp]	Handy-Guthaben aufladen	
	I'm out of credit. [ˈkredɪt]	Ich habe kein Guthaben mehr auf meinem Handy.	
	cash machine [ˈkæʃməʃiːn]	Geldautomat	
	bank account [ˈbæŋkəkaʊnt]	Bankkonto	
	ATM [eɪtiːˈem]	Geldautomat	→ The queue at the *ATM* was simply awful!
	have a shower [ˈʃaʊə]	duschen	
	yogurt [ˈjɒgət]	Jogurt	

	mango, mangoes ['mæŋgəʊ, 'mæŋgəʊz]	Mango, Mangos	
	I'm thirsty ['θɜ:sti]	ich habe Durst	→ I'm not hungry, but *I'm* really *thirsty*.
	fizzy ['fɪzi]	sprudelnd	
	change money	Geld wechseln, Geld umtauschen	→ Before you go to Canada, you should *change* some *money* at the bank.
43	**I can't think of the right word.**	Mir fällt das richtige Wort nicht ein.	→ *I can't think of the right word* at the moment. It's a sort of machine for making normal water fizzy.
	gas [gæs]	Gas	
	typical ['tɪpɪkl]	typisch	→ The weather isn't *typical* for spring. It's too hot.

Writing

44	**Who with?**	Mit wem?	→ I'm going to the prom next week. – *Who with?*
	***fly** [flaɪ]	fliegen	
	if-clause ['ɪfklɔ:z]	If-Satz	
	give an opinion	eine Meinung abgeben	
45	**clear** [klɪə]	deutlich	

Reading

46	**miss** [mɪs]	versäumen, verpassen	→ Although I ran, I *missed* the bus.
	empty ['empti]	leer	
	stairs [steəz]	Treppe	→ The children came down the *stairs* to say hello.
	almost ['ɔ:lməʊst]	fast, beinahe	→ Oh no – the bag of crisps is *almost* empty!
	husband ['hʌzbənd]	Ehemann	
	sit down	sich (hin)setzen	→ Hello, Mr Fox. Please come in and *sit down*.
	peaceful ['pi:sfl]	friedlich	
	look around	sich umschauen	→ We got out of the car and *looked around*.
	thick [θɪk]	dick	
	bomb [bɒm]	Bombe	→ ! *bomb* [bɒm], climb [klaɪm]
	explode [ɪk'spləʊd]	explodieren	
47	**knife, knives** [naɪf, naɪvz]	Messer →	
	criminal ['krɪmɪnl]	Verbrecher/in, Kriminelle/r	
	I don't mind. [maɪnd]	Das ist mir egal.	→ Her parents were angry, but *she didn't mind*.
	dark [dɑ:k]	dunkel	
	I want to **thank you for being** with me.	Ich möchte Ihnen dafür danken, dass Sie bei mir waren.	→ He *thanked everybody for coming* to his party.
	I can't help laughing.	Ich kann nicht anders, ich muss lachen.	→ The film was so frightening, *they couldn't help* screaming.
	star [stɑ:]	Stern	
	***shine** [ʃaɪn]	scheinen, glänzen	→ The sun *is shining* brilliantly today.
49	**protest** ['prəʊtest]	Protest	
	extremist [ɪk'stri:mɪst]	Extremist/in	
	salt [sɔ:lt]	Salz	
	march [mɑ:tʃ]	(Protest-)Marsch	
	non-violent [nɒn'vaɪələnt]	gewaltfrei	
	peace [pi:s]	Frieden →	

→ **-f(e), -ves**
knife, knives
life, lives
shelf, shelves

→ peace
peaceful
non-violent

Look at language

50	**turbine** ['tɜ:baɪn]	Turbine	→ These wind *turbines* produce
	wind farm ['wɪndfɑ:m]	Windpark	→ electricity on a *wind farm*.
	indirect speech ['ɪndərekt'spi:tʃ]	indirekte Rede	

*Irregular verbs

Infinitive form	Simple past form	Present perfect form
build [bɪld]	I built [bɪlt]	I've built [bɪlt]
cost [kɒst]	it cost [kɒst]	it has cost [kɒst]
fly [flaɪ]	I flew [flu:]	I've flown [fləʊn]
shine [ʃaɪn]	I shone [ʃɒn]	I've shone [ʃɒn]

Test yourself

1 Word families: Find the new words and write them in your exercise book.

1 **India** (noun) – ... (adjective)
2 **married** (adjective) – ... (noun)
3 **building** (noun) – ... (verb)
4 **flight** (noun) – ... (verb)
5 **empty** (verb) – ... (adjective)
6 **peaceful** (adjective) – ... (noun)

Tipp: Schau dir die vorangegangenen Wortlisten gut an.

2 Definitions: Find and write in your exercise book a word for:

1 a person who is very, very rich
2 one thousand million
3 somebody who doesn't eat meat
4 something that makes a drink fizzy
5 a married man
6 something that you put on your food if you want it to taste better

3 Make sentences with these words and write them in your exercise book.

1 **second – director – this is – the – best – by – film – this**
2 **at the – can't – right – I – word – think of – moment – the**
3 **thanked – they – coming – the – for – guests**
4 **help – was – the story – couldn't – sad, – crying – so – I**

Do you remember?

Pick the right word and finish the sentences in your exercise book.

annoyed • carry • platform • seat • shake • strong

1 If I don't wake up, ... me, please.
2 Can you ... this heavy bag for me?
3 Sorry, I'm not ... enough.
4 Everything went wrong. I'm so ... .
5 What ... does the train go from?
6 I put my bag on the ... next to me.

Are your answers right? Check on page 193.

Unit 4

Lerntipp 4: Englische Rechtschreibung

Bei folgenden Buchstabenkombinationen kommt es oft zu Fehlern:

- **-al**: Weil im Englischen die Endung -al nicht betont gesprochen wird, verwechselt man sie leicht mit -le oder -el. Markiere dir jede al-Endung deutlich, z.B. in Wörtern wie *alphabetical, financial, general, informal, medical* oder *multicultural*.

- **-or**: Wenn man einen Menschen benennen will, der etwas Bestimmtes tut, hängt man entweder ein -er an das Verb (z.B. *teacher*) oder ein -or: *actor, counsellor, director* oder *visitor*. Vorsicht: Die Endungen werden gleich ausgesprochen, deshalb solltest du jedes -or deutlich markieren!

52	**What next?**	Was nun?	
	I'll keep my fingers crossed for you. ['fɪŋgəz, krɒst]	Ich drücke dir die Daumen.	
	course [kɔːs]	Kurs, Lehrgang	
	childcare ['tʃaɪldkeə]	Kinderbetreuung, Kinderpflege	→ My sister works in *childcare*. She loves kids.
	web page design ['webpeɪdʒdɪzaɪn]	Webseiten-Design	
	abroad [ə'brɔːd]	im/ins Ausland	→ My brother worked *abroad* for a year.
	work out [wɜːk'aʊt]	sich (gut) entwickeln, (gut) laufen	→ Unfortunately, my first job didn't *work out*.

Speaking

54	**Better luck next time!**	Nächstes Mal hast du bestimmt mehr Glück!	→ I didn't pass my driving test. – Poor you. *Better luck next time!*
	All's well that ends well.	Ende gut, alles gut.	
	do well	gut abschneiden	→ I've always *done well* in maths. It's my favourite subject.
	still [stɪl]	trotzdem	→ Were they invited? – No, but they *still* went to the party.
	I'm fed up. [fed'ʌp]	Ich habe die Nase voll.	
	something comes up	etwas ergibt sich	→ Nothing *came up* for me abroad, so I went home.
	Guess what!	Stell dir vor!	
	DIY store [diːaɪ'waɪstɔː]	Heimwerkermarkt	→ You can buy everything in a *DIY* (= do it yourself) *store*.
	seem [siːm]	scheinen	→ The trip *seemed* awfully long.
	you can have your holiday **after all** ['ɑːftərɔːl]	du kannst doch noch Urlaub machen	→ Congratulations! I heard that you passed your driving test *after all*.
	I'm serious. ['sɪəries]	Ich meine es ernst.	→ What – Alice and Sasha? You can't *be serious*!
	I don't know what to say.	Ich weiß nicht, was ich sagen soll.	
	get over something	über etwas hinwegkommen	
	gap [gæp]	Lücke	
55	**electrician** [ɪlek'trɪʃn]	Elektriker/in →	
	mechanic [mə'kænɪk]	Mechaniker/in	

→ electric
electronic
electricity
electrician

Reading

56	**first floor room** [flɔː]	Zimmer im ersten Stockwerk	
	wardrobe ['wɔːdrəʊb]	Kleiderschrank →	→ My brother and I have to share a *wardrobe* – it's so full!
	dining room ['daɪnɪŋruːm]	Esszimmer	→ We don't have a *dining room*, so we eat our meals in the kitchen.
	including [ɪn'kluːdɪŋ]	einschließlich	
	TV licence ['tiː'viːlaɪsns]	Fernsehgebühr	
	Wi-Fi ['waɪfaɪ]	*umgangssprachlich für:* Funknetzwerk (z.B. WLAN)	
	one-bedroom apartment	Einzimmerwohnung	
	entrance hall ['entrənshɔːl]	Diele, Hausflur	
	cooker ['kʊkə]	Herd	→ Mum, can you show me how to use a gas *cooker*?
	fridge [frɪdʒ]	Kühlschrank	
	freezer ['friːzə]	Gefriertruhe, -schrank	
	washing machine ['wɒʃɪŋməʃiːn]	Waschmaschine	

→ **Furniture**
bed
chair
cupboard
shelf
table
wardrobe

	toilet ['tɔɪlət]	Toilette	→ The *toilet* is next to the bathroom.
	deposit [dɪ'pɒzɪt]	Kaution	→ They normally ask you to pay £100 *deposit*.
	required [rɪ'kwaɪəd]	erforderlich	→ I didn't get the *required* number of points.
	upstairs [ʌp'steəz]	oben (im Haus); nach oben	→ My bedroom is *upstairs*.
	extra ['ekstrə]	extra, zusätzlich	→ The article is going to be a lot of *extra* work.
	fire instructions ['faɪəɪnstrʌkʃnz]	Vorschriften für das Verhalten im Brandfall	
	phone for help	telefonisch Hilfe holen	
57	**saying** ['seɪɪŋ]	Sprichwort	→ Have you ever heard the *saying* "Accidents will happen"? It's true!
	disaster [dɪ'zɑːstə]	Katastrophe	→ Losing your job doesn't have to be a *disaster*.

Listening

58	**event** [ɪ'vent]	Veranstaltung; Ereignis	
	give blood [blʌd]	Blut spenden	
	relationship [rɪ'leɪʃnʃɪp]	Beziehung, Verhältnis	→ I have a very good *relationship* with my boss.
59	**disabled** [dɪs'eɪbld]	behindert	→ I want to work with *disabled* children.

Reading

60	**book** [bʊk]	buchen, reservieren (lassen)	→ You can *book* everything online.
	budget ['bʌdʒɪt]	Budget	→ My parents helped me with my holiday *budget*.
	choice [tʃɔɪs]	Wahl →	→ choose / choice
	comfortable ['kʌmftəbl]	komfortabel, bequem	
	Who cares? [huː'keəz]	Ist doch egal! Na und?	
	ferry ['feri]	Fähre	
	view(s) [vjuː, vjuːz]	Aussicht, Sicht	→ The *view* from our hotel was fantastic.
	a last-minute decision	eine Entscheidung in letzter Minute	
	perfect ['pɜːfɪkt]	vollkommen, perfekt	
	further ['fɜːðə]	weiter →	→ far – further – furthest
	make sure (that) ... [ʃʊə]	dafür sorgen, dass ...	→ I'll *make sure* nobody finds out about this.
	local ['ləʊkl]	örtlich, einheimisch	
61	**away match** [ə'weɪmætʃ]	Auswärtsspiel	
	accommodation [əkɒmə'deɪʃn]	Unterkunft; Unterbringung	
	uncomfortable [ʌn'kʌmftəbl]	unbequem, ungemütlich	→ This chair is so *uncomfortable*!
	flexible ['fleksəbl]	flexibel	
	expression [ɪk'spreʃn]	Ausdruck	→ He used *expressions* that I've never heard before.
	sum up [sʌm'ʌp]	zusammenfassen →	→ sum up / summary

Writing

62	**X-ray assistant** ['eksreɪəsɪstənt]	Röntgenassistent/in	
	quality ['kwɒləti]	Eigenschaft	→ I don't have the right *qualities* for that job.
63	**chief librarian** [tʃiːflaɪ'breərɪən]	leitende/r Bibliothekar/in	
	Polish ['pəʊlɪʃ]	polnisch; Polnisch; Pole/Polin →	→ Can you speak *Polish*? → Poland / Polish
	serve [sɜːv]	bedienen	
	be happy to do something	etwas gern tun	→ He'*ll be happy to* show us his house.
	reference ['refərəns]	Referenz, Zeugnis	

title ['taɪtl]	Anrede	
gender ['dʒendə]	Geschlecht	→ What does "*Gender*: m/f" mean? – Male/female.
date/country of birth [bɜːθ]	Geburtsdatum/-land	
postcode ['pəʊstkəʊd]	Postleitzahl	

Look at language

64 **embarrassing** [ɪm'bærəsɪŋ]	peinlich	→ It was so *embarrassing* – I had to dance with my teacher!
midnight ['mɪdnaɪt]	Mitternacht	
alarm clock [ə'lɑːmklɒk]	Wecker	→ 
dress [dres]	(sich) anziehen	
second ['sekənd]	Sekunde →	→ second, minute, hour
slipper ['slɪpə]	Hausschuh	
half my breakfast [hɑːf]	mein halbes Frühstück	→ We met *half* our class at the cinema.

Test yourself

1 Pick the right word/spelling and write the sentences in your exercise book.

1 My sister lives aboard/abroad.
2 My brother works in a DIY/DYI store.
3 Your friend seams/seems to be nice.
4 You can't be series/serious!
5 The hurricane was a disaster/desaster.
6 I want to learn Polnish/Polish.

Tipp:
Schau dir die vorangegangenen Wortlisten gut an.

2 Pick the right word and finish the sentences in your exercise book.

for • of • out • over • to • up

1 I tried hairdressing, but it didn't work ...
2 I'm really fed ...
3 Don't worry – you'll get ... it.
4 If you notice a fire, you have to phone ... help.
5 My teacher will be happy to talk ... you.
6 My country ... birth is Portugal.

3 Pick the three words that you could use to finish each sentence and write them in your exercise book.

cooker • date of birth • dining room • DIY store • embarrassing • entrance hall • freezer • fridge • gender • perfect • postcode • uncomfortable

1 Bad news: The ... is broken!
2 Where's Andy? – I think he's in the ...
3 Please fill in your personal details. Start with your ...
4 My new slippers are ...

Do you remember?

a) Add the missing letters (•) to these words and write them in your exercise book.

a••ident • a•res• • apprenti••ship • b••becue • beautif•• • bro••ure • competi••on • equi••ent • ••perience • rec••ve • succe••ful • supp••t

b) Look at a) and pick the right words to finish these sentences.

1 Quick, please! There was an ... in Hill Street. I don't know the full ...
2 My brother took part in a skiing ... last winter. He was quite ...
3 Did you ... the holiday ... that I sent you last month?
4 The weather is ... today. Let's get our swimming ... and go to the lake.

Are your answers right? Check on page 193.

Extra Practice · Unit 1

68	*barbecue* ['bɑːbɪkjuː]	Grillfest; Grill	→
	extra ['ekstrə]	extra, zusätzlich	
69	*race* [reɪs]	(Wett-)Rennen	
70	*peaceful* ['piːsfl]	friedlich	
	protest ['prəʊtest]	Protest	
	military ['mɪlətri]	militärisch	
	sabotage ['sæbətɑːʒ]	Sabotage	
	before that	davor	
	get married [get'mærid]	heiraten	
72	*Table Mountain*	Tafelberg	
	cable car ['keɪblkɑː]	Seilbahn	
	car [kɑː]	Wagen, Gondel	→
	every 15 minutes	alle 15 Minuten	
	trip takes 5-6 minutes	Fahrt dauert 5-6 Minuten	
	wind [wɪnd]	Wind	

Extra Practice · Unit 2

76	*if-clause* ['ɪfklɔːz]	If-Satz
	type [taɪp]	Typ
	agony aunt ['ægəniɑːnt]	„Kummerkastentante"
	not ... anybody ['enibɒdi]	niemand ➔
77	*if-clause* ['ɪfklɔːz]	If-Satz
	type [taɪp]	Typ
	agony aunt ['ægəniɑːnt]	„Kummerkastentante"
	main clause ['meɪnklɔːz]	Hauptsatz
78	*not ... anybody* ['enibɒdi]	niemand ➔

➔ not ... any
not ... anybody
not ... anything
not ... anywhere

Extra Practice · Unit 3

84	*colony* ['kɒləni]	Kolonie	
	leader ['liːdə]	Führer/in ➔	
	campaign [kæm'peɪn]	Kampagne, Aktion	
	for free	umsonst	
	independent [ɪndɪ'pendənt]	unabhängig	
	snow storm ['snəʊstɔːm]	Schneesturm	→
85	*independent* [ɪndɪ'pendənt]	unabhängig	
	leader ['liːdə]	Führer/in	
	disaster [dɪ'zɑːstə]	Katastrophe	
	prime minister [praɪm'mɪnɪstə]	Premierminister/in, Ministerpräsident/in ➔	
86	*I'm lucky* ['lʌki]	ich habe Glück ➔	

➔ lead
leader

➔ president
prime minister

➔ Good luck!
Lucky thing!
I'm lucky.
luckily

Extra Practice · Unit 4

92	*youth camp* ['juːθkæmp]	Jugendferienlager
	train [treɪn]	ausbilden ➔
	service motorbikes ['sɜːvɪs]	Motorräder instand halten
	repair [rɪ'peə]	reparieren
93	*revise (for an exam)* [rɪ'vaɪz]	(für eine Prüfung) lernen

➔ I trained as a ...
I was trained as a ...
I did my training as a ...

NUMBERS, SOUNDS, ABC

ENGLISH NUMBERS

1	one [wʌn]	1st	first [fɜːst]
2	two [tuː]	2nd	second ['sekənd]
3	three [θriː]	3rd	third [θɜːd]
4	four [fɔː]	4th	fourth [fɔːθ]
5	five [faɪv]	5th	fifth [fɪfθ]
6	six [sɪks]	6th	sixth [sɪksθ]
7	seven ['sevn]	7th	seventh ['sevnθ]
8	eight [eɪt]	8th	eighth [eɪtθ]
9	nine [naɪn]	9th	ninth [naɪnθ]
10	ten [ten]	10th	tenth [tenθ]
11	eleven [ɪ'levn]	11th	eleventh [ɪ'levnθ]
12	twelve [twelv]	12th	twelfth [twelfθ]
13	thirteen ['θɜː'tiːn]	13th	thirteenth ['θɜː'tiːnθ]
14	fourteen ['fɔː'tiːn]	14th	fourteenth ['fɔː'tiːnθ]
15	fifteen ['fɪf'tiːn]	15th	fifteenth ['fɪf'tiːnθ]
16	sixteen ['sɪks'tiːn]	16th	sixteenth ['sɪks'tiːnθ]
17	seventeen ['sevn'tiːn]	17th	seventeenth ['sevn'tiːnθ]
18	eighteen ['eɪ'tiːn]	18th	eighteenth ['eɪ'tiːnθ]
19	nineteen ['naɪn'tiːn]	19th	nineteenth ['naɪn'tiːnθ]
20	twenty ['twenti]	20th	twentieth ['twentiəθ]
21	twenty-one ['twenti'wʌn]	21st	twenty-first ['twenti'fɜːst]
...		...	
30	thirty ['θɜːti]	30th	thirtieth ['θɜːtiəθ]
40	forty ['fɔːti]	40th	fortieth ['fɔːtiəθ]
50	fifty ['fɪfti]	50th	fiftieth ['fɪftiəθ]
60	sixty ['sɪksti]	60th	sixtieth ['sɪkstiəθ]
70	seventy ['sevnti]	70th	seventieth ['sevntiəθ]
80	eighty ['eɪti]	80th	eightieth ['eɪtiəθ]
90	ninety ['naɪnti]	90th	ninetieth ['naɪntiəθ]
100	a hundred [ə'hʌndrəd] one hundred ['wʌn'hʌndrəd]	100th	hundredth ['hʌndrədθ]
101	one hundred and one [wʌnhʌndrədn'wʌn]	101st	one hundred and first [wʌnhʌndrədn'fɜːst]
...		...	
1000	a thousand [ə'θaʊznd] one thousand ['wʌn'θaʊznd]	1000th	thousandth ['θaʊznθ]

ENGLISH SOUNDS

[iː]	eat, see, he
[ɑː]	ask, class, car
[ɔː]	or, ball, door, four
[uː]	ruler, blue, too, two, you
[ɜː]	early, her, girl, work
[ɪ]	in, big, England
[e]	yes, bed, again, breakfast
[æ]	animal, cat, black
[ʌ]	bus, colour
[ɒ]	on, dog, what
[ʊ]	put, good
[ə]	again, sister, today
[i]	radio, video, happy
[u]	July, museum, usually
[eɪ]	eight, name, play, great
[aɪ]	I, time, right, my
[ɔɪ]	boy, toy
[əʊ]	old, no, road, yellow
[aʊ]	our, house, now
[ɪə]	near, here, we're
[eə]	airport, share, there, their
[ʊə]	poor, you're, sure
[b]	bike, table, verb
[p]	pen, pupil, shop
[d]	day, window, good
[t]	ten, matter, at
[k]	kitchen, car, back, book
[g]	go, again, bag
[ŋ]	wrong, morning, bank
[l]	like, old, small
[r]	ruler, friend, sorry
[v]	very, seven, have
[w]	we, where, quarter
[s]	six, poster, yes
[z]	present, quiz, his, please
[ʃ]	she, station, English
[tʃ]	child, teacher, match
[dʒ]	job, German, orange
[ʒ]	usually
[j]	yes, you, young
[θ]	thing, bathroom, month
[ð]	the, father, with

[iː] [ɑː] [ɔː]

THE ENGLISH ALPHABET

A B C

a	[eɪ]	n	[en]
b	[biː]	o	[əʊ]
c	[siː]	p	[piː]
d	[diː]	q	[kjuː]
e	[iː]	r	[ɑː]
f	[ef]	s	[es]
g	[dʒiː]	t	[tiː]
h	[eɪtʃ]	u	[juː]
i	[aɪ]	v	[viː]
j	[dʒeɪ]	w	['dʌbljuː]
k	[keɪ]	x	[eks]
l	[el]	y	[waɪ]
m	[em]	z	[zed]

Alphabetische Liste der Wörter aus den Bänden 1–6 (Englisch – Deutsch)

mit Fundstellenangaben für den Lernwortschatz aus Band 6, z. B. U1: 13 = Unit 1, S.13

WF (wahlfrei): nicht zum Lernwortschatz gehörende Wörter
→ verweist auf die Grundform eines Wortes
(AE): überwiegend im amerikanischen Englisch benutzte Vokabeln; Schreibweise und Aussprache entsprechen generell dem britischen Englisch.

A

a [ə] ein/e; **she's a bus driver** sie ist Busfahrerin; **24 hours a day** 24 Stunden am/pro Tag
able ['eɪbl]**: I'm not able to come** ich kann nicht kommen U2: 25; **able to deal with stress** belastbar WF
Aboriginal [æbə'rɪdʒənl] zur Urbevölkerung zählend
about [ə'baʊt] **1** über; **ask them about something** sie nach etwas fragen; **hear about ...** von ... erfahren, von ... hören; **I'm embarrassed about ...** ich schäme mich wegen ...; **The text is about ...** Der Text handelt von ...; **What about you?** Und du?/Was ist mit dir? **2** ungefähr
above [ə'bʌv] über
abroad [ə'brɔːd] im/ins Ausland U4: 52
abuse [ə'bjuːs] Missbrauch WF
accent ['æksənt] Akzent U1: 13
accessories [ək'sesəriz] Accessoires WF
accident ['æksɪdənt] Unfall
accommodation [əkɒmə'deɪʃn] Unterkunft U4: 61
account [ə'kaʊnt] Konto U3: 42
across [ə'krɒs] über; hinüber/herüber
act [ækt] (in einem Film/Theaterstück) spielen U1: 20; **Act the dialogue.** Spielt das Gespräch nach.
action ['ækʃn] Handlung U1: 20
action film ['ækʃnfɪlm] Actionfilm
activity [æk'tɪvəti] Beschäftigung, Aktivität
actor ['æktə] Schauspieler/in
actually ['æktʃuəli] eigentlich U2: 34
address [ə'dres] Adresse
adjective ['ædʒɪktɪv] Adjektiv, Eigenschaftswort
adult ['ædʌlt] Erwachsene/Erwachsener
advance [əd'vaːns] Vorverkauf WF; **in advance** im Voraus WF
adventure [əd'ventʃə] Abenteuer
adverb ['ædvɜːb] Adverb, Umstandswort
advert ['ædvɜːt] Anzeige
advertising company ['ædvətaɪzɪŋkʌmpəni] Werbefirma WF
advice [əd'vaɪs] Rat, Ratschläge; **give (some) advice** Rat(schläge) geben, beraten
adviser [əd'vaɪzə] Berater/in WF
afraid [ə'freɪd]**: be afraid (of)** Angst haben (vor) U1: 9; **I'm afraid ...** Leider ...
Africa ['æfrɪkə] Afrika
African ['æfrɪkən] afrikanisch; Afrikaner/in
African National Congress ['æfrɪkənæʃnəl'kɒngres] Afrikanischer Nationalkongress *(südafrikanische Partei)* WF
after ['ɑːftə] **1** nach; **after school** nach der Schule; **after a ball** hinter einem Ball her; **you can have your holiday after all** ['ɑːftərɔːl] du kannst doch noch Urlaub machen U4: 54; **2** nachdem
afternoon ['ɑːftə'nuːn] Nachmittag; **in the afternoon** am Nachmittag, nachmittags
afterwards ['ɑːftəwədz] danach WF
again [ə'gen] noch einmal, (schon) wieder
against [ə'genst] gegen; **for and against** dafür und dagegen
age [eɪdʒ] Alter; **at the age of ...** im Alter von ... WF; **between the ages of 20–24** im Alter von 20–24 Jahren WF; **under the age of 14** unter 14 WF
aged [eɪdʒd]**: girls aged 13 to 15** Mädchen im Alter von 13 bis 15 WF
age limit ['eɪdʒlɪmɪt] Altersgrenze WF
aggressive [ə'gresɪv] aggressiv, angriffslustig U2: 22
ago [ə'gəʊ]**: two years ago** vor zwei Jahren
agony aunt ['ægəniɑːnt] „Kummerkastentante" WF
agree [ə'griː]**: I agree (with you).** Ich stimme (dir) zu. Ich bin derselben Meinung (wie du). **I agree to help her** ich erkläre mich bereit, ihr zu helfen
ahead [ə'hed]**: Go ahead.** Mach(t) nur. **look ahead** vorausschauen, die Zukunft planen
aid [eɪd]**: first aid** erste Hilfe
ain't [eɪnt] = isn't WF
airport ['eəpɔːt] Flughafen; **at Exeter Airport** am Flughafen Exeter
alarm [ə'lɑːm] Alarmanlage; **sound the alarm** Alarm auslösen WF
alarm clock [ə'lɑːmklɒk] Wecker U4: 64
alcohol ['ælkəhɒl] Alkohol
alcoholic [ælkə'hɒlɪk] alkoholisch WF
alive [ə'laɪv]**: stay alive** am Leben bleiben WF
all (the) [ɔːl] alle; **all in all** insgesamt; **all over** überall in/auf; **all the time** die ganze Zeit; **all weekend** das ganze Wochenende; **All's well that ends well.** Ende gut, alles gut. U4: 54; **at all times** jederzeit, immer U3: 40; **no work at all** überhaupt keine Arbeit WF; **not at all** überhaupt nicht WF
allow [ə'laʊ] erlauben, gestatten, zulassen U1: 11; **allow 3 hours** 3 Stunden einplanen WF
allowed [ə'laʊd]**: I'm allowed to go** ich darf gehen; **they were allowed visits** ihnen wurden Besuche zugestanden WF
almost ['ɔːlməʊst] fast, beinahe U3: 46
alone [ə'ləʊn] allein
along [ə'lɒŋ] entlang
alphabet ['ælfəbet] Alphabet
alphabetical [ælfə'betɪkl] alphabetisch
already [ɔːl'redi] schon U1: 9
also ['ɔːlsəʊ] auch; **Also, ...** Außerdem ... U1: 18
alternative [ɔːl'tɜːnətɪv] alternativ WF

although [ɔːl'ðəʊ] obwohl U1: 8
always ['ɔːlweɪz] immer
a.m. [eɪ'em] morgens, vormittags
am [æm] bin; **I'm (= I am) Sarah.** Ich heiße Sarah. **I'm from London.** Ich komme aus London. **How are you? - I'm fine, thanks.** Wie geht's? - Danke, gut. **Are you ...? - Yes, I am./ No, I'm not.** Bist du ...? - Ja./ Nein.
amazing [ə'meɪzɪŋ] unglaublich, erstaunlich U1: 10
America [ə'merɪkə] Amerika
American [ə'merɪkən] amerikanisch; Amerikaner/in
amongst [ə'mʌŋst] unter WF
amusement arcade [ə'mjuːzməntɑːkeɪd] Spielhalle
an [ən] ein/e
and [ænd, ənd] und
Angola [æŋ'gəʊlə] Angola
angry (with) ['æŋgri] böse, wütend (auf)
animal ['ænɪml] Tier; **animal rights** Tierrechte, Tierschutz-
announcement [ə'naʊnsmənt] Durchsage
annoyed [ə'nɔɪd] verärgert
anorak ['ænəræk] Anorak WF
another [ə'nʌðə] **1** noch ein, eine, einer, eins; **2** ein anderer/anderes, eine andere
answer ['ɑːnsə] **1** (be)antworten; **answer the phone** ans Telefon gehen; **2** Antwort; **3 answer to a problem** Lösung eines Problems U2: 31
antelope ['æntɪləʊp] Antilope WF
anti-social [ænti'səʊʃl] unsozial WF
any ['eni] irgendwelche; **not ... any** kein/e; **not any more** nicht mehr WF
anybody ['enibɒdi]: **not ... anybody** niemand WF
anything ['eniθɪŋ]: **not ... anything** nichts; **no drugs or anything like that** keine Drogen oder so etwas WF; **be the first to try anything** alles als Erste/r ausprobieren wollen WF
anyway ['eniweɪ] sowieso, ohnehin U2: 24
anywhere ['eniweə]: **not ... anywhere** nirgendwo(-hin/-her)
apartheid [ə'pɑːtaɪt] Apartheid U1: 12
apartment [ə'pɑːtmənt] (AE) Wohnung
apple ['æpl] Apfel
applicant ['æplɪkənt] Bewerber/in WF
application (form) [æplɪ'keɪʃn] Bewerbung(sformular) U2: 32
apply (for/to) [ə'plaɪ] sich bewerben (um/bei)
appointment [ə'pɔɪntmənt] Termin, Verabredung; **appointment card** (Patienten-)Terminkärtchen
apprenticeship [ə'prentɪsʃɪp] Lehre; **do an apprenticeship** eine Lehre machen
April ['eɪprəl] April
are [ɑː] bist; seid; sind; **aren't (= are not)** bist/seid/sind nicht; **How are you?** Wie geht's? **What are they in German?** Wie heißen sie auf Deutsch?
area ['eəriə] Gegend
argument ['ɑːgjumənt] **1** Argument U2: 27; **2** Streit; **have an argument** Streit haben
arm [ɑːm] Arm
around [ə'raʊnd] um, herum; **look around** sich umschauen U3: 46
arrange [ə'reɪndʒ] arrangieren WF
arrangement [ə'reɪndʒmənt] Absprache; **make an arrangement** eine Absprache treffen
arrive [ə'raɪv] ankommen
art [ɑːt] Kunst
article ['ɑːtɪkl] Artikel
artist ['ɑːtɪst] Künstler/in U1: 20
as [æz, əz] **1** als; **2** wie WF; **as many/... as** so viele/... wie; **as small as two years old** erst zwei Jahre alt WF
asap [eɪeseɪ'piː] **(= as soon as possible)** so bald wie möglich U1: 18
ashamed [ə'ʃeɪmd]: **feel ashamed** sich schämen WF
Asia ['eɪʃə] Asien
Asian ['eɪʃn] asiatisch; Asiat/in
ask [ɑːsk] fragen; **ask for** bitten um; **ask a question** eine Frage stellen; **ask them about something** sie nach etwas fragen
assistant [ə'sɪstənt] Assistent/in; **shop assistant** Verkäufer/in
astronaut ['æstrənɔːt] Astronaut/in
at [æt, ət] bei; an; in; **at eight o'clock** um acht/zwanzig Uhr; **at 16 (years old)** mit 16 (Jahren), im Alter von 16 Jahren; **at all times** jederzeit, immer U3: 40; **at Exeter Station** im Bahnhof Exeter; **at first** zunächst; **at home** zu Hause, daheim; **at last** endlich, schließlich; **at least** mindestens, wenigstens; **at night** nachts, in der Nacht; **at the moment** zurzeit, im Moment; **at the weekend** am Wochenende; **she's at school** sie ist in der Schule; sie geht zur Schule; **travel at 65 miles per hour** mit 65 Meilen pro Stunde fahren WF
ate [et] (→ eat): **I ate** ich aß, ich habe gegessen
athletics [æθ'letɪks] Leichtathletik
Atlantic Ocean [ət'læntɪk'əʊʃn] Atlantik
ATM [eɪtiː'em] Geldautomat U3: 42
atmosphere ['ætməsfɪə] Atmosphäre, Stimmung WF
attack [ə'tæk] **1** angreifen; **attack something** gegen etwas vorgehen WF; **2** Angriff WF
attention [ə'tenʃn] Beachtung U3: 40
attic ['ætɪk] Dachboden, Speicher WF
attract [ə'trækt] anlocken, anziehen WF
audition [ɔː'dɪʃn] Vorsprechen, Vorsingen
August ['ɔːgəst] August; **August 20th** 20. August
aunt [ɑːnt] Tante
Australia [ɒ'streɪliə] Australien
Australian [ɒ'streɪliən] australisch; Australier/in(nen)
Aussie Rules ['ɒzi'ruːlz] Australian Rules Football *(ähnl. wie Rugby)*
Austria ['ɒstriə] Österreich
autograph ['ɔːtəgrɑːf] Autogramm
autumn ['ɔːtəm] Herbst
avoid [ə'vɔɪd] vermeiden WF
award [ə'wɔːd] Preis, Auszeichnung
away [ə'weɪ] weg, fort
away match [ə'weɪmætʃ] Auswärtsspiel U4: 61
awesome ['ɔːsəm] (AE) irre, toll
awful ['ɔːfl] furchtbar, schrecklich U2: 30

B

baboon [bə'buːn] Pavian WF
baby ['beɪbi] Baby
back [bæk] **1** zurück; **back from school** aus der Schule zurück; **I'm back!** Ich bin wieder da! **at the back of the book** hinten im Buch
background ['bækgraʊnd] Hintergrund
bad [bæd] schlecht; schlimm; **Too bad!** Schade!

badminton ['bædmɪntən] Badminton, Federball(spiel)
bag [bæg] (Schul-)Tasche
baggage handler ['bægɪdʒhændlə] Gepäckabfertiger/in
balcony ['bælkəni] Balkon WF
ball [bɔːl] Ball
ballet ['bæleɪ] Ballett WF
ban [bæn] verbieten U2: 31
banana [bə'nɑːnə] Banane
band [bænd] Band, (Musik-)Gruppe
bank [bæŋk] Bank, Sparkasse
bank account ['bæŋkəkaʊnt] Bankkonto U3: 42
bapu ['bɑːpuː] *Hindi für „Vater"* WF
bar [bɑː] Bar WF
barbecue ['bɑːbɪkjuː] Grill; Grillfest U2: 24
baseball ['beɪsbɔːl] Baseball
basement ['beɪsmənt] Kellergeschoss WF
basket ['bɑːskɪt] Korb WF
basketball ['bɑːskɪtbɔːl] Basketball
bathroom ['bɑːθruːm] Badezimmer, Bad
battery ['bætri] Batterie WF
bay [beɪ] Bucht WF
BBC [biːbiː'siː] BBC (British Broadcasting Corporation; britische Rundfunkanstalt) WF
be [biː, bi] (I/he was, you were; I've been) sein
beach [biːtʃ] Strand; **on the beach** am Strand
bear [beə] Bär
beard [bɪəd] Bart
beat [biːt] schlagen WF
beaten ['biːtn]: **be beaten** geschlagen werden WF
beautician [bjuː'tɪʃn] Kosmetiker/Kosmetikerin WF
beautiful ['bjuːtɪfl] (wunder)schön
beauty ['bjuːti] Schönheit(s-) WF
beaver ['biːvə] Biber
became [bɪ'keɪm] (→ become): **I became** ich wurde, ich bin geworden
because [bɪ'kɒz] weil
become [bɪ'kʌm] (I became, I've become) werden; **I've become** ich bin geworden
bed [bed] Bett
bedroom ['bedruːm] Schlafzimmer **one-bedroom apartment** Einzimmerwohnung U4: 56
beef [biːf] Rindfleisch
been [biːn, bɪn] (→ be): **I've been** ich bin gewesen
beep [biːp] piepsen
beer [bɪə] Bier
before [bɪ'fɔː] **1** bevor; **2** vor; **before that** davor WF
beg [beg]: **beg for money** Geld erbetteln WF
begin [bɪ'gɪn] beginnen WF
behave [bɪ'heɪv] sich verhalten
behaviour [bɪ'heɪvjə] Verhalten WF
behind [bɪ'haɪnd] **1** hinter; **2** „Außentor"
Belgium ['beldʒəm] Belgien
believe [bɪ'liːv] glauben; **believe in** glauben an WF
belong [bɪ'lɒŋ]: **belong to** gehören WF; **belong together** zusammengehören WF
belongings [bɪ'lɒŋɪŋz] Sachen, Besitz WF
below [bɪ'ləʊ] unter, unterhalb (von); unten U2: 26
belt [belt] Gürtel WF
beside [bɪ'saɪd] neben WF
best [best] beste/r/s; am besten; **Best wishes, ...** Viele Grüße ...
better ['betə] besser; **Better luck next time!** Nächstes Mal hast du bestimmt mehr Glück! U4: 54; **better to be poor ...** lieber arm sein ... WF
between [bɪ'twiːn] zwischen
beverage ['bevərɪdʒ] Getränk WF
biased ['baɪəst]: **be biased against somebody** gegen jemanden voreingenommen sein U2: 22
big [bɪg] groß
bike [baɪk] Fahrrad, Rad
bikini [bɪ'kiːni] Bikini WF
billion ['bɪljən] Milliarde U3: 37
bird [bɜːd] Vogel
birth [bɜːθ]: **date/country of birth** Geburtsdatum/-land U4: 63
birthday ['bɜːθdeɪ] Geburtstag; **It's my birthday.** Ich habe Geburtstag.
bit [bɪt]: **a bit (of)** ein bisschen, ein wenig
black [blæk] schwarz; **black people** Schwarze
Blacks [blæks] Schwarze WF
blind [blaɪnd] blenden, blind machen WF
block [blɒk] Häuserblock
blog [blɒg] Blog *(von Weblog; hier eine Art Online-Tagebuch)*
blogger ['blɒgə] Blogger/in *(Autor/Autorin eines Blogs)*
blogging ['blɒgɪŋ] Bloggen *(ein Blog führen, auf Blogs reagieren)*
blonde [blɒnd] blond
blood [blʌd] Blut U4: 58; **give blood** Blut spenden U4: 58
blouse [blaʊz] Bluse WF
blow [bləʊ] blasen WF
blue [bluː] blau
board [bɔːd] **1** Tafel; **2** Board, Brett; **3** Behörde WF; **4** einsteigen WF
boarding pass ['bɔːdɪŋpɑːs] Bordkarte, Einsteigekarte
boarding school ['bɔːdɪŋskuːl] Internat
boardwalk ['bɔːdwɔːk] **1** (hölzerne) Strandpromenade; **2** Steg WF
boat [bəʊt] Boot; Schiff
body ['bɒdi] Körper
bomb [bɒm] Bombe U3: 46
book [bʊk] **1** Buch; Heft; **2** buchen, reservieren (lassen) U4: 60
book cover ['bʊkʌvə] Bucheinband, -umschlag
bookshop ['bʊkʃɒp] Buchladen, -handlung
boot [buːt] Stiefel WF
border ['bɔːdə] Grenze
bored [bɔːd] gelangweilt; **I'm bored** ich langweile mich
boring ['bɔːrɪŋ] langweilig
born [bɔːn]: **I was born ...** ich wurde ... geboren
borrow ['bɒrəʊ]: **borrow a pen** sich einen Füller (aus)leihen
boss [bɒs] Boss, Chef/in
both [bəʊθ]: **both ... and ...** sowohl ... als auch ... WF; **they both buy ...** sie kaufen beide ... WF
bottle ['bɒtl] Flasche WF
bought [bɔːt] (→ buy): **I bought** ich kaufte, ich habe gekauft; **I've bought** ich habe gekauft
boutique [buː'tiːk] Boutique
bow tie [bəʊ'taɪ] Fliege *(Kleidungsstück)* WF
box [bɒks] Kiste, Kasten
boy [bɔɪ] Junge; **boys placking cricket** Jungen, die Kricket spiel(t)en WF
boyfriend ['bɔɪfrend] (fester) Freund
brand [brænd] Marke
brave [breɪv] mutig, tapfer
bread [bred] Brot
break [breɪk] **1** Pause; **2** brechen, zerbrechen WF
break up (with him) [breɪk'ʌp] (I broke up, I've broken up) (mit ihm) Schluss machen
breakfast ['brekfəst] Frühstück; **have breakfast** frühstücken
bridge [brɪdʒ] Brücke
bright [braɪt] leuchtend WF
brighten up [braɪtn'ʌp] aufhellen WF

brilliant ['brɪliənt] toll, glänzend, großartig U1: 8
bring [brɪŋ] (I brought, I've brought) bringen
Britain ['brɪtn] Großbritannien
British ['brɪtɪʃ] britisch; Brite/Britin
brochure ['brəʊʃə] Broschüre
broke up [brəʊk'ʌp] (→ break up): **I broke up** ich machte Schluss, ich habe Schluss gemacht
broken ['brəʊkən] kaputt, zerbrochen U1: 18
broken up [brəʊkən'ʌp] (→ break up): **I've broken up** ich habe Schluss gemacht
brother ['brʌðə] Bruder; **brothers and sisters** Geschwister
brought [brɔːt] (→ bring): **I brought** ich brachte, ich habe gebracht; **I've brought** ich habe gebracht
brown [braʊn] braun; **brown bread** Graubrot
bubble ['bʌbl] Blase
bucket ['bʌkɪt] Eimer WF
buddy ['bʌdi] „Kumpel" *(ältere/r Schüler/in, der/die jüngeren hilft)*
budget ['bʌdʒɪt] Budget U4: 60
buffalo ['bʌfələʊ] Büffel WF
build [bɪld] (I built, I've built) bauen U3: 41
building ['bɪldɪŋ] Gebäude
built [bɪlt] (→ build): **I built** ich baute, ich habe gebaut U3: 41; **I've built** ich habe gebaut U3: 41
bully ['bʊli] **1** tyrannisieren, einschüchtern; **2** Tyrann, „Mobber/in"
bullying ['bʊliɪŋ] Schikanieren, Mobbing; **text bullying** SMS-Terror
burka ['bʊəkə] Burka U3: 46
bus [bʌs] Bus
bus driver ['bʌsdraɪvə] Busfahrer/in
bush [bʊʃ]: **the bush** der (australische) Busch
business ['bɪznəs] Betrieb, Geschäft(s-); **I plan to start my own business.** Ich habe vor, mich selbstständig zu machen.
business adviser ['bɪznəsədvaɪzə] Unternehmensberater/in WF
bus station ['bʌsteɪʃn] Bushof, Busbahnhof
bus stop ['bʌstɒp] Bushaltestelle
busy ['bɪzi] beschäftigt; hektisch, belebt; **a busy road** eine viel befahrene Straße
but [bʌt] aber
button ['bʌtn] Knopf; Taste
buy [baɪ] (I bought, I've bought) kaufen
buzz off [bʌz'ɒf] „abschwirren", „abzischen" WF
by [baɪ] **1** an, in der Nähe von, neben; **2** von; durch; **by bike/bus/...** mit dem Rad/Bus/...; **by day** tagsüber WF; **by his arms** an den Armen; **by May 15th** bis zum 15. Mai; **by the way** übrigens U1: 10; **Learn it by heart.** Lerne es auswendig. **play by the rules** sich an die Spielregeln halten
Bye. [baɪ] Tschüs. Wiedersehen.

C

cabin ['kæbɪn] Hütte
cable car ['keɪblkɑː] Seilbahn WF
cafe ['kæfeɪ] Café
cake [keɪk] Kuchen
California [kælə'fɔːniə] Kalifornien
call [kɔːl] **1** anrufen; (herbei)rufen; **call back** zurückrufen; **call out** ausrufen WF; **2** nennen, bezeichnen; **they called me names** sie beschimpften mich; **3 final call** letzter Aufruf; **4 phone call** Anruf
call centre ['kɔːlsentə] Callcenter U3: 36
called [kɔːld]: **it's called ...** er/sie/es heißt ... U2: 30
calling ['kɔːlɪŋ]: **Thanks for calling.** Danke für den Anruf.
calorie ['kæləri] Kalorie
came [keɪm] (→ come): **I came** ich kam, ich bin gekommen
camera ['kæmərə] Fotoapparat, Kamera
campaign [kæm'peɪn] Kampagne, Aktion WF
campfire ['kæmpfaɪə] Lagerfeuer
campground ['kæmpgraʊnd] (AE) Campingplatz, Zeltplatz
camping ['kæmpɪŋ] Camping
campsite ['kæmpsaɪt] Campingplatz, Zeltplatz U1: 19
can [kæn, kən] **1** können, dürfen; **can't** [kɑːnt] nicht können; **Can you ...? - Yes, I can./No, I can't.** Kannst du ...? - Ja./Nein. **2** Dose, Büchse U2: 30
canal [kə'næl] Kanal
cannabis ['kænəbɪs] Haschisch U2: 26
canoe [kə'nuː] Kanu
canoeing [kə'nuːɪŋ] Kanufahren, Paddeln
cap [kæp] Kappe
cape [keɪp]: **Cape of Good Hope** Kap der guten Hoffnung WF
Cape Town ['keɪptaʊn] Kapstadt U1: 6
capital ['kæpɪtl] Hauptstadt
car [kɑː] **1** Auto; **2** Wagen, Gondel WF
car boot sale [kɑː'buːtseɪl] *(eine Art)* Flohmarkt WF
card [kɑːd] Karte
cardigan ['kɑːdɪgən] Strickjacke WF
care [keə]: **Take care.** Mach's gut. U1: 10; **Who cares?** Ist doch egal! Na und? U4: 60
career [kə'rɪə] **1** Beruf, Berufs-; **2 career (in TV)** (Fernseh-)Karriere, berufliche Laufbahn (im Fernsehen)
careful ['keəfl] vorsichtig
carefully ['keəfli] sorgfältig, aufmerksam U2: 27
carnival ['kɑːnɪvl] Karneval
car park ['kɑːpɑːk] (großer) Parkplatz
car racing ['kɑːreɪsɪŋ] Autorennen
carry ['kæri] tragen U2: 28
cartoon [kɑː'tuːn] Cartoon, Karikatur
cash machine ['kæʃməʃiːn] Geldautomat U3: 42
cashier [kæ'ʃɪə] Kassierer/in
castle ['kɑːsl] Schloss; Burg
cat [kæt] Katze
catch [kætʃ] (I caught, I've caught) fangen; fassen; erwischen
category ['kætəgəri] Kategorie WF
cattle station ['kætlsteɪʃn] *große australische Viehfarm* WF
catwalk ['kætwɔːk] Laufsteg WF
caught [kɔːt] (→ catch): **I caught** ich fing, ich habe gefangen; **I've caught** ich habe gefangen
caution ['kɔːʃn] Vorsicht WF
cave [keɪv] Höhle WF
CD [siː'diː] CD
ceiling ['siːlɪŋ] (Zimmer-)Decke WF
celebrity [sə'lebrəti] Prominente/r
cellar ['selə] Keller WF
cellphone ['selfəʊn] (AE) Handy, Mobiltelefon
cent [sent] Cent
centimetre ['sentɪmiːtə] Zentimeter
central ['sentrəl] zentral, Zentral- WF
centre ['sentə] Zentrum; Mitte
centre post ['sentəpəʊst] Mittelpfosten
certainly ['sɜːtnli] sicher, bestimmt WF

chair [tʃeə] Stuhl; Sessel
chairperson ['tʃeəpɜ:sn] Vorsitzende/r
chalk [tʃɔ:k] mit Kreide schreiben WF
chance [tʃɑ:ns] Chance WF
change [tʃeɪndʒ] **1** (sich) ändern, (sich) verändern; **change money** Geld wechseln, Geld umtauschen U3: 42; **change schools** die Schule wechseln; **I change my mind** ich ändere meine Meinung U2: 24; **2** umsteigen; **change at 42nd Street to line 7** an der 42. Straße in die Linie 7 umsteigen; **3** sich umziehen WF; **4** Veränderung WF
chaos ['keɪɒs] Chaos WF
character ['kærəktə] Figur, Person
charged up [tʃɑ:dʒd'ʌp]**: it's charged up** es ist aufgeladen
charger ['tʃɑ:dʒə] (Batterie-)Ladegerät
chat [tʃæt] sich unterhalten, plaudern U1: 10; **have a chat** sich unterhalten
chat room ['tʃætru:m] (Internet-) Chatroom
chat show ['tʃætʃəʊ] Talkshow
cheap [tʃi:p] billig, preiswert
cheat [tʃi:t] schummeln, betrügen WF
check [tʃek] kontrollieren, überprüfen
checklist ['tʃeklɪst] Checkliste
cheer [tʃɪə] (zu)jubeln, hurra rufen
cheerleader ['tʃɪəli:də] *Person, die das Publikum bei einem Wettkampf zum Beifall anfeuert*
cheese [tʃi:z] Käse
cheque [tʃek] Scheck WF; **the cheque was for $2,700** der Scheck war auf 2.700$ ausgestellt WF
cherry ['tʃeri] Kirsche
chicken ['tʃɪkɪn] Huhn; (Brat-) Hähnchen; **chicken tikka masala** ['tɪkəmə'sɑ:lə] *indisches Currygericht* WF
chief executive [tʃi:fɪg'zekjətɪv] Geschäftsführer/in WF
chief librarian [tʃi:flaɪ'breərɪən] leitende/r Bibliothekar/in U4: 63
child, children [tʃaɪld, 'tʃɪldrən] Kind, Kinder
childcare Kinderbetreuung, Kinderpflege U4: 52
chimney ['tʃɪmni] Schornstein WF
chips [tʃɪps] Pommes frites
chocolate ['tʃɒklət] Schokolade

choice [tʃɔɪs] Wahl U4: 60
choir ['kwaɪə] Chor U1: 13
choose [tʃu:z] (I chose, I've chosen) (aus)wählen, aussuchen U1: 7
chose [tʃəʊz] (→ choose)**: I chose** ich wählte aus, ich habe ausgewählt U1: 7
chosen ['tʃəʊzn] (→ choose)**: I've chosen** ich habe ausgewählt U1: 7
Christmas ['krɪsməs] Weihnachten
church [tʃɜ:tʃ] Kirche
cider ['saɪdə] Apfelwein
cigarette [sɪgə'ret] Zigarette
cinema ['sɪnəmə] Kino
circus ['sɜ:kəs] Zirkus
citizen ['sɪtɪzn] Staatangehörige/r, Bürger/in WF
citizen card ['sɪtɪznkɑ:d] *(inoffizieller)* Identitätsausweis WF
city ['sɪti] Stadt, Großstadt
civil war [sɪvl'wɔ:] Bürgerkrieg
class [klɑ:s] Klasse; **extra classes** Förderunterricht
classroom ['klɑ:sru:m] Klassenzimmer
class teacher ['klɑ:'ti:tʃə] Klassenlehrer/in
clause [klɔ:z]**: if-clause** If-Satz WF; **main clause** Hauptsatz WF
clean [kli:n] **1** sauber; **2** sauber machen, putzen
cleaner ['kli:nə] Putzhilfe, Raumpfleger/in
clear [klɪə] deutlich U3: 45; **stand clear (of ...)** zurücktreten (von ...) U3: 40
clever ['klevə] schlau, klug
cliff [klɪf] Klippe, Felsen
climb (a hill) [klaɪm] (auf einen Hügel) klettern
climber ['klaɪmə] Kletterer, Kletterin
clinic ['klɪnɪk] Klinik U1: 13
clock [klɒk] Uhr
close [kləʊs] **1** nahe, dicht WF; **close to** in der Nähe von WF; **2** genau, sorgfältig WF
close [kləʊz] zumachen, schließen
closed [kləʊzd] geschlossen, zu
clothes [kləʊðz] Kleidung, Kleider
cloud [klaʊd] Wolke
cloudy ['klaʊdi] bewölkt
club [klʌb] **1** Klub, Arbeitsgemeinschaft; Verein; **2** Disko
coach [kəʊtʃ] **1** Coach; **2** Reisebus WF
coast [kəʊst] Küste; **on the coast** an der Küste WF

coat [kəʊt] Mantel WF
coffee shop ['kɒfiʃɒp] Selbstbedienungscafé
cola ['kəʊlə] Cola
cold [kəʊld] kalt
collar ['kɒlə] Kragen WF
colleague ['kɒli:g] Kollege/Kollegin WF
collect [kə'lekt] **1** sammeln; **2** holen, abholen WF
college ['kɒlɪdʒ] Berufsschule, Fach(hoch)schule
Cologne [kə'ləʊn] Köln WF
Colombia [kə'lɒmbiə] Kolumbien
colony ['kɒləni] Kolonie WF
colour ['kʌlə] Farbe; **What colour is your room?** Welche Farbe hat dein Zimmer?
coloured ['kʌləd] Farbige/r *(Südafrikaner/in mit schwarzen und weißen Vorfahren)* WF
colourful ['kʌləfl] bunt, farbenfroh WF
come [kʌm] (I came, I've come) kommen; mitkommen; **I've come** ich bin gekommen; **come first in ...** Erste/r werden bei ...; **come in** hereinkommen; **Come on!** Komm schon! U2: 24; **something comes up** etwas ergibt sich U4: 54
comedy ['kɒmədi] Komödie, humorvoller Film/Roman
comfortable ['kʌmftəbl] komfortabel, bequem U4: 60
comment ['kɒment] Äußerung, Kommentar
commit [kə'mɪt]**: commit a crime** ein Verbrechen begehen U2: 23
community [kə'mju:nəti] Gemeinschaft WF
commuter [kə'mju:tə] Pendler/in WF
company ['kʌmpəni] Firma, Unternehmen
compare [kəm'peə] vergleichen
compared [kəm'peəd]**: compared with** im Vergleich zu WF
compartment [kəm'pɑ:tmənt] Abteil WF
competition [kɒmpə'tɪʃn] Wettbewerb
complain [kəm'pleɪn] sich beschweren
complaint [kəm'pleɪnt] Beschwerde WF
complete [kəm'pli:t] **1** vollständig; **2** vervollständigen U1: 9
computer [kəm'pju:tə] Computer, Rechner

computer geek [kəm'pju:təgi:k] Computerfreak WF
computer program [kəm'pju:təprəʊgræm] Computerprogramm U3: 39
computer programmer [kəmpju:tə'prəʊgræmə] Computerprogrammierer/in U3: 39
concert ['kɒnsət] Konzert
conditions [kən'dɪʃnz] Verhältnisse, Zustände U2: 30
confident ['kɒnfɪdənt] zuversichtlich, selbstsicher
Congratulations! [kəngrætʃu'leɪʃnz] Herzlichen Glückwunsch!
consider [kən'sɪdə] berücksichtigen WF
contact ['kɒntækt] sich in Verbindung setzen mit WF
context ['kɒntekst] Zusammenhang, Kontext
continent ['kɒntɪnənt] Kontinent, Erdteil
conversation [kɒnvə'seɪʃn] Unterhaltung, Gespräch
cook [kʊk] **1** kochen; **2** Koch/Köchin
cooker ['kʊkə] Herd U4: 56
cool [ku:l] cool, toll
copy ['kɒpi] abschreiben; kopieren
correct [kə'rekt] **1** richtig, korrekt U1: 6; **2** korrigieren, berichtigen
cost [kɒst] **1** (it cost, it has cost) (Geld) kosten U3: 39; **it cost** es kostete, es hat gekostet U3: 39; **it has cost** es hat gekostet U3: 39; **2** Kosten WF
cougar ['ku:gə] (AE) Puma
could [kʊd]: **I could(n't)** **1** ich konnte (nicht); **2** ich könnte (nicht)
counsellor ['kaʊnsələ] Berater/in
country ['kʌntri] Land; **in the country** auf dem Land
countryside ['kʌntrisaɪd] Landschaft WF
courier ['kʊriə] Kurier/in, Bote/Botin
course [kɔ:s] **1** Kurs, Lehrgang U4: 52; **2** **of course** natürlich, selbstverständlich
court [kɔ:t] Spielfeld, Platz
cousin ['kʌzn] Cousin, Cousine
cover ['kʌvə] Umschlag, Einband
cover letter ['kʌvəletə] Anschreiben, Begleitbrief
cow [kaʊ] Kuh
cow dung ['kaʊdʌŋ] Kuhmist WF
crawl [krɔ:l] kriechen; **crawl in** hineinkriechen
credit ['kredɪt] Guthaben; **I'm out of credit.** Ich habe kein Guthaben mehr auf meinem Handy. U3: 42
cricket ['krɪkɪt] Kricket U1: 6
crime [kraɪm] Verbrechen
criminal ['krɪmɪnl] **1** kriminell WF; **2** Verbrecher/in, Kriminelle/r U3: 47
crisps [krɪsps] Kartoffelchips
critic ['krɪtɪk] Kritiker/in WF
crocodile ['krɒkədaɪl] Krokodil
cross [krɒs]: **cross (over)** überqueren WF; **I'll keep my fingers crossed for you.** Ich drücke dir die Daumen. U4: 52
crowd [kraʊd] (Menschen-)Menge WF
crowded ['kraʊdɪd] voll, überfüllt WF
crown [kraʊn] Krone WF
cry [kraɪ] weinen
culture ['kʌltʃə] Kultur U1: 6
cup [kʌp] Tasse; **a cup of tea** eine Tasse Tee
cupboard ['kʌbəd] Schrank
customer ['kʌstəmə] Kunde/Kundin U2: 26
cut [kʌt] (I cut, I've cut) **1** schneiden; „ritzen"; **2** reduzieren WF; **I cut** ich schnitt, ich habe geschnitten; **I've cut** ich habe geschnitten
CV (curriculum vitae) [si:'vi:, kə'rɪkjələm'vi:taɪ] Lebenslauf U3: 39
cyberbully ['saɪbəbʊli] „Cybermobber/in"
cyberbullying ['saɪbəbʊliɪŋ] „Cybermobbing" *(Mobbing über Internet/Mobiltelefon)*
cycle rickshaw Fahrradrikscha WF
cycling ['saɪklɪŋ] Radfahren
cyclist ['saɪklɪst] Radfahrer/in WF
Czech Republic [tʃekrɪ'pʌblɪk] Tschechische Republik

D

dad [dæd] Papa, Vati
daily ['deɪli] täglich WF
damaged ['dæmɪdʒd] beschädigt U1: 18
damn [dæm]: **Damn!** Verdammt! WF
dance [dɑ:ns] tanzen
dancer ['dɑ:nsə] Tänzer/in
danger ['deɪndʒə]: **in danger** bedroht WF
dangerous ['deɪndʒərəs] gefährlich
dare [deə] Mutprobe
dark [dɑ:k] dunkel U3: 47
date [deɪt] **1** Datum; **2** Verabredung
daughter ['dɔ:tə] Tochter
day [deɪ] Tag
day centre ['deɪsentə] Tagesstätte WF
deaf [def] taub
deal [di:l] (I dealt, I've dealt): **deal with bags** sich um Taschen kümmern; **deal with problems** mit Problemen umgehen
dealt [delt] (→ deal): **I dealt** ich ging um, ich bin umgegangen; **I've dealt** ich bin umgegangen
Dear ... [dɪə] Liebe/Lieber ...; **Dear Sir/Madam, ...** Sehr geehrte Damen und Herren, ...
December [dɪ'sembə] Dezember
decide [dɪ'saɪd] beschließen, (sich) entscheiden
decision [dɪ'sɪʒn] Entscheidung; **make a decision** eine Entscheidung treffen
deer [dɪə] Hirsch, Hirsche
definition [defɪ'nɪʃn] Definition
degree [dɪ'gri:] Grad
delete [dɪ'li:t] löschen *(Computer)*
deli ['deli] (AE) Feinkostgeschäft und -imbiss
denim ['denɪm]: **denim jacket** Jeansjacke WF
Denmark ['denmɑ:k] Dänemark
densely ['densli]: **densely populated** dicht besiedelt WF
dentist ['dentɪst] Zahnarzt/-ärztin
department [dɪ'pɑ:tmənt] Abteilung
department store [dɪ'pɑ:tməntstɔ:] Kaufhaus
deposit [dɪ'pɒzɪt] Kaution U4: 56
depressed [dɪ'prest] deprimiert
Deputy Head [depjəti'hed] stellvertretende/r Schulleiter/in WF
describe [dɪ'skraɪb] beschreiben; **Describe them to your partner.** Beschreibe sie deinem Partner / deiner Partnerin.
description [dɪ'skrɪpʃn] Beschreibung
desert ['dezət] Wüste WF
desert [dɪ'zɜ:t] verlassen WF
design [dɪ'zaɪn] **1** entwerfen WF; **2** Design
detachable [dɪ'tætʃəbl] abnehmbar WF
detail ['di:teɪl] Detail, Einzelheit U2: 32; **personal details** Angaben zur Person
detective [dɪ'tektɪv] Detektiv/in

devastated ['devəsteɪtɪd] erschüttert, am Boden zerstört
develop [dɪ'veləp] entwickeln WF
dhaba ['dɑ:bə] *einfaches indisches Restaurant* WF
diagram ['daɪəgræm] Diagramm, schematische Darstellung
dialogue ['daɪəlɒg] Dialog, Gespräch
diary ['daɪəri] Tagebuch; **homework diary** Hausaufgabenheft; Schülerkalender
dictionary ['dɪkʃənri] Wörterbuch; Wörterverzeichnis
did [dɪd] (→ do): **I did** ich machte, ich habe gemacht
die [daɪ] sterben
different ['dɪfrənt] verschieden; anders; andere/r/s; **different from** anders als
difficult ['dɪfɪkəlt] schwierig, schwer
digest [daɪ'dʒest] verdauen WF
digital ['dɪdʒɪtl] Digital-; digital
dining room ['daɪnɪŋru:m] Esszimmer U4: 56
dinner ['dɪnə] Abendessen
dinner suit ['dɪnəsu:t] Abendanzug WF
direct [də'rekt]: **direct speech** direkte Rede U2: 33
director [də'rektə] Regisseur/in
dirty ['dɜ:ti] schmutzig
disability [dɪsə'bɪləti] (Körper-)Behinderung WF
disabled [dɪs'eɪbld] behindert U4: 59
disappear [dɪsə'pɪə] verschwinden
disappointed [dɪsə'pɔɪntɪd] enttäuscht
disaster [dɪ'zɑ:stə] Katastrophe U4: 57
discover [dɪ'skʌvə] entdecken WF
discriminate [dɪ'skrɪmɪneɪt]: **discriminate against somebody** jemanden diskriminieren WF
discrimination [dɪskrɪmɪ'neɪʃn] Diskriminierung WF
discussion [dɪ'skʌʃn] Diskussion
dishwasher ['dɪʃwɒʃə] Geschirrspülmaschine
dislike [dɪs'laɪk] Abneigung
dismount [dɪs'maʊnt] absteigen WF
district ['dɪstrɪkt] Bezirk, Gebiet
dive [daɪv] einen Kopfsprung machen
diversion [daɪ'vɜ:ʃn] Umleitung WF
divorced [dɪ'vɔ:st]: **get divorced** sich scheiden lassen; **they were divorced** sie waren geschieden
DIY store [di:aɪ'waɪstɔ:] Heimwerkermarkt U4: 54
DJ ['di:dʒeɪ] DJ (= Discjockey)
do [du:] (he does; I did, I've done) **1** tun, machen; schaffen; **do research** Forschung betreiben, forschen WF; **do something to somebody** jemandem etwas antun WF; **do well** gut abschneiden U4: 54; **2 I don't (= do not)/He doesn't (= does not) live here.** Ich wohne/Er wohnt nicht hier. **Do you/Does he live here? - Yes, I do./No, I don't. / Yes, he does./No, he doesn't.** Wohnst du/Wohnt er hier? - Ja./Nein. **Don't eat.** Iss nicht.
doctor ['dɒktə] Arzt/Ärztin
document ['dɒkjumənt] Dokument, Beleg WF
does [dʌz] → do
dog [dɒg] Hund
doing ['du:ɪŋ]: **What are you doing?** Was machst du (da)?
dollar ($) ['dɒlə] Dollar *(Währung)*
dolphin ['dɒlfɪn] Delfin
done [dʌn] (→ do): **I've done** ich habe gemacht
door [dɔ:] **1** Tür; **2** Abendkasse WF
down [daʊn] **1** hinunter/herunter, hinab/herab; **2** niedergeschlagen, deprimiert WF
download [daʊn'ləʊd] herunterladen
downloaded [daʊn'ləʊdɪd]: **most downloaded film star** der am häufigsten heruntergeladene Filmstar WF
downstairs [daʊn'steəz] unten (im Haus); nach unten WF
down under [daʊn'ʌndə]: **a land down under** ein Land auf der anderen Seite der Erde
drank [dræŋk] (→ drink): **I drank** ich trank, ich habe getrunken
draw [drɔ:] (I drew, I've drawn) zeichnen
dream [dri:m] **1** träumen; **2** Traum
dress [dres] **1** (sich) anziehen U4: 64; **2** Kleid U2: 24
drink [drɪŋk] **1** (I drank, I've drunk) trinken; **2** Getränk
drive [draɪv] (I drove, I've driven) fahren; **drive off** losfahren WF
driven ['drɪvn] (→ drive): **I've driven** ich bin gefahren
driver ['draɪvə] (Auto-)Fahrer/in
driving lesson ['draɪvɪŋlesn] Fahrstunde U2: 22
driving test ['draɪvɪŋtest] Führerscheinprüfung U2: 34
drove [drəʊv] (→ drive): **I drove** ich fuhr, ich bin gefahren
drug [drʌg] Droge
Dubliner ['dʌblɪnə] Dubliner/in
duke [dju:k] Herzog WF
during ['djʊərɪŋ] während U1: 8
DVD [di:vi:'di:] DVD; **DVD player** DVD-Player

E

each [i:tʃ] jede/r/s; **each other** einander, sich WF
eagle ['i:gl] Adler WF
ear [ɪə] Ohr
early ['ɜ:li] früh
earn [ɜ:n] verdienen
east [i:st] Osten; Ost-; östlich
east coast ['i:stkəʊst] Ostküste
easy ['i:zi] einfach, leicht
eat [i:t] (I ate, I've eaten) essen; fressen; **eat out** essen gehen
eaten ['i:tn] (→ eat): **I've eaten** ich habe gegessen
economy [ɪ'kɒnəmi] Wirtschaft
ecstasy ['ekstəsi] Ecstasy U2: 26
education [edʒu'keɪʃn] Bildung, Ausbildung
egg [eg] Ei
Egypt ['i:dʒɪpt] Ägypten
either ... or ['aɪðə] entweder ... oder U2: 25
elect [ɪ'lekt] wählen WF
election [ɪ'lekʃn] Wahl WF
electric [ɪ'lektrɪk] elektrisch
electrician [ɪlek'trɪʃn] Elektriker/in U4: 55
electricity [ɪlek'trɪsəti] Strom, Elektrizität
electronic [ɪlek'trɒnɪk] elektronisch
elephant ['elɪfənt] Elefant U1: 6
else [els]: **anything else** sonst noch etwas WF
e-mail ['i:meɪl] E-Mail
embarrassed [ɪm'bærəst] verlegen; **I'm embarrassed about ...** ich schäme mich wegen ...
embarrassing [ɪm'bærəsɪŋ] peinlich U4: 64
emergency exit [i'mɜ:dʒənsieksɪt] Notausgang WF
employee [ɪm'plɔɪi:] Angestellte/r, Arbeitnehmer/in WF
employer [ɪm'plɔɪə] Arbeitgeber/in
empty ['empti] **1** leer U3: 46; **2** ausräumen, leeren

encourage [ɪn'kʌrɪdʒ] ermutigen, ermuntern
end [end] Ende; **in the end** letztendlich; schließlich; **All's well that ends well.** Ende gut, alles gut. U4: 54
ending ['endɪŋ] Schluss; **happy ending** Happy End
energy ['enədʒi] Energie; Kraft
England ['ɪŋglənd] England
English ['ɪŋglɪʃ] englisch; Englisch; Engländer/in(nen)
enjoy [ɪn'dʒɔɪ] genießen, Spaß haben an, gern haben/tun; **enjoy working** Spaß am Arbeiten haben, gern arbeiten; **I enjoy myself** ich amüsiere mich, ich habe viel Spaß
enormous [ɪ'nɔːməs] ungeheuer groß WF
enough [ɪ'nʌf] genug U2: 34
entertainer [entə'teɪnə]: **street entertainer** Straßenkünstler/in WF
entrance fee ['entrənsfiː] Eintrittspreis
entrance hall ['entrənshɔːl] Diele, Hausflur U4: 56
entry ['entri] **1** Eintrag; **2 on entry** am Eingang, beim Betreten U1: 11
environment [ɪn'vaɪrənmənt] Umwelt; Umgebung
equip [ɪ'kwɪp] ausstatten WF
equipment [ɪ'kwɪpmənt] Ausstattung, Ausrüstung
escape [ɪ'skeɪp] fliehen, flüchten
etc. [et'setərə] etc., usw. WF
EU [iː'juː] EU (Europäische Union) WF
euro (€) ['jʊərəʊ] Euro
Europe ['jʊərəp] Europa
European [jʊərə'piːən] europäisch; Europäer/in
even ['iːvn] sogar; **never even** nicht einmal WF
evening ['iːvnɪŋ] Abend; **in the evening** am Abend, abends
event [ɪ'vent] Veranstaltung; Ereignis U4: 58
ever ['evə] schon einmal, jemals
every ['evri] jede/r/s; **every 15 minutes** alle 15 Minuten WF
everybody ['evribɒdi] jeder, alle
everything ['evriθɪŋ] alles
everywhere ['evriweə] überall, überallhin/-her; **everywhere she goes** überall, wo sie hingeht WF
exam [ɪg'zæm] Prüfung; **take an exam** eine Prüfung machen
example [ɪg'zɑːmpl] Beispiel; **for example** zum Beispiel

excellent ['eksələnt] ausgezeichnet WF
except [ɪk'sept] außer WF
exchange [ɪks'tʃeɪndʒ] **1** tauschen, austauschen WF; **2** Austausch-; Tausch-
excited [ɪk'saɪtɪd] aufgeregt, begeistert
exciting [ɪk'saɪtɪŋ] aufregend, spannend
excuse [ɪk'skjuːs] Entschuldigung, Ausrede, Vorwand U2: 25; **Excuse me, ...** Entschuldigen Sie, ...
executive [ɪg'zekjətɪv]: **chief executive** Geschäftsführer/in WF
exercise ['eksəsaɪz] **1** Übung; **2** Ausgleichssport; **do exercise** Ausgleichssport treiben
exercise book ['eksəsaɪzbʊk] Schulheft
exhibition [eksɪ'bɪʃn] Ausstellung
exist [ɪg'zɪst] existieren, vorkommen WF
exotic [ɪg'zɒtɪk] exotisch WF
expect [ɪk'spekt] erwarten; **they expect teenagers to ...** sie erwarten von Teenagern, dass sie ...
expedition [ekspə'dɪʃn] Expedition
expensive [ɪk'spensɪv] teuer
experience [ɪk'spɪəriəns] Erfahrung
experiment [ɪk'sperɪmənt] Experiment, Versuch
expert ['ekspɜːt] Fachmann/-frau, Experte/Expertin
explain [ɪk'spleɪn] erklären; **explain something to her** ihr etwas erklären
explode [ɪk'spləʊd] explodieren U3: 46
explore [ɪk'splɔː] erkunden WF
export ['ekspɔːt] Export WF
expression [ɪk'spreʃn] Ausdruck U4: 61
extra ['ekstrə] extra, zusätzlich U4: 56; **extra classes** Förderunterricht
extremist [ɪk'striːmɪst] Extremist/in U3: 49
eye [aɪ] Auge
eyebrow ['aɪbraʊ] Augenbraue

F

face [feɪs] Gesicht
fact [fækt] Tatsache; **In fact, it was better.** Es war sogar besser.

factfile ['fæktfaɪl] Faktensammlung U3: 37
factory ['fæktri] Fabrik
fair [feə] fair, gerecht
fair play [feə'pleɪ] Fair Play
Fairtrade [feə'treɪd] *Organisation für fairen Handel mit Entwicklungsländern* WF
faithfully ['feɪθfəli]: **Yours faithfully, ...** Mit freundlichen Grüßen ...
fake [feɪk] gefälscht, unecht
fall [fɔːl] (I fell, I've fallen) fallen; **fall to the ground** auf den Boden fallen
false [fɔːls] falsch, unwahr
family ['fæməli] Familie; **family name** Nachname, Familienname
famous ['feɪməs] berühmt
fan [fæn] Fan, Anhänger/in; **fans waiting** Fans, die warteten WF
fantastic [fæn'tæstɪk] fantastisch
far [fɑː] weit
farm [fɑːm] Bauernhof, Hof; Farm
farmer ['fɑːmə] Bauer/Bäuerin
fascinating ['fæsɪneɪtɪŋ] faszinierend WF
fashion ['fæʃn] Mode
fast [fɑːst] schnell
fast food [fɑːst'fuːd] Fastfood *(schnell verzehrbare Gerichte)*
fat [fæt] dick
father ['fɑːðə] Vater
favourite ['feɪvərɪt] Lieblings-; Favorit/in
February ['februəri] Februar
fed up [fed'ʌp]: **I'm fed up.** Ich habe die Nase voll. U4: 54
feed [fiːd] (I fed, I've fed) füttern, zu essen geben; **feeding equipment** Geräte zur Nahrungsaufnahme WF
feel [fiːl] (I felt, I've felt) (sich) fühlen; **feel a different person** sich wie ein anderer Mensch fühlen WF; **feel an outsider** sich als Außenseiter/in fühlen WF; **feel ashamed** sich schämen WF; **feel sorry for me** mit mir Mitleid haben, mich bemitleiden
feeling ['fiːlɪŋ] Gefühl
feet [fiːt] (→ foot) **1** Füße; **2** Fuß *(Längenmaß; 30,48 cm)*
fell [fel] (→ fall): **I fell** ich fiel, ich bin gefallen
felt [felt] (→ feel): **I felt** ich fühlte (mich), ich habe (mich) gefühlt; **I've felt** ich habe (mich) gefühlt
female ['fiːmeɪl] weiblich
fence [fens] Zaun

ferry ['feri] Fähre U4: 60
festival ['festɪvl] Festival; Fest
fetch [fetʃ] holen WF
few [fju:] wenige WF; **a few** ein paar U1: 18
field [fi:ld] Feld, Wiese
fight [faɪt] **1** (I fought, I've fought) kämpfen; sich streiten; **fight for something** um etwas kämpfen U1: 8; **he fights him** er bekämpft ihn WF; **2** Kampf WF
file [faɪl] Karteikarte; Akte
fill in [fɪl'ɪn] ausfüllen
film [fɪlm] Film; **film studies** Filmwissenschaft WF; **film trailer** Filmtrailer, Filmvorschau
final ['faɪnl] letzte/r/s WF; **final call** letzter Aufruf; **final round** Schlussrunde, Finale WF
finally ['faɪnəli] schließlich WF
financial [faɪ'nænʃl] finanziell, Finanz-
find [faɪnd] (I found, I've found) finden; **find out** herausfinden
fine [faɪn] **1** gut, schön; **How are you? – I'm fine, thanks.** Wie geht's? – Danke, gut. **2** fein
finger ['fɪŋgə]: **I'll keep my fingers crossed for you.** Ich drücke dir die Daumen. U4: 52
finish ['fɪnɪʃ] aufhören (mit); beenden; **To finish, ...** Um zum Ende zu kommen, ...
finished ['fɪnɪʃt]: **I'm finished** ich bin fertig
fire ['faɪə] Feuer; Brand
fire brigade ['faɪəbrɪgeɪd] Feuerwehr WF
firefighter ['faɪəfaɪtə] Feuerwehrfrau/Feuerwehrmann
fire instructions ['faɪəɪnstrʌkʃnz] Vorschriften für das Verhalten im Brandfall U4: 56
fireworks ['faɪəwɜ:ks] Feuerwerk
first [fɜ:st] **1** erste/r/s; **the first to try anything** die Erste, die etwas versucht WF; **first aid** erste Hilfe; **first language** Muttersprache; **first name** Vorname; **2** zuerst; **at first** zunächst
firstly ['fɜ:stli] erstens
fish [fɪʃ] **1** Fisch, Fische; **2** fischen, angeln
fish and chip shop [fɪʃən'tʃɪpʃɒp] *Schnellimbiss für Fisch und Pommes frites*
fishing ['fɪʃɪŋ] Fischen, Angeln
fit [fɪt] **1** fit; **2** passen WF; **It fits tightly.** Er/Sie/Es sitzt eng. WF
fitting service ['fɪtɪŋsɜ:vɪs] Änderungsservice WF
fix [fɪks] reparieren
fizzy ['fɪzi] sprudelnd U3: 42
flag [flæg] Fahne, Flagge
flat [flæt] Wohnung
flew [flu:] (→ fly): **I flew** ich flog, ich bin geflogen U3: 44
flexible ['fleksəbl] flexibel U4: 61
flight [flaɪt] Flug
flight attendant ['flaɪtətendənt] Flugbegleiter/in, Steward/ess
flip phone ['flɪpfəʊn] Klapphandy
floor [flɔ:] **1** Fußboden, Boden; **2** Stockwerk U4: 56; **on the ground floor/first floor** im Erdgeschoss/ersten Stock
flow [fləʊ] fließen WF
flown [fləʊn] (→ fly): **I've flown** ich bin geflogen U3: 44
fly [flaɪ] fliegen U3: 44
follow ['fɒləʊ] folgen, verfolgen
food [fu:d] Essen; Lebensmittel
foot, feet [fʊt, fi:t] **1** Fuß, Füße; **on foot** zu Fuß; **2** Fuß *(Längenmaß; 30,48 cm)*
football ['fʊtbɔ:l] Fußball; **American football** American Football *(ähnlich wie Rugby)*
for [fɔ:, fə] **1** für; **2** zu; **for 14 years** 14 Jahre lang; **for a long time** lange; **for and against** dafür und dagegen; **for breakfast/...** zum Frühstück/...; **for ever** für immer, auf ewig WF; **for example** zum Beispiel; **fight for something** um etwas kämpfen U1: 8; **stay for long** lange bleiben
force [fɔ:s] zwingen U1: 20
foreground ['fɔ:graʊnd] Vordergrund
foreign ['fɒrən]: **foreign language** Fremdsprache; fremdsprachig U1: 20
forest ['fɒrɪst] Wald, Waldgebiet
forget [fə'get] (I forgot, I've forgotten) vergessen
forgot [fə'gɒt] (→ forget): **I forgot** ich vergaß, ich habe vergessen
forgotten [fə'gɒtn] (→ forget): **I've forgotten** ich habe vergessen
form [fɔ:m] **1** Form; **2** Formular
formula ['fɔ:mjələ] Formel
fort [fɔ:t] Fort WF
forward ['fɔ:wəd] **1** weiterleiten; **2 I'm looking forward to hearing from you** ich freue mich darauf, von Ihnen zu hören
fought [fɔ:t] (→ fight): **I fought** ich kämpfte, ich habe gekämpft; **I've fought** ich habe gekämpft
foul [faʊl] Foul
found [faʊnd] (→ find): **I found** ich fand, ich habe gefunden; **I've found** ich habe gefunden
France [frɑ:ns] Frankreich
freak [fri:k] Freak *(jemand, der sich sehr für etwas begeistert)*
free [fri:] **1** frei; **2** kostenlos; **free throw** Freiwurf U3: 40; **free time** Freizeit; **for free** umsonst WF
freedom ['fri:dəm] Freiheit
freeway ['fri:weɪ] Autobahn *(in den USA)*
freezer ['fri:zə] Gefriertruhe, -schrank U4: 56
French [frentʃ] französisch; Französisch; Franzose(n)/Französin(nen)
fresh [freʃ] frisch WF
Friday ['fraɪdeɪ, 'fraɪdi] Freitag
fridge [frɪdʒ] Kühlschrank U4: 56
friend [frend] Freund/in
friendly ['frendli] freundlich
frighten ['fraɪtn] Angst machen, erschrecken WF
frightened ['fraɪtnd]: **I'm frightened** ich habe Angst; **look frightened** verängstigt aussehen
frightening ['fraɪtnɪŋ] beängstigend, furchterregend
from [frɒm, frəm] **1** aus; von; **I'm from London.** Ich komme aus London. **2** ab WF
front [frʌnt]: **in front of** vor
fruit [fru:t] Obst, Früchte
fruit picker ['fru:tpɪkə] Obstpflücker/in
full [fʊl] ganz; voll; vollständig U1: 9; **full of clouds** voller Wolken WF
full board [fʊl'bɔ:d] Vollpension WF
full-time [fʊl'taɪm] ganztags, Ganztags-
fun [fʌn] Spaß; **It's fun.** Es macht Spaß. **have good fun** viel Spaß haben WF
funfair ['fʌnfeə] Kirmes, Jahrmarkt
fun-packed ['fʌnpækt] „spaßgeladen" WF
funny ['fʌni] lustig, komisch
furniture ['fɜ:nɪtʃə] Möbel
further ['fɜ:ðə] weiter U4: 60
future ['fju:tʃə] Zukunft

G

Gaelic ['gælɪk] Gälisch *(keltische Sprache)*
game [geɪm] Spiel
gang [gæŋ] Gang, Bande, Clique
gang leader ['gæŋliːdə] Bandenführer/in WF
gap [gæp] Lücke U4: 54
garage ['gærɑːʒ] Garage WF
garden ['gɑːdn] Garten
gardener ['gɑːdnə] Gärtner/in
gas [gæs] Gas U3: 43
gate [geɪt] **1** Tor; **2** Flugsteig, Ausgang
gave [geɪv] (→ give): **I gave** ich gab, ich habe gegeben
gear [gɪə] **1** Gang *(Fahrrad, Auto)*; **2** Ausrüstung; **safety gear** Sicherheitsausrüstung; **3** Kleidung, Klamotten
geek [giːk]: **computer geek** Computerfreak WF
gender ['dʒendə] Geschlecht U4: 63
general ['dʒenrəl] allgemein
generation [dʒenə'reɪʃn] Generation
geography [dʒi'ɒgrəfi] Geografie
German ['dʒɜːmən] deutsch; Deutsch; Deutsche/r
Germany ['dʒɜːməni] Deutschland
get [get] (I got, I've got) **1** bekommen; **2** holen; **3** kommen, gelangen; **4** werden; **get divorced** sich scheiden lassen; **get lost** sich verirren; **get married** heiraten U3: 38; **get into a car/...** in ein Auto/... einsteigen WF; **get on a plane/...** in ein Flugzeug/... einsteigen; **get out (of the car/...)** (aus dem Auto/...) aussteigen; **I have to get out of this place.** Ich muss hier raus. **get over something** über etwas hinwegkommen U4: 54; **get up** aufstehen
ghost [gəʊst] Geist, Gespenst
giraffe [dʒə'rɑːf] Giraffe WF
girl [gɜːl] Mädchen
girlfriend ['gɜːlfrend] (feste) Freundin
girly girl ['gɜːligɜːl] *Mädchen, das sich traditionell feminin kleidet und benimmt* WF
give [gɪv] (I gave, I've given) geben; **Give the book to Tim.** Gib Tim das Buch. **give a talk** einen Vortrag halten WF; **give an opinion** eine Meinung abgeben U3: 44; **give blood** Blut spenden U4: 58; **give it a go** es probieren WF; **give notice** kündigen WF; **give somebody a hug** jemanden umarmen U1: 8; **give way** die Vorfahrt beachten WF; **give up** aufgeben
given ['gɪvn] (→ give): **I've given** ich habe gegeben
giving ['gɪvɪŋ]: **Giving orders** Anweisungen geben, Befehle erteilen
glad [glæd]: **I'm glad** ich bin froh WF
glass [glɑːs] Glas, Trinkglas
glasses ['glɑːsɪz] Brille
glove [glʌv] Handschuh WF
glue [gluː] Klebstoff WF
go [gəʊ] **1** (I went, I've gone) gehen; fahren; fliegen; führen; **Go ahead.** Mach(t) nur. **go down** untergehen WF; **go in** hineingehen; **go on** weitergehen WF; **go out** aus-/weggehen; **go out with somebody** mit jemandem gehen; **go wrong** schiefgehen; **2 give it a go** es (aus)probieren WF
goal [gəʊl] Tor
God [gɒd] Gott WF; **God be with you.** Gott sei bei dir. WF; **Good God!** O Gott! WF; **Thank God.** Gott sei Dank. WF
going to ['gəʊɪŋtu, 'gəʊɪŋtə]: **I'm going to win** ich werde gewinnen, ich gewinne; **I'm going to be a ranger.** Ich werde Ranger.
gold [gəʊld] Gold WF
golf [gɒlf] Golf
gone [gɒn] (→ go): **I've gone** ich bin gegangen
good [gʊd] gut; **good at** gut in; **Good evening/morning/night.** Gute(n) Abend/Morgen/Nacht. **Good God!** O Gott! WF; **Good luck!** Viel Glück!
Goodbye. [gʊd'baɪ] Auf Wiedersehen.
good-looking [gʊd'lʊkɪŋ] gut aussehend
gorilla [gə'rɪlə] Gorilla WF
gospel ['gɒspl] Gospel(musik) U1: 13
got [gɒt]: **1** (→ get) **I got** ich bekam, ich habe bekommen; **I've got** ich habe bekommen; **2 you've got** du hast WF; **I've got to ...** ich muss ... U1: 10
government ['gʌvənmənt] Regierung
grade [greɪd] (AE) (Schul-)Klasse
grandad ['grændæd] Opa, Großvater
grandchildren ['græntʃɪldrən] Enkelkinder U1: 12
grandma ['grænmɑː] Oma, Großmutter
grandmother ['grænmʌðə] Großmutter
grandparents ['grænpeərənts] Großeltern
grass [grɑːs] Gras, Rasen
grave [greɪv] Grab
great [greɪt] **1** toll, großartig; **2** groß WF
green [griːn] grün
grew [gruː] (→ grow): **I grew** ich wuchs, ich bin gewachsen
grey [greɪ] grau U2: 31
ground [graʊnd] Boden
ground floor [graʊnd'flɔː] Erdgeschoss, Parterre WF
grounded ['graʊndɪd]: **I'm grounded** ich habe Hausarrest/Stubenarrest
group [gruːp] Gruppe
grow [grəʊ] (I grew, I've grown) **1** wachsen; **grow things** etwas anbauen; **2 grow older/...** älter/... werden WF
grown [grəʊn] (→ grow): **I've grown** ich bin gewachsen
guard [gɑːd]: **security guard** Wachfrau/Wachmann
guess [ges] raten; erraten; **Guess what!** Stell dir vor! U4: 54
guest [gest] Gast; **guest room** Gästezimmer WF
guide [gaɪd] **1** führen, leiten WF; **2** Führer/in *(für Sehenswürdigkeiten)*
guitar [gɪ'tɑː] Gitarre
gun [gʌn] Waffe WF
guy [gaɪ] Kerl, Typ WF
guys [gaɪz]: **Hi you guys.** (AE) Hallo Leute.
gym [dʒɪm] Turnhalle; Fitnessstudio

H

habitat ['hæbɪtæt] Habitat, Lebensraum WF
hack [hæk]: **hack into a computer** in einen Computer eindringen
had [hæd, həd] (→ have): **I had** ich hatte, ich habe gehabt; **I had listened** ich hatte zugehört; **I've had** ich habe gehabt
hair [heə] Haar, Haare
hairdresser ['heədresə] Friseur/in

hairdressing ['heədresɪŋ] das Frisieren
half [hɑːf]: **half an hour** eine halbe Stunde U2: 33; **half my breakfast** mein halbes Frühstück U4: 64; **half past nine** halb zehn; **three and a half** dreieinhalb
half-time [hɑːf'taɪm] Halbzeit
Halloween [hæləʊ'iːn] Halloween
ham [hæm] Schinken
hamburger ['hæmbɜːgə] Hamburger
hamster ['hæmstə] Hamster
hand [hænd] Hand; **On the one hand, ... On the other hand, ...** Einerseits ... Andererseits ...
handbag ['hændbæg] Handtasche WF
handle ['hændl] Kurbel(griff) WF
hand signal ['hændsɪgnəl] Handzeichen
hang [hæŋ]: **hang around** (I hung around, I've hung around) herumhängen U2: 22
hanged [hæŋd]: **he was hanged** er wurde gehängt
happen ['hæpən] passieren, geschehen
happy ['hæpi] glücklich, froh; **I'm happy for her** ich freue mich für sie; **be happy to do something** etwas gern tun U4: 63; **Happy birthday!** Herzlichen Glückwunsch zum Geburtstag! **happy ending** Happy End
hard [hɑːd] hart; schwer
hard-working [hɑːd'wɜːkɪŋ] fleißig WF
has [hæz, həz] → have
hate [heɪt] hassen, nicht ausstehen können
Havana [hə'vænə] Havanna
have [hæv, həv] (he has; I had, I've had) **1** haben; **I'll have ...** Ich nehme ... *(Bestellung)*; **have a chat** sich unterhalten; **have a cola** eine Cola trinken; **have a look around** sich umschauen WF; **have a party** eine Party geben; **have a picnic** ein Picknick machen; **have a rest** eine Pause machen WF; **have a test** einen Test machen lassen U1: 13; **have an ice cream** ein Eis essen; **have breakfast** frühstücken; **Have a nice day!** (AE) (Einen) Schönen Tag noch! **2 I've (= I have)/he has finished** ich habe/er hat beendet; **I haven't (= have not)/he hasn't (= has not) finished** ich habe/er hat nicht beendet;
Have you ever ...? - Yes, I have./No, I haven't. Bist/Hast du schon einmal ...? - Ja./Nein.
have to ['hævtu, 'hævtə] (I had to, I've had to) müssen
he [hiː] er; **he's (= he is)** er ist
head [hed] Kopf
heading ['hedɪŋ] Rubrik; Überschrift
headline ['hedlaɪn] Schlagzeile
health [helθ] Gesundheit WF
healthy ['helθi] gesund
hear [hɪə] (I heard, I've heard) hören; **hear about ...** von ... erfahren, von ... hören
heard [hɜːd] (→ hear): **I heard** ich hörte, ich habe gehört; **I've heard** ich habe gehört
heart [hɑːt]: **Learn it by heart.** Lerne es auswendig.
heavy ['hevi] schwer, dick WF
height [haɪt] Größe; Höhe
held [held] (→ hold): **I held** ich hielt, ich habe gehalten; **I've held** ich habe gehalten
Hello. [hə'ləʊ] Hallo. (Guten) Tag.
helmet ['helmɪt] Helm
help [help] **1** helfen; **Can I help you?** Kann ich Ihnen behilflich sein? **I can't help laughing.** Ich kann nicht anders, ich muss lachen. U3: 47; **2** Hilfe
helper ['helpə] Helfer/in
her [hɜː] **1** ihr/e; **2** ihr, sie
here [hɪə] hier; hierher; **Here you are.** Hier, bitte.
hero, heroes ['hɪərəʊ, 'hɪərəʊz] Held/in, Helden/Heldinnen
herself [hɜː'self] sich (selbst); selbst
Hi. [haɪ] Hallo.
high [haɪ] hoch; **high-frequency** [haɪ'friːkwənsi] Hochfrequenz- WF; **high jump** Hochsprung; **high mountains** Hochgebirge WF; **high school** Oberschule *(in den USA)*
hike [haɪk] **1** wandern; **2** Wanderung U2: 28
hiker ['haɪkə] Wanderer/Wanderin
hill [hɪl] Hügel, (kleiner) Berg
him [hɪm] ihm, ihn
Himalayas [hɪmə'leɪəz]: **the Himalayas** der Himalaya WF
himself [hɪm'self] sich (selbst); selbst
Hindi ['hɪndi] Hindi U3: 37
Hindu ['hɪnduː] Hindu U3: 37
hip [hɪp] Hüfte
hippo ['hɪpəʊ] Nilpferd WF
hire ['haɪə] **1** (ver)mieten; **2** Verleih WF; **3** anstellen WF
hire department ['haɪədɪpɑːtmənt] Verleih *(Firma)* WF
his [hɪz] sein/e
Hispanic [hɪ'spænɪk] Hispano-Amerikaner/in; hispanisch; spanischsprachig
history ['hɪstri] Geschichte
hit [hɪt] **1** (I hit, I've hit) schlagen; **2** (I hit, I've hit) treffen U1: 8; **I hit** ich schlug/traf, ich habe geschlagen/getroffen; **I've hit** ich habe geschlagen/getroffen; **2** Hit
hobby ['hɒbi] Hobby
hockey ['hɒki] Hockey
hold [həʊld] (I held, I've held) halten; (MP3-Player:) speichern; **hold somebody back** jemanden aufhalten WF
holiday, holidays ['hɒlədeɪ, -z] Ferien, Urlaub; **go on holiday** in den Urlaub fahren; **she's on holiday** sie macht Urlaub, sie ist im Urlaub
home [həʊm] **1** Heim, Zuhause; **2** Kinderheim U1: 9; **at home** zu Hause, daheim; **go home** nach Hause gehen
homeless ['həʊmləs] heimatlos; obdachlos
home-made [həʊm'meɪd] selbst gemacht
homework ['həʊmwɜːk] Hausaufgaben, Schularbeiten; **I do my homework.** Ich mache (meine) Hausaufgaben.
homework diary [həʊmwɜːk'daɪəri] Hausaufgabenheft; Schülerkalender
hood [hʊd] Kapuze WF
hoody ['hʊdi] Kapuzensweatshirt/-jacke U2: 26
hoop [huːp] (Basketball-)Korb
hope [həʊp] hoffen; **I hope so.** Das hoffe ich. U1: 10
horn [hɔːn] Horn WF
horrible ['hɒrəbl] scheußlich U2: 29
horror ['hɒrə] Horror
horse [hɔːs] Pferd
horse riding ['hɔːsraɪdɪŋ] Reiten
hospital ['hɒspɪtl] Krankenhaus
host [həʊst] Moderator/in WF
hot [hɒt] heiß
hotel [həʊ'tel] Hotel
hound [haʊnd] (Jagd-)Hund WF
hour ['aʊə] Stunde
hours ['aʊəz] Arbeitszeit(en)

house [haʊs] **1** Haus; **at Tim's house** bei Tim (zu Hause); **Let's go to my house.** Gehen wir zu mir (nach Hause). **2** House *(Musikrichtung)*
how [haʊ] wie; **how to find us** wie man uns findet; **How much is/are ...?** Was kostet/kosten ...?
hug [hʌg]: **give somebody a hug** jemanden umarmen U1: 8
human ['hju:mən] Mensch WF
humour ['hju:mə]: **a great sense of humour** Sinn für Humor WF
hundred ['hʌndrəd] hundert
hung [hʌŋ] (→ hang): **I hung around** ich hing herum, ich habe herumgehangen U2: 22; **I've hung around** ich habe herumgehangen U2: 22
hungry ['hʌŋgri] hungrig; **I'm hungry.** Ich habe Hunger.
hunt [hʌnt] jagen
hunter ['hʌntə] Jäger/in
hurling ['hɜ:lɪŋ] Hurling *(irische Sportart; ähnlich wie Hockey)*
hurricane ['hʌrɪkən] Orkan
hurry ['hʌri]: **Hurry up!** Beeil dich!
hurt [hɜ:t] **1** (I hurt, I've hurt) verletzen, wehtun; **I hurt my hand** ich verletzte mir die Hand, ich habe mir die Hand verletzt; **2** verletzt
husband ['hʌzbənd] Ehemann U3: 46
hyena [haɪ'i:nə] Hyäne WF

I

I [aɪ] ich; **I'd like ...** Ich möchte .../Ich hätte gern ...; **I'd like to go/...** Ich möchte gehen/...; **I'll (= I will) go** ich werde gehen; **I'll give you your invitations in the break.** Ich gebe euch eure Einladungen in der Pause. **I'll have ...** Ich nehme ... *(Bestellung)*; **I'm (= I am)** ich bin
ice cream [aɪs'kri:m] (Speise-)Eis
idea [aɪ'dɪə] Idee, Einfall
identity [aɪ'dentəti] Identität
if [ɪf] **1** wenn, falls; **2** ob
if-clause ['ɪfklɔ:z] If-Satz WF
ill [ɪl] krank
illegal [ɪ'li:gl] ungesetzlich, illegal
illness ['ɪlnəs] Krankheit
illuminations [ɪlu:mɪ'neɪʃnz] Festbeleuchtung
imagine [ɪ'mædʒɪn] sich (etwas) vorstellen
immigrant ['ɪmɪgrənt] Immigrant/in, Einwanderer/Einwanderin
imperative [ɪm'perətɪv] Befehlsform, Imperativ
important [ɪm'pɔ:tnt] wichtig
in [ɪn] in; **in 1971** (im Jahre) 1971; **in April** im April; **in Dean Road** in der Dean Road; **In fact, it was better.** Es war sogar besser. **in front of** vor; **in German** auf Deutsch; **in minutes** innerhalb weniger Minuten WF; **in the car park** auf dem Parkplatz; **in the country** auf dem Land; **in the foreground/background** im Vordergrund/Hintergrund; **in the morning/afternoon/evening** am Morgen/Nachmittag/Abend; **in the picture** auf dem Bild; **in the playground** auf dem Schulhof; **in the same place** am selben Ort; **in the street** auf der Straße; **in the world** auf der (ganzen) Welt; **in winter** im Winter; **come in** hereinkommen; **go in** hineingehen
inch [ɪntʃ] *Längenmaß* (= 2,54 cm)
include [ɪn'klu:d] einschließen WF
included [ɪn'klu:dɪd]: **included (in the price)** (im Preis) enthalten U3: 40
including [ɪn'klu:dɪŋ] einschließlich U4: 56
independence [ɪndɪ'pendəns] Unabhängigkeit U3: 36
independent [ɪndɪ'pendənt] unabhängig WF
India ['ɪndiə] Indien U3: 36
Indian ['ɪndiən] indisch; Inder/in U3: 37
indirect [ɪndə'rekt]: **indirect speech** indirekte Rede U3: 50
Indonesia [ɪndə'ni:ziə] Indonesien
indoor ['ɪndɔ:]: **indoor and outdoor use** Innen- und Außengebrauch WF
indoors [ɪn'dɔ:z] in der Halle, drinnen
industry ['ɪndəstri] Industrie U3: 36
influence ['ɪnfluəns]: **they could be a bad influence** sie könnten einen schlechten Einfluss haben WF
informal [ɪn'fɔ:ml] formlos, informell, „locker" U1: 18
information [ɪnfə'meɪʃn] Informationen, Informations-
in-line skate [ɪnlaɪn'skeɪt] Inlineskate, Inliner
in-line skating [ɪnlaɪn'skeɪtɪŋ] Inlineskating WF
inside [ɪn'saɪd] innerhalb (von); in; (nach) drinnen U2: 26
insist [ɪn'sɪst] beharren WF
inspector [ɪn'spektə] Kontrolleur/in WF
inspiration [ɪnspə'reɪʃn] Inspiration WF
instead of [ɪn'stedəv] statt
institute ['ɪnstɪtju:t] Institut WF
instructions [ɪn'strʌkʃnz] Gebrauchsanweisung
instructor [ɪn'strʌktə] Ausbilder/in WF
instrument ['ɪnstrəmənt] Instrument
insurance [ɪn'ʃʊərəns] Versicherung U2: 34
intercom ['ɪntəkɒm] Sprechanlage
interest ['ɪntrəst] Interesse
interested (in) ['ɪntrəstɪd] interessiert (an)
interesting ['ɪntrəstɪŋ] interessant
international [ɪntə'næʃnəl] international
Internet ['ɪntənet] Internet; **on the Internet** im Internet
Internet kiosk ['ɪntənetki:ɒsk] Internet-Kiosk *(öffentlich zugängliches Internet-Terminal)*
interpret [ɪn'tɜ:prɪt] dolmetschen
interpreting [ɪn'tɜ:prɪtɪŋ] Dolmetschen
interview ['ɪntəvju:] **1** Interview; **2 (job) interview** Vorstellungsgespräch
interviewer ['ɪntəvju:ə] Leiter/in des Vorstellungsgesprächs
into ['ɪntu, 'ɪntə] in (... hinein/herein); **into the street** auf die Straße (hinaus)
invent [ɪn'vent] erfinden WF
invention [ɪn'venʃn] Erfindung WF
invitation [ɪnvɪ'teɪʃn] Einladung
invite (for) [ɪn'vaɪt] einladen (zu)
Ireland ['aɪələnd] Irland
Irish ['aɪrɪʃ] irisch; Irisch; Ire(n), Irin(nen)
is [ɪz] ist; **isn't (= is not)** ist nicht; **he's six feet one (inch)** er ist einsfünfundachtzig groß; **What colour is your room?** Welche Farbe hat dein Zimmer? **... but is it?** ... aber ist es das auch? WF
island ['aɪlənd] Insel
it [ɪt] **1** es (*nicht bei Personen:* er, sie); **2** ihm, es (*nicht bei Personen*: ihm, ihn; ihr, sie); **it's (= it is)** es ist; **it's 24–18 to North**

es steht 24:18 für North; **It's my birthday.** Ich habe Geburtstag. **It's Sarah.** Hier spricht Sarah.
Italy ['ɪtəli] Italien
item ['aɪtəm] Artikel, Gegenstand WF
its [ɪts] sein/e; ihr/e
itself [ɪt'self] sich (selbst); selbst

J

jackal ['dʒækl] Schakal WF
jacket ['dʒækət] Jacke
January ['dʒænjuəri] Januar
Japanese [dʒæpə'ni:z] japanisch WF
jealous (of) ['dʒeləs] neidisch (auf); eifersüchtig (auf)
jeans [dʒi:nz] Jeans
job [dʒɒb] **1** Aufgabe, Arbeit; **2** Arbeitsstelle; Beruf
jog [dʒɒg] joggen
jogger ['dʒɒgə] Jogger/in
jogging ['dʒɒgɪŋ] Jogging
join [dʒɔɪn]: **join a circus** sich einem Zirkus anschließen; **join a club** einem Klub beitreten, Mitglied in einem Klub werden; **join in (with)** mitmachen (bei)
joke [dʒəʊk] Witz, Scherz
joking ['dʒəʊkɪŋ]: **You must be joking.** Du machst wohl Witze. U2: 24
journalist ['dʒɜ:nəlɪst] Journalist/in
journey ['dʒɜ:ni] Fahrt, Reise U2: 28
judge [dʒʌdʒ] urteilen WF
judo ['dʒu:dəʊ] Judo
juice [dʒu:s] Saft
July [dʒu'laɪ] Juli
jump [dʒʌmp] springen; **(the) high jump** Hochsprung
June [dʒu:n] Juni
junior ['dʒu:niə]: **junior ranger** Junior-Ranger
just [dʒʌst] **1** gerade, soeben; **2** einfach, nur; **Just a minute.** Einen Augenblick. **just before** kurz (be)vor; **just over 2000 euros** etwas mehr als 2000 Euro WF; **just so that ...** nur damit ... WF

K

karate [kə'rɑ:ti] Karate WF
kayak ['kaɪæk] Kajak
kayaking ['kaɪækɪŋ] Kajakfahren
keen [ki:n]: **I'm not keen on it** ich habe nicht viel dafür übrig
keep [ki:p] (I kept, I've kept) **1** halten, behalten; **2** erhalten WF; **keep a diary** Tagebuch führen WF; **keep your head together** einen kühlen Kopf bewahren WF; **Let's keep in touch.** Wir hören voneinander. *(Lass uns in Verbindung bleiben.)* U1: 10; **keep out** draußen bleiben WF; **keep out of the farms** von den Farmen fernhalten
kept [kept] (→ keep): **I kept** ich hielt, ich habe gehalten; **I've kept** ich habe gehalten
key [ki:] Schlüssel
keyboard ['ki:bɔ:d] Tastatur U1: 19
keyword ['ki:wɜ:d] Schlüsselwort; Stichwort U1: 16
kick [kɪk] **1** kicken, treten; **2** Kick, Hochgefühl U2: 22
kid [kɪd] Kind; Jugendliche/r
kill [kɪl] töten, umbringen
killing ['kɪlɪŋ] Mord WF
kilogram ['kɪləgræm] Kilogramm
kilometre ['kɪləmi:tə] Kilometer
kilt [kɪlt] Kilt *(Schottenrock)*
kind [kaɪnd] **1** freundlich, nett U2: 24; **2 What kind of programmes?** Was für Sendungen?
kingdom ['kɪŋdəm] Königreich WF
kiosk ['ki:ɒsk]: **Internet kiosk** Internet-Kiosk *(öffentlich zugängliches Internet-Terminal)*
kip [kɪp]: **kip down** schlafen gehen WF
kiss [kɪs] (sich) küssen
kitchen ['kɪtʃɪn] Küche
knew [nju:] (→ know): **I knew** ich wusste, ich habe gewusst
knife, knives [naɪf, naɪvz] Messer U3: 47
knock [nɒk] klopfen WF
know [nəʊ] (I knew, I've known) wissen, kennen; **let me know** geben Sie mir Bescheid U1: 18
known [nəʊn]: **she's known as ... to her friends** ihre Freundinnen und Freunde kennen sie als ... WF
koala [kəʊ'ɑ:lə] Koala(bär)
kwaito ['kwaɪtəʊ] Kwaito *(südafrikanische Musikrichtung)* U1: 13

L

label ['leɪbl] Schildchen, Etikett
lady ['leɪdi] Dame WF
laid [leɪd] (→ lay): **I laid the table** ich deckte den Tisch, ich habe den Tisch gedeckt; **I've laid ...** ich habe ... gedeckt
lain [leɪn] (→ lie): **I've lain** ich habe gelegen U1: 16
lake [leɪk] (Binnen-)See
land [lænd] **1** landen WF; **2** Land
language ['læŋgwɪdʒ] Sprache **first language** Muttersprache
laptop ['læptɒp] Laptop
large [lɑ:dʒ] groß U3: 36
lassi ['læsi] *indisches Jogurtgetränk* WF
last [lɑ:st] **1** letzte/r/s: **a last-minute decision** eine Entscheidung in letzter Minute U4: 60; **at last** endlich, schließlich; **2** dauern WF
late [leɪt] spät; zu spät, verspätet; **He's late (for school).** Er kommt zu spät (zur Schule). **be in your/... late 20s** Ende zwanzig sein WF
later ['leɪtə] später
latest ['leɪtɪst] neueste/r/s
laugh [lɑ:f] lachen; **laugh at** auslachen
law [lɔ:] Gesetz WF
lawyer ['lɔ:jə] Rechtsanwalt/-anwältin WF
lay [leɪ] **1** (I laid, I've laid) **lay the table** den Tisch decken; **2** (→ lie) **I lay** ich lag, ich habe gelegen U1: 16
layout ['leɪaʊt] Layout WF
lazy ['leɪzi] faul
lead [li:d] (I led, I've led) führen; **leading them into ...** indem sie es in ... führen WF
lead actor ['li:dæktə] Hauptdarsteller/in WF
leader ['li:də] Führer/in WF
learn [lɜ:n] lernen; **learn about London** etwas über London erfahren; **Learn it by heart.** Lerne es auswendig.
least [li:st] am wenigsten WF; **at least** mindestens, wenigstens
leave [li:v] (I left, I've left) **1** verlassen, weggehen (von); **2** abfahren, abfliegen, abreisen; **3** (stehen/liegen) lassen, vergessen
led [led] (→ lead): **I led** ich führte, ich habe geführt; **I've led** ich habe geführt
leek [li:k] Lauch, Porree
left [left] links; **on the left** auf der linken Seite; **on your left** links (von Ihnen)

left [left] (→ leave): **I left** ich verließ, ich habe verlassen; **I've left** ich habe verlassen; **What's left of you?** Was bleibt von dir übrig? **she was left behind** sie blieb zurück WF
leg [leg] Bein
lemonade [lemə'neɪd] (Zitronen-) Limonade
lens [lens] Objektiv WF
leopard ['lepəd] Leopard WF
less [les] weniger
lesson ['lesn] (Unterrichts-)Stunde
let [let]: **Let's finish.** Lasst uns aufhören./Hören wir auf. **let me know** geben Sie mir Bescheid U1: 18
letter ['letə] **1** Brief; **letter of application** Bewerbungsschreiben; **2** Buchstabe
letterboxing ['letəbɒksɪŋ] „Letterboxing" *(eine Art Schatzsuche)*
lettuce ['letɪs] (Kopf-)Salat
librarian [laɪ'breərɪən] Bibliothekar/in U4: 63
library ['laɪbrəri] Bücherei
licence ['laɪsns]: **TV licence** Fernsehgebühr U4: 56
lie [laɪ] **1** lügen; **2** (I lay, I've lain) liegen U1: 16
life, lives [laɪf, laɪvz] Leben, (die) Leben
lift [lɪft] Aufzug, Fahrstuhl WF
light [laɪt] Licht, Lampe
lighthouse ['laɪthaʊs] Leuchtturm WF
light switch ['laɪtswɪtʃ] Lichtschalter
like [laɪk] **1** mögen, gern haben; **I like it.** Ich mag es./Es gefällt mir. **I (don't) like walking.** Ich laufe (nicht) gern. **I'd like ...** Ich möchte .../Ich hätte gern ...; **I'd like to go/...** Ich möchte gehen/...; **Who likes it best?** Wem gefällt es am besten? **2** wie; als ob WF; **like that/this** so; **a job like that/this** so ein Job; **things like that** solche Dinge, so etwas WF; **What does she look like?** Wie sieht sie aus? **what the book is like** wie das Buch ist
likes and dislikes ['laɪksən'dɪslaɪks] Vorlieben und Abneigungen
limit ['lɪmɪt]: **age limit** Altersgrenze WF
limo ['lɪməʊ] Luxuslimousine U2: 25
line [laɪn] **1** Zeile; **2** Linie; (AE) (Warte-)Schlange; **wait in line** (AE) Schlange stehen
linen ['lɪnɪn] Wäsche WF
link [lɪŋk] **1** Link; Verbindung; **2 link (to/with)** in Verbindung bringen (mit); verbinden (mit) U2: 26
lion ['laɪən] Löwe U1: 6
lip [lɪp] Lippe
list [lɪst] Liste
listen ['lɪsn] zuhören; **listen to** hören, sich anhören
litter ['lɪtə] Abfall
little ['lɪtl] klein
live [lɪv] wohnen, leben
live [laɪv] live; Live- WF
lives [laɪvz] (die) Leben (→ life)
living room ['lɪvɪŋru:m] Wohnzimmer
loads [ləʊdz] Unmengen WF
local ['ləʊkl] örtlich, einheimisch U4: 60
locker ['lɒkə] Schließfach, Spind
log [lɒg]: **reading log** Lesetagebuch WF
lonely ['ləʊnli] einsam
long [lɒŋ] lang; lange; **(for) a long time** lange; **as long as** solange WF
look [lʊk] **1** schauen, sehen; **look after** [lʊk'ɑ:ftə] sich kümmern um, aufpassen auf; **look ahead** vorausschauen, die Zukunft planen; **look around** sich umschauen U3: 46; **look at** ansehen, sich ansehen; **look for** suchen; **I'm looking forward to hearing from you** ich freue mich darauf, von Ihnen zu hören; **look out for something** auf etwas achten WF; **look up** nachschlagen, nachsehen; **2** aussehen; **What does she look like?** Wie sieht sie aus? **have a look around** sich umschauen WF
looks [lʊks] (das) Aussehen WF
loosely ['lu:sli]: **It fits loosely.** Er/Sie/Es sitzt weit. WF
lose [lu:z] (I lost, I've lost) verlieren; **lose weight** abnehmen, Gewicht verlieren
lost [lɒst] **1** (→ lose) **I lost** ich verlor, ich habe verloren; **I've lost** ich habe verloren; **2 get lost** sich verirren
lot [lɒt]: **a lot** viel; sehr U1: 9
lots [lɒts]: **lots of** viele; viel
lotto ['lɒtəʊ] Lotto; **win the lotto** im Lotto gewinnen
loud [laʊd] laut
love [lʌv] lieben, sehr mögen; **I love reading.** Ich lese sehr gern. **I'd love to ...** ich würde sehr gern ... U2: 24; **2** Liebe; **(Lots of) Love, ...** (Viele) Liebe Grüße ...
low [ləʊ] niedrig WF
lower ['ləʊə] untere/r/s WF
luck [lʌk]: **Better luck next time!** Nächstes Mal hast du bestimmt mehr Glück! U4: 54; **Good luck!** Viel Glück!
luckily ['lʌkɪli] glücklicherweise U2: 30
lucky ['lʌki]: **I'm lucky** ich habe Glück WF; **Lucky thing!** Der/Die Glückliche! Du Glückliche/r!
lunch [lʌntʃ] Mittagessen
lunch break ['lʌntʃbreɪk] Mittagspause
lunchtime ['lʌntʃtaɪm] Mittagszeit; Mittagspause
Luxembourg ['lʌksəmbɜ:g] Luxemburg
luxury ['lʌkʃəri] Luxus WF

M

machine [mə'ʃi:n] Maschine, Gerät
mad [mæd] verrückt WF
madam ['mædəm]: **Dear Sir/Madam, ...** Sehr geehrte Damen und Herren, ...
made [meɪd] (→ make): **I made** ich machte, ich habe gemacht; **I've made** ich habe gemacht; **made of metal/...** aus Metall/...; **if they made me say goodbye** wenn man mich zwänge, mich zu verabschieden; **it made me think about ...** er brachte mich dazu, darüber nachzudenken ... WF
magazine [mægə'zi:n] Zeitschrift
main ... [meɪn] Haupt- U2: 23; **main clause** Hauptsatz WF; **main point** Schwerpunkt
Majorca [mə'jɔ:kə] Mallorca WF
make [meɪk] (I made, I've made) machen, herstellen; **make a decision/an arrangement** eine Entscheidung/Absprache treffen; **make friends** Freundschaft/en schließen; **make groups** Gruppen bilden; **Make notes.** Mach dir Notizen. **make sure (that) ...** dafür sorgen, dass ... U4: 60; **Make sure you know ...** Sorgen Sie dafür, dass Sie wissen ... WF;

make the world a better place die Welt verbessern WF; **make us do what we can** uns dazu bringen, zu tun, was wir können WF; **nobody can make me eat this** keiner kann mich dazu zwingen, dies zu essen
make up [meɪk'ʌp] erfinden, sich ausdenken U2: 33
make-up ['meɪkʌp] Make-up
make-up artist ['meɪkʌpɑ:tɪst] Visagist/in
male [meɪl] männlich
mall [mɔ:l] (AE) Einkaufszentrum
man, men [mæn, men] Mann, Männer
manager ['mænɪdʒə] Manager/in, Geschäftsführer/in; **office manager** Büroleiter/in
mango, mangoes ['mæŋgəʊ, 'mæŋgəʊz] Mango, Mangos U3: 42
many ['meni] viele
map [mæp] Landkarte, Karte; Plan
March [mɑ:tʃ] März
march [mɑ:tʃ] (Protest-)Marsch U3: 49
mark [mɑ:k] Note, Zensur
market ['mɑ:kɪt] Markt
marriage ['mærɪdʒ] Ehe U3: 38
married ['mærid] verheiratet; **get married** heiraten U3: 38
massacre ['mæsəkə] Massaker WF
match [mætʃ] **1** Spiel, Wettkampf; **2 Match the words with the pictures.** Ordne den Wörtern die Bilder zu.
maths [mæθs] Mathe(matik)
May [meɪ] Mai
may [meɪ]: **I may not follow** ich werde vielleicht nicht folgen WF; **it may be drunk** es darf getrunken werden WF
maybe ['meɪbi] vielleicht
me [mi:] **1** mir, mich; **2** ich
meal [mi:l] Mahlzeit, (zubereitetes) Essen
mean [mi:n] (I meant, I've meant) meinen; bedeuten
meaning ['mi:nɪŋ] Bedeutung
meant [ment] (→ mean): **I meant** ich meinte, ich habe gemeint; **I've meant** ich habe gemeint
meat [mi:t] Fleisch
mechanic [mə'kænɪk] Mechaniker/in U4: 55
media ['mi:diə]: **the media** die Medien
mediate ['mi:dieɪt] vermitteln
medical ['medɪkl] Medizin-; medizinisch
meet [mi:t] (I met, I've met) **1** (sich) treffen (mit); **2** kennen lernen; **Nice to meet you.** Schön, dich/Sie kennen zu lernen.
megapixel ['megəpɪksl] Megapixel WF
memory card ['meməríkɑ:d] Speicherkarte U1: 18
men [men] Männer (→ man)
menu ['menju:] Speisekarte
message ['mesɪdʒ] **1** Mitteilung, Nachricht; **2** Botschaft; **phone message** Telefonnotiz; telefonische Nachricht; **Can I take a message?** Kann ich (ihm/ihr) etwas ausrichten?
met [met] (→ meet): **I met** ich traf, ich habe getroffen; **I've met** ich habe getroffen
metal ['metl] **1** Metall; **2** Metal *(Musikrichtung)*
metre ['mi:tə] Meter
Mexico ['meksɪkəʊ] Mexiko
middle ['mɪdl] Mitte WF
midnight ['mɪdnaɪt] Mitternacht U4: 64
mile [maɪl] Meile
military ['mɪlətri] militärisch WF
milk [mɪlk] Milch
million ['mɪljən] Million
millionaire [mɪljə'neə] Millionär/in U3: 37
mind [maɪnd]: **Do you mind if I sit here?** Haben Sie etwas dagegen, wenn ich mich hier hinsetze? **I don't mind.** Das ist mir egal. U3: 47; **I don't mind using ...** mir macht es nichts aus, ... zu benutzen WF
mind map ['maɪndmæp] Mindmap *(eine Art Gedankenkarte)*
mine [maɪn] Bergwerk, Mine WF
minimum ['mɪnɪməm] Minimum WF
minute ['mɪnɪt] Minute
mirror ['mɪrə] Spiegel
miserable ['mɪzrəbl] unglücklich, elend
miss [mɪs] **1** vermissen; **2** daneben treffen; daneben gehen; **3** versäumen, verpassen U3: 46
missing ['mɪsɪŋ]: **it's missing** es fehlt; **the missing words** die fehlenden Wörter
mistake [mɪ'steɪk] Fehler
mix up [mɪks'ʌp] durcheinander bringen, mischen
mobile (phone) ['məʊbaɪl, məʊbaɪl'fəʊn] Handy, Mobiltelefon
mobile home [məʊbaɪl'həʊm] (Stand-)Wohnwagen
model ['mɒdl] (Foto-)Modell
modern ['mɒdn] modern
mom [mɒm] (AE) Mama, Mutti
moment ['məʊmənt] Moment; **at the moment** zurzeit, im Moment; **The moment I see somebody, ...** In dem Moment, wo ich jemanden sehe, ... WF
Monday ['mʌndeɪ, 'mʌndi] Montag
money ['mʌni] Geld
monster ['mɒnstə] Monster
month [mʌnθ] Monat
monument ['mɒnjumənt] Denkmal U3: 37; **a monument to ...** ein Denkmal für ... WF
moon [mu:n] Mond
moor [mɔ:] (Hoch-)Moor
more [mɔ:] mehr, weitere; **more expensive** teurer
morning ['mɔ:nɪŋ] Morgen; **in the morning** am Morgen, morgens; **Monday morning** Montagmorgen
mosquito [məs'ki:təʊ] Stechmücke, Moskito U2: 29
most [məʊst] der/die/das meiste, die meisten; **most expensive** teuerste/r/s, am teuersten; **most of the guests** die meisten Gäste
mother ['mʌðə] Mutter
motor ['məʊtə] Motor U3: 41
motorbike ['məʊtəbaɪk] Motorrad
motorway ['məʊtəweɪ] Autobahn WF
mountain ['maʊntən] Berg; **high mountains** Hochgebirge WF; **in the mountains** im Gebirge
mountain bike ['maʊntənbaɪk] Mountainbike
mountain biking ['maʊntənbaɪkɪŋ] Mountainbikefahren
mountain board ['maʊntənbɔ:d] Mountainboard *(eine Art Gelände-Skateboard)*
mountain boarding ['maʊntənbɔ:dɪŋ] Mountainboardfahren
mouse [maʊs] (Computer-)Maus U1: 19
mouth [maʊθ] Mund
move [mu:v] **1** (sich) bewegen; **2** umziehen
movie ['mu:vi] (AE) Film
Mozambique [məʊzæm'bi:k] Mosambik WF
MP3 player [empi:'θri:pleɪə] MP3-Player
Mr ['mɪstə]: **Mr Dunn** Herr Dunn

Mrs ['mɪsɪz]: **Mrs Dunn** Frau Dunn
Ms [mɪz, məz]: **Ms Brown** Frau Brown
much [mʌtʃ] **1** viel; **2 (very) much** sehr U3: 38
muffin ['mʌfɪn] Muffin
multicultural [mʌlti'kʌltʃərəl] multikulturell
mum [mʌm] Mama, Mutti
museum [mju'zi:əm] Museum
music ['mju:zɪk] Musik
musical instrument [mju:zɪkl'ɪnstrəmənt] Musikinstrument
musician [mju'zɪʃn] Musiker/in
Muslim ['mʊzlɪm] Muslim/in; muslimisch WF
must [mʌst] müssen
mustn't ['mʌsnt] nicht dürfen
my [maɪ] mein/e
myself [maɪ'self] mir/mich (selbst); selbst

N

name [neɪm] Name; **What's your name?** Wie heißt du?
narrow ['nærəʊ] schmal, eng
nation ['neɪʃn] Nation U1: 6
national ['næʃnəl] national, landesweit U2: 30
national anthem [næʃnəl'ænθəm] Nationalhymne WF
nationality [næʃə'næləti] Nationalität; Staatsbürgerschaft
national park [næʃnəl'pɑ:k] Nationalpark
national team [næʃnəl'ti:m] Nationalmannschaft U1: 8
Native American ['neɪtɪvə'merɪkən] amerik. Ureinwohner/in, Indianer/in
natural ['nætʃrəl] natürlich WF
near [nɪə] in der Nähe (von); nah
nearest ['nɪərɪst]: **the nearest airport** der nächste Flughafen
nearly ['nɪəli] fast, beinahe
need [ni:d] brauchen
needs [ni:dz] Bedürfnisse WF
negative ['negətɪv] negativ U2: 34
neighbour ['neɪbə] Nachbar/in
neighbourhood ['neɪbəhʊd] Viertel, Gegend
neighbouring ['neɪbərɪŋ]: **neighbouring country** Nachbarland WF
nervous ['nɜ:vəs] nervös, ängstlich
Netherlands ['neðələndz] Niederlande
network ['netwɜ:k] Netz; Wortnetz, Wörternetz
never ['nevə] (noch) nie, niemals
new [nju:] neu
New Delhi [nju:'deli] Neu-Delhi U3: 36
news [nju:z] Nachricht(en); Neuigkeit(en)
newspaper ['nju:zpeɪpə] Zeitung
next [nekst] nächste/r/s; **What next?** Was nun? U4: 52
next to ['nekstu, 'nekstə] neben
nice [naɪs] nett; schön
night [naɪt] Nacht; **at night** nachts, in der Nacht
no [nəʊ] **1** nein; **2** kein/e; **There's no such thing.** So etwas gibt es nicht.
Nobel Peace Prize [nəʊbəl'pi:spraɪz] Friedensnobelpreis WF
nobody ['nəʊbədi] niemand
noise [nɔɪz] Lärm; Geräusch
non-alcoholic ['nɒnælkəhɒlɪk] alkoholfrei WF
nonsense ['nɒnsns] Unsinn, Blödsinn
non-violent [nɒn'vaɪələnt] gewaltfrei U3: 49
normal ['nɔ:ml] normal WF
north [nɔ:θ] Norden; Nord-; nördlich; **in the north** im Norden; **to the north of ...** nördlich von ... WF
North America [nɔ:θə'merɪkə] Nordamerika
north-east [nɔ:θ'i:st]: **in north-east Africa** im Nordosten von Afrika
northern ['nɔ:ðən] Nord-, nördlich
Northern Ireland ['nɔ:ðən'aɪələnd] Nordirland
north-west [nɔ:θ'west]: **(the) north-west** (der) Nordwesten
nose [nəʊz]: **pay through the nose (for something)** viel zu viel (für etwas) bezahlen WF
not [nɒt] nicht
note [nəʊt] **1** Notiz; **2** Geldschein U3: 36; **3** beachten WF
nothing ['nʌθɪŋ] (gar) nichts
notice ['nəʊtɪs] **1** bemerken, merken; **2 give notice** kündigen WF
noticeboard ['nəʊtɪsbɔ:d] Anschlagbrett, Schwarzes Brett
noun [naʊn] Nomen
November [nəʊ'vembə] November
now [naʊ] nun, jetzt
number ['nʌmbə] Nummer; Zahl; Ziffer
nurse [nɜ:s] Krankenpfleger, Krankenschwester

O

obese [əʊ'bi:s] fettleibig
obesity [əʊ'bi:səti] Fettleibigkeit
obviously ['ɒbviəsli] offensichtlich
ocean ['əʊʃn] Ozean; Meer
o'clock [ə'klɒk]: **at eight o'clock** um acht/zwanzig Uhr
October [ɒk'təʊbə] Oktober
of [ɒv, əv] von; **a picture of my dog** ein Bild meines Hundes; **a cup of tea** eine Tasse Tee; **think of** denken an
of course [əv'kɔ:s] natürlich, selbstverständlich
off [ɒf] von
offer ['ɒfə] **1** anbieten; **2** Angebot; **special offer** Sonderangebot
office ['ɒfɪs] Büro; **office manager** Büroleiter/in; **tourist office** Touristeninformation, Fremdenverkehrsbüro
officer ['ɒfɪsə]: **police officer** Polizist/in, Polizeibeamter/-beamtin
official language [əfɪʃl'læŋgwɪdʒ] Amtssprache U3: 37
off-road ['ɒfrəʊd] abseits der Straße, im Gelände
often ['ɒfn] oft
OK [əʊ'keɪ] okay, (schon) gut, in Ordnung; **Are you OK?** Ist alles in Ordnung bei dir? **That's OK.** Schon gut./Bitte.
old [əʊld] alt
Olympics [ə'lɪmpɪks]: **the Olympics** die Olympischen Spiele
on [ɒn] **1** auf; **2** an, eingeschaltet; **3** über U2: 33; **on August 5th** am 5. August; **on a reservation** in einer Reservation; **on Dartmoor** in Dartmoor; **on entry** am Eingang, beim Betreten WF; **on foot** zu Fuß; **on holiday** in/im Urlaub; **on sale** erhältlich WF; **on Saturdays** samstags; **on school days** an Schultagen; **on special offer** im Sonderangebot; **on the beach** am Strand; **on the board** an der Tafel; **on the bus** im Bus; **on the coast** an der Küste WF; **on the first floor** im ersten Stock WF; **on the intercom** über die Sprechanlage; **on the Internet** im Internet; **On the one hand, ... On the other hand, ...** Einerseits ... Andererseits ...;

on the phone am Telefon; **on the road** unterwegs; **on time** pünktlich; **on TV** im Fernsehen; **get on the team** in die Mannschaft kommen; **go on** weitergehen WF; **phone/text on 071...** anrufen/eine SMS schicken unter 071... U1: 10; **he's on it** er ist dabei WF
once [wʌns] **1** einmal; **2** früher U1: 9; **3** sobald, wenn WF
one [wʌn] **1** ein, eine, einer, eines; **one day** eines Tages; **2** man WF
online [ɒn'laɪn] online
only ['əʊnli] nur, bloß; erst; **for women only** nur für Frauen WF
onto ['ɒntʊ, 'ɒntə] auf (... hinauf/herauf)
open ['əʊpən] **1** öffnen, aufmachen; **2** sich öffnen, aufgehen; **3** offen, geöffnet
operation [ɒpə'reɪʃn] Operation WF
opinion [ə'pɪnjən] Meinung; **give an opinion** eine Meinung abgeben U3: 44; **in my opinion** meiner Meinung nach
opposite ['ɒpəzɪt] **1** Gegenteil; **2** gegenüber (von)
option ['ɒpʃn] (Wahl-)Möglichkeit WF
or [ɔ:] oder
orange ['ɒrɪndʒ] Orange
orchard ['ɔ:tʃəd] Obstgarten
order ['ɔ:də] **1** bestellen U1: 18; **2** Reihenfolge; **3** Anweisung, Befehl; **in order to see him** um ihn zu sehen WF
ordinary ['ɔ:dnri] normal, gewöhnlich U2: 30
organization [ɔ:gənaɪ'zeɪʃn] Organisation U1: 9
organize ['ɔ:gənaɪz] ordnen; organisieren
organizer ['ɔ:gənaɪzə] Veranstalter/in, Organisator/in WF
other ['ʌðə] andere, weitere
our ['aʊə] unser/e
ourselves [aʊə'selvz] uns (selbst); selbst
out [aʊt] hinaus/heraus; aus; **out and about** unterwegs; **out there** da draußen; **find out** herausfinden
out of ['aʊtəv] aus (... hinaus/heraus); **I have to get out of this place.** Ich muss hier raus. **I'm out of credit.** Ich habe kein Guthaben mehr auf meinem Handy. U3: 42
outback ['aʊtbæk]: **the outback** das Outback *(das Landesinnere Australiens)* WF
outdoor ['aʊtdɔ:]: **outdoor activity** Beschäftigung im Freien; **outdoor store** (AE) Geschäft mit Artikeln für Sport/Freizeit im Freien
outdoors [aʊt'dɔ:z] im Freien, draußen
outer ['aʊtə] äußere/r/s WF
outlaw ['aʊtlɔ:] Bandit/in
outside [aʊt'saɪd] **1** außerhalb (von), vor U2: 29; **2** draußen WF
outside post ['aʊtsaɪdpəʊst] Außenpfosten
outsider [aʊt'saɪdə] Außenseiter/in WF
oval ['əʊvl] oval
over ['əʊvə] **1** vorbei, zu Ende, aus; **2** über WF; **3** über, mehr als WF; **over 18s** über 18-jährige WF; **over there** da drüben, dort drüben (hin); **all over** überall in/auf
overhead mirror [əʊvəhed'mɪrə] „Spiegelhimmel" WF
overtime ['əʊvətaɪm]: **work overtime** Überstunden machen WF
overweight [əʊvə'weɪt] übergewichtig
own [əʊn]: **your own room** dein eigenes Zimmer
owner ['əʊnə] Besitzer/in, Eigentümer/in U2: 26
Oz [ɒz] *Spitzname für Australien*

P

pack [pæk] packen, einpacken
package deal ['pækɪdʒdi:l] Pauschalangebot WF
packet ['pækɪt] Paket WF
page [peɪdʒ] Seite
paid [peɪd] **1** bezahlt; **2** (→ pay) **I paid** ich zahlte, ich habe gezahlt
pain [peɪn] Schmerzen; **Parents are a pain!** Eltern nerven!
pair [peə]: **a pair of** ein Paar WF
pale [peɪl] blass
panic ['pænɪk] durchdrehen, in Panik geraten
paper ['peɪpə] Papier
papers ['peɪpəz] (Ausweis-)Papiere
paragraph ['pærəgrɑ:f] Absatz
paramedic [pærə'medɪk] Rettungssanitäter/in
parent, parents ['peərənt, 'peərənts] Elternteil, Eltern
parenting ['peərəntɪŋ] Kindererziehung, Kindererziehungs- WF
park [pɑ:k] Park
part [pɑ:t] **1** Teil; **2** sich trennen WF; **take part (in)** teilnehmen (an), mitmachen (bei) U2: 28
part-time [pɑ:t'taɪm] Teilzeit(-)
participle [pɑ:'tɪsɪpl]: **past participle** Partizip Perfekt, Mittelwort der Vergangenheit
partner ['pɑ:tnə] Partner/in
party ['pɑ:ti] Party
pass [pɑ:s] **1** bestehen U2: 34; **2** Ausweis U1: 12
passage ['pæsɪdʒ] Gang, Korridor
passenger ['pæsɪndʒə] Fahrgast, Passagier/in U3: 40
passive ['pæsɪv] Passiv
passport ['pɑ:spɔ:t] (Reise-)Pass WF
past [pɑ:st]: **past the house** am Haus vorbei; **five past ten** fünf nach zehn; **half past nine** halb zehn
past participle [pɑ:stpɑ:'tɪsɪpl] Partizip Perfekt, Mittelwort der Vergangenheit
past perfect [pɑ:st'pɜ:fɪkt] vollendete Vergangenheit U1: 20
past progressive [pɑ:stprə'gresɪv] Verlaufsform der Vergangenheit
pavement ['peɪvmənt] Bürgersteig, Gehsteig
pay [peɪ] **1** (I paid, I've paid) zahlen, bezahlen; **pay through the nose (for something)** viel zu viel (für etwas) bezahlen WF; **2** Bezahlung, Lohn, Gehalt
peace [pi:s] Frieden U3: 49
peaceful ['pi:sfl] friedlich U3: 46
peach [pi:tʃ] Pfirsich
pear [peə] Birne
pedal boat ['pedlbəʊt] Tretboot
pen [pen] Füller
pence (p) [pens] Pence *(britische Währung)*
pencil ['pensl] Bleistift
pencil case ['penslkeɪs] Federmäppchen, Schreibetui
penguin ['peŋgwɪn] Pinguin WF
peninsula [pe'nɪnsjʊlə] Halbinsel WF
people ['pi:pl] Leute, Menschen; **black/white people** Schwarze/Weiße; **people using the street** Menschen, die die Straße benutzen WF
per [pɜ:] pro
per cent [pə'sent] Prozent
perfect ['pɜ:fɪkt] vollkommen, perfekt U4: 60; **past perfect** vollendete Vergangenheit U1: 20

perhaps [pə'hæps] vielleicht
permitting [pə'mɪtɪŋ]**: weather permitting** bei gutem Wetter *(wenn es das Wetter erlaubt)* WF
person ['pɜːsn] Person, Mensch
personal ['pɜːsənl] persönlich WF
personal details [pɜːsənl'diːteɪlz] Angaben zur Person
pet [pet] Haustier, zahmes Tier
pet shop ['petʃɒp] Zoohandlung, Tierhandlung
petrol station ['petrəlsteɪʃn] Tankstelle WF
Philippines ['fɪlɪpiːnz]**: the Philippines** die Philippinen WF
phone [fəʊn] **1** anrufen, telefonieren; **phone back** zurückrufen; **phone for help** telefonisch Hilfe holen U4: 56; **2** Telefon; **on the phone** am Telefon
phone call ['fəʊnkɔːl] Anruf
phone message ['fəʊnmesɪdʒ] Telefonnotiz; telefonische Nachricht
photo ['fəʊtəʊ] Foto; **take photos** Fotos machen, fotografieren
photographer [fə'tɒgrəfə] Fotograf/in
photo shoot ['fəutəuʃuːt] Fotosession, Fotoshooting
phrase [freɪz] Ausdruck
physical ['fɪzɪkl] körperlich WF
piano [pi'ænəʊ] Klavier
pick [pɪk] **1** aussuchen, wählen; **2** pflücken
pick up [pɪk'ʌp] **1** aufheben, hochheben; **2** abholen
picnic ['pɪknɪk] Picknick
picture ['pɪktʃə] Bild, Foto
piece [piːs] Stück
pier [pɪə] Pier, Anlegestelle
piercing ['pɪəsɪŋ] Piercing
pig [pɪg] Schwein
pilot ['paɪlət] Pilot/in WF
pink [pɪŋk] rosa, pink
pirate ['paɪrət] Pirat/in
pity ['pɪti]**: That's a pity.** Das ist schade. U2: 24
pizza ['piːtsə] Pizza
pizzeria [piːtsə'riːə] Pizzeria U2: 25
place [pleɪs] Ort, Stelle, Platz; **a place to meet** ein Treffpunkt; **take place** stattfinden WF
plain [pleɪn] Ebene WF
plan [plæn] **1** planen, vorhaben; **2** Plan
plane [pleɪn] Flugzeug
planner ['plænə] Planer/in
platform ['plætfɔːm] **1** Bahnsteig, Gleis; **2** Podium WF

play [pleɪ] spielen; **play by the rules** sich an die Spielregeln halten; **play sports** Sport treiben; **play the guitar** Gitarre spielen; **men playing games** Männer, die Spiele spielen
player ['pleɪə] **1** Spieler/in; **2** Abspielgerät
playground ['pleɪgraʊnd] Schulhof; **in the playground** auf dem Schulhof
please [pliːz] bitte
pleasure ['pleʒə] Freude WF
plum [plʌm] Pflaume
plumber ['plʌmə] Installateur/in, Klempner/in
p.m. [piː'em] nachmittags, abends
pocket ['pɒkɪt] Tasche
pocket money ['pɒkɪtmʌni] Taschengeld
podcast ['pɒdkɑːst] Podcast U3: 37
poem ['pəʊɪm] Gedicht
poet ['pəʊɪt] Dichter/in
point [pɔɪnt] Punkt
Poland ['pəʊlənd] Polen
police [pə'liːs] Polizei; Polizei-
police officer [pə'liːsɒfɪsə] Polizist/in, Polizeibeamter/-beamtin
Polish ['pəʊlɪʃ] polnisch; Polnisch; Pole/Polin U4: 63
polish ['pɒlɪʃ] putzen, polieren WF
polite [pə'laɪt] höflich
political [pə'lɪtɪkl] politisch WF
politics ['pɒlətɪks] Politik WF
polo-neck sweater ['pəʊləʊnekswetə] Rollkragenpullover WF
pony ['pəʊni] Pony
pool [puːl] Schwimmbecken
poor [pʊə] arm; **Poor you!** Du Arme/r!
pop [pɒp] Pop(musik)
popcorn ['pɒpkɔːn] Popcorn
popular ['pɒpjələ] beliebt
populated ['pɒpjuleɪtɪd]**: densely populated** dicht besiedelt WF
population [pɒpju'leɪʃn] Bevölkerung, Bevölkerungszahl
portfolio [pɔːt'fəʊliəʊ] Portfolio
positive ['pɒzətɪv] positiv U2: 34; **be HIV positive** HIV-positiv sein U1: 13
post [pəʊst] **1** Pfosten; **2 post comments** (im Internet) Kommentare abgeben
postcard ['pəʊstkɑːd] Postkarte, Ansichtskarte
postcode ['pəʊstkəʊd] Postleitzahl U4: 63

poster ['pəʊstə] Poster
post office ['pəʊstɒfɪs] Post(amt)
potato, potatoes [pə'teɪtəʊ, pə'teɪtəʊz] Kartoffel, Kartoffeln
potato chips [pə'teɪtəʊtʃɪps] (AE) Kartoffelchips
pound [paʊnd] **1** Pfund *(Gewichtseinheit)*; **2** (£) Pfund *(britische Währung)*
poverty ['pɒvəti] Armut WF
power ['paʊə] Macht; Stärke
power cable ['paʊəkeɪbl] Stromkabel U1: 18
practise ['præktɪs] üben; trainieren
prefer [prɪ'fɜː] vorziehen
pregnant ['pregnənt] schwanger
premature ['premətʃə] vorzeitig, zu früh WF
prepare (for something) [prɪ'peə] (sich auf etwas) vorbereiten
preposition [prepə'zɪʃn] Präposition, Verhältniswort
present [prɪ'zent] präsentieren
present ['preznt] **1** Geschenk; **2 simple present** einfache Gegenwart
present progressive [prezntprə'gresɪv] Verlaufsform der Gegenwart
president ['prezɪdənt] Präsident/in U1: 21
pressure ['preʃə] Druck
pretty ['prɪti]**: pretty awful** ziemlich furchtbar WF
prey [preɪ]**: prey on children** Kinder ausnutzen WF
price [praɪs] Preis
prime minister [praɪm'mɪnɪstə] Premierminister/in, Ministerpräsident/in WF
primitive ['prɪmətɪv] primitiv WF
prince [prɪns] Prinz WF
princess [prɪn'ses] Prinzessin WF
print out [prɪnt'aʊt] ausdrucken
printer ['prɪntə] Drucker
priority list [praɪ'ɒrətilɪst] Prioritätenliste, Rangliste
prison ['prɪzn] Gefängnis; **go to prison** ins Gefängnis kommen; **in prison** im Gefängnis
prisoner ['prɪznə] Gefangene/r WF
prize [praɪz] Preis, Gewinn
probably ['prɒbəbli] wahrscheinlich U2: 26
problem ['prɒbləm] Problem
produce [prə'djuːs] herstellen, produzieren
product ['prɒdʌkt] Produkt, Erzeugnis WF

program ['prəʊgræm]**: computer program** Computerprogramm U3: 39
programme ['prəʊgræm] (Radio-, Fernseh-)Sendung
programmer ['prəʊgræmə] Programmierer/in U3: 39
programming language ['prəʊgræmɪŋlæŋgwɪdʒ] Programmiersprache WF
progressive [prə'gresɪv]**: past/ present progressive** Verlaufsform der Vergangenheit/Gegenwart
prohibit [prə'hɪbɪt] verbieten
prohibited [prə'hɪbɪtɪd] verboten
project ['prɒdʒekt] Projekt(arbeit)
prom [prɒm]**: (school) prom** (Schul-)Abschlussball
promote [prə'məʊt]**: promote the idea** die Ansicht fördern WF
pronoun ['prəʊnaʊn] Pronomen, Fürwort
pronunciation [prənʌnsi'eɪʃn] Aussprache
prospectus [prə'spektəs] Prospekt WF
prostitute ['prɒstɪtju:t] Prostituierte/r WF
protector [prə'tektə] Protektor, Schützer
protest ['prəʊtest] Protest U3: 49
proud [praʊd]**: feel proud of ...** stolz sein auf ... WF
prove [pru:v] beweisen WF
proverb ['prɒvɜ:b] Sprichwort WF
provide [prə'vaɪd] zur Verfügung stellen U3: 39
provocative [prə'vɒkətɪv] provozierend, herausfordernd U2: 22
public ['pʌblɪk]**: the public** die Öffentlichkeit WF
punctual ['pʌŋktʃuəl] pünktlich WF
punk [pʌŋk] Punk(musik)
pupil ['pju:pl] Schüler/in
push [pʊʃ] drücken
put [pʊt] (I put, I've put) stellen; legen; (an einen Platz) tun; **I put** ich tat, ich habe getan; **I've put** ich habe getan; **put in the right order** in die richtige Reihenfolge bringen; **put something on** etwas anziehen WF
put in [pʊt'ɪn] ein-/hinzufügen
put up [pʊt'ʌp] anbringen, aufhängen WF; **put up a tent** ein Zelt aufstellen; **Put up your hand.** Heb(t) die Hand.
puzzled ['pʌzld] verblüfft, verwundert
pyjamas [pə'dʒɑ:məz] Schlafanzug

Q

quad (bike) [kwɒd] Quad *(eine Art vierrädriges Gelände-Motorrad)*
qualification [kwɒlɪfɪ'keɪʃn] Abschluss WF
quality ['kwɒləti] Eigenschaft U4: 62
quarter ['kwɔ:tə]**: quarter to/past one** Viertel vor/nach eins
queen [kwi:n] Königin
question ['kwestʃən] **1** verhören; befragen U2: 22; **2** Frage
questionnaire [kwestʃə'neə] Fragebogen
queue [kju:] (Warte-)Schlange U1: 8; **queue (up)** Schlange stehen
quickly ['kwɪkli] schnell
quiet ['kwaɪət] ruhig
quite [kwaɪt] ziemlich, recht U2: 22
quiz [kwɪz] Quiz
quote [kwəʊt] Zitat

R

R & B [ɑ:rən'bi:] R & B *(Musikrichtung)*
rabbit ['ræbɪt] Kaninchen
rabbit-proof ['ræbɪtpru:f] kaninchensicher
race [reɪs] (Wett-)Rennen WF
racing driver ['reɪsɪŋdraɪvə] Rennfahrer/in
radiator ['reɪdieɪtə] Heizkörper
radio ['reɪdiəʊ] Radio
railcard ['reɪlkɑ:d] Rabattkarte für Bahnreisen *(wie BahnCard)* WF
railings ['reɪlɪŋz] Geländer
railway line ['reɪlweɪlaɪn] Eisenbahnstrecke, Gleis
railway station ['reɪlweɪsteɪʃn] Bahnhof U2: 32
rain [reɪn] regnen
rainbow ['reɪnbəʊ] Regenbogen U1: 6
rainforest ['reɪnfɒrɪst] Regenwald WF
ran [ræn] (→ run)**: I ran** ich rannte, ich bin gerannt
rand [rænd] Rand *(südafrikanische Währung)* U1: 11
range [reɪndʒ] Reichweite WF
ranger ['reɪndʒə] Ranger *(Aufseher/in in Nationalparks)*
rank [ræŋk] einstufen WF
rap [ræp] Rap(musik)
rapid ['ræpɪd] schnell WF
rapper ['ræpə] Rapper/in, Rapsänger/in

rat [ræt] Ratte
react (to) [ri'ækt] reagieren (auf) U2: 24
read [ri:d] (I read, I've read) lesen, vorlesen; **read something to her** ihr etwas vorlesen; **read out** vorlesen, ablesen
read [red] (→ read)**: I read** ich las, ich habe gelesen; **I've read** ich habe gelesen
reader ['ri:də] Leser/in
reading log ['ri:dɪŋlɒg] Lesetagebuch WF
reading week ['ri:dɪŋwi:k] Lesewoche
ready ['redi] fertig, bereit
real ['ri:əl] wahr, echt, richtig U2: 31
realize ['ri:əlaɪz] erkennen, sich klar werden über U2: 33
really ['ri:əli] wirklich, eigentlich
reason ['ri:zn] Grund
receive [rɪ'si:v] erhalten, bekommen U1: 18
reception [rɪ'sepʃn]**: work in reception** am Empfang arbeiten WF
receptionist [rɪ'sepʃənɪst] Empfangschef/-dame
recommend [rekə'mend] empfehlen
record [rɪ'kɔ:d] aufnehmen, aufzeichnen
red [red] rot
referee [refə'ri:] Schiedsrichter/in
reference ['refərəns] Referenz, Zeugnis U4: 63
refreshment [rɪ'freʃmənt] Erfrischung WF
regulations [regju'leɪʃnz] Vorschriften WF
relationship [rɪ'leɪʃnʃɪp] Beziehung, Verhältnis U4: 58
relax [rɪ'læks] (sich) entspannen
relaxed [rɪ'lækst] entspannt U2: 22
relaxing [rɪ'læksɪŋ] entspannend WF
reliable [rɪ'laɪəbl] zuverlässig WF
relieved [rɪ'li:vd] erleichtert
religion [rɪ'lɪdʒən] Religion, Glaube U3: 37
remain [rɪ'meɪn] bleiben WF
remember [rɪ'membə] **1** sich erinnern (an); **2** daran denken
removal [rɪ'mu:vl] Umzug
rent [rent] mieten; ausleihen
repair [rɪ'peə] reparieren WF
repeat [rɪ'pi:t] nachsprechen
replacement [rɪ'pleɪsmənt] Ersatz U1: 18
report [rɪ'pɔ:t] Bericht
reporter [rɪ'pɔ:tə] Reporter/in

required [rɪ'kwaɪəd] erforderlich U4: 56
research [rɪ'sɜːtʃ]: **do research** Forschung betreiben, forschen WF
reservation [rezə'veɪʃn] (Indianer-)Reservation, Reservat; **on a reservation** in einer Reservation
resistance (to) [rɪ'zɪstəns] Widerstand (gegen) WF
respect [rɪ'spekt] respektieren, achten
responsibility [rɪspɒnsə'bɪləti] Verantwortung
responsible [rɪ'spɒnsəbl] verantwortlich
rest [rest]: **have a rest** eine Pause machen WF
restaurant ['restrɒnt] Restaurant
result [rɪ'zʌlt] Ergebnis, Folge
résumé ['rezjumeɪ] (AE) Lebenslauf
return [rɪ'tɜːn] zurückkehren WF
review [rɪ'vjuː] Besprechung, Rezension
revise (for an exam) [rɪ'vaɪz] (für eine Prüfung) lernen WF
Rhine [raɪn] Rhein
rhino ['raɪnəʊ] Nashorn WF
rhyme (with) [raɪm] (sich) reimen (auf)
rhythm ['rɪðəm] Rhythmus
rich [rɪtʃ] reich
ridden ['rɪdn] (→ ride): **I've ridden** ich bin gefahren
ride [raɪd] **1** (I rode, I've ridden) **ride a bike/quad/...** (mit einem) Rad/Quad fahren; **2** Fahrt; **3** Fahrgeschäft, „Fahrattraktion"
riding ['raɪdɪŋ]: **horse riding** Reiten; **quad/Trikke/... riding** Quadfahren/Trikkefahren/...
right [raɪt] **1** richtig; **You're right.** Du hast Recht. **2** Recht; **animal rights** Tierrechte, Tierschutz-; **3** rechts; **on the right** auf der rechten Seite; **on your right** rechts (von Ihnen)
ringtone ['rɪŋtəʊn] Klingelton
riot ['raɪət] Aufstand WF
risk [rɪsk] Risiko WF; **take risks** Risiken eingehen WF
river ['rɪvə] Fluss; **the River Exe** der Exe
road [rəʊd] Straße; **in Dean Road** in der Dean Road; **on the road** unterwegs
road safety ['rəʊdseɪfti] Verkehrssicherheit
rob [rɒb]: **rob a bank** eine Bank ausrauben
rock [rɒk] Fels, großer Stein
rock climber ['rɒkklaɪmə] Kletterer/Kletterin
rock climbing ['rɒkklaɪmɪŋ] Klettern
role [rəʊl] Rolle; **role card** Rollen(spiel)karte
roll [rəʊl] Brötchen
roller coaster ['rəʊləkəʊstə] Achterbahn
romance [rəʊ'mæns] Liebesfilm, Liebesroman
romantic [rəʊ'mæntɪk] romantisch
Rome [rəʊm] Rom
roof [ruːf] Dach U2: 30
room [ruːm] Raum, Zimmer; **first floor room** Zimmer im ersten Stockwerk U4: 56
root [ruːt] Wurzel
RSVP [ɑːresviː'piː] u.A.w.g. (= um Antwort wird gebeten)
rubber ['rʌbə] Radiergummi
rubbish ['rʌbɪʃ] Abfall, Müll
rubbish tip ['rʌbɪʃtɪp] Müllkippe WF
rucksack ['rʌksæk] Rucksack U2: 28
rugby ['rʌgbi] Rugby
rule [ruːl] Regel, Vorschrift; **play by the rules** sich an die Spielregeln halten
ruler ['ruːlə] Lineal
run [rʌn] (I ran, I've run) rennen, laufen; **run a business** ein Unternehmen führen WF
runner ['rʌnə] Läufer/in
running ['rʌnɪŋ] Laufen
running water [rʌnɪŋ'wɔːtə] fließendes Wasser U1: 12
rupee [ruː'piː] Rupie U3: 36

S

sabotage ['sæbətɑːʒ] Sabotage WF
sad [sæd] traurig
safari [sə'fɑːri] Safari WF
safe [seɪf] sicher, in Sicherheit
safety ['seɪfti]: **road safety** Verkehrssicherheit
safety gear ['seɪftigɪə] Sicherheitsausrüstung
said [sed] (→ say): **I said** ich sagte, ich habe gesagt; **I've said** ich habe gesagt
sailing ['seɪlɪŋ] Segeln WF
salad ['sæləd] Salat
salary ['sæləri] Gehalt WF
sale [seɪl]: **on sale** erhältlich WF
sales clerk ['seɪlzklɑːk] (AE) Verkäufer/in
salmon ['sæmən] Lachs
salt [sɔːlt] Salz U3: 49
same [seɪm]: **the same** der-/die-/dasselbe, der/die/das gleiche
sandboard ['sændbɔːd] sandboarden WF
sandboarder ['sandbɔːdə] Sandboardfahrer/in WF
sandwich ['sænwɪtʃ] Sandwich *(belegtes Brot)*
sandy ['sændi] sandig WF
sang [sæŋ] (→ sing): **I sang** ich sang, ich habe gesungen
sat [sæt] (→ sit): **I sat** ich saß, ich habe gesessen
Saturday ['sætədeɪ, 'sætədi] Samstag, Sonnabend
sausage ['sɒsɪdʒ] Wurst, Würstchen
save [seɪv] **1** sparen; **2** retten
saw [sɔː] (→ see): **I saw** ich sah, ich habe gesehen
say [seɪ] (I said, I've said) sagen; **say something to her** ihr etwas sagen; **say goodbye to ...** sich von ... verabschieden; **Say hi to her, please.** Grüße sie, bitte. **say sorry** sich entschuldigen
saying ['seɪɪŋ] Sprichwort U4: 57
scandal Skandal U2: 31
scarf [skɑːf] Schal WF
scene [siːn] Szene; Ansicht
school [skuːl] Schule; **she's at school** sie ist in der Schule; sie geht zur Schule
school day ['skuːldeɪ] Schultag
science ['saɪəns] Naturwissenschaft
scientist ['saɪəntɪst] Wissenschaftler/in
score [skɔː] **1** (Punkte) erzielen, (Tor) schießen; **2** Spielstand, Punktzahl; **What's the score?** Wie steht's?
Scotland ['skɒtlənd] Schottland
Scots [skɒts] Schottisch *(engl. Dialekt)*
Scottish ['skɒtɪʃ] schottisch; Schotte(n)/Schottin(nen)
scream [skriːm] schreien
screen [skriːn] Bildschirm U1: 18
sea [siː] Meer
search [sɜːtʃ] durchsuchen WF
search engine ['sɜːtʃendʒɪn] Suchmaschine
seashell ['siːʃel] Muschel
seashore ['siːʃɔː] Küste, Strand
season ['siːzn] Jahreszeit
seat [siːt] Sitz, Platz U1: 10
second ['sekənd] **1** Sekunde U4: 64; **2** **English as a Second Language** Englisch als Zweitsprache; **the second largest/...** der/die/das zweitgrößte/... U3: 37

second-hand shop [sekəndhændʃɒp] Secondhand-shop *(Laden, in dem gebrauchte Sachen verkauft werden)* WF
secret ['si:krət] **1** heimlich WF; **2** Geheimnis WF
security check [sɪ'kjʊərətitʃek] Sicherheitskontrolle
security guard [sɪ'kjʊərətigɑ:d] Wachfrau/-mann
see [si:] (I saw, I've seen) sehen; **See you.** Bis dann. **See you tomorrow/...** Bis morgen/...; **See you again some time?** Sieht man sich mal wieder? U1: 10; **..., you see.** ..., verstehst du?
seem [si:m] scheinen U4: 54
seen [si:n] (→ see): **I've seen** ich habe gesehen
selection [sɪ'lekʃn] Auswahl WF
self-confidence [self'kɒnfɪdəns] Selbstvertrauen
self-confident [self'kɒnfɪdənt] selbstsicher
self-control [selfkən'trəʊl] Selbstbeherrschung
sell [sel] (I sold, I've sold) verkaufen
send [send] (I sent, I've sent) senden, schicken
sensation [sen'seɪʃn] Sensation WF
sense [sens]: **a great sense of humour** Sinn für Humor WF
sent [sent] (→ send): **I sent** ich sendete, ich habe gesendet; **I've sent** ich habe gesendet
sentence ['sentəns] Satz
September [sep'tembə] September
series ['sɪəri:z] Serie; Reihe
serious ['sɪəries] ernst(haft) U4: 54
serve [s3:v] bedienen U4: 63
service ['s3:vɪs]: **service motorbikes** Motorräder instand halten WF
serving ['s3:vɪŋ]: **a serving of fruit** eine Portion Obst
set [set]: **a film set in ...** ein Film, der in ... spielt WF
several ['sevrəl] mehrere WF
sex [seks] Sex U1: 12
sex worker ['sekswɜ:kə] Sexarbeiter/in WF
sexist ['seksɪst] sexistisch WF
shake [ʃeɪk] (I shook, I've shaken) schütteln; **she shakes her head** sie schüttelt den Kopf
shaken ['ʃeɪkən] (→ shake): **I've shaken** ich habe geschüttelt
shall [ʃəl]: **we shall ...** wir werden ... WF
shanty town ['ʃæntitaʊn] Slum, Elendsviertel WF
share [ʃeə]: **share a room** sich ein Zimmer teilen
shark [ʃɑ:k] Hai WF
she [ʃi:] sie; **she's (= she is)** sie ist
sheep [ʃi:p] Schaf, Schafe
shelf, shelves [ʃelf, ʃelvz] Regal, Regale
shift [ʃɪft] (Arbeits-)Schicht WF
shine [ʃaɪn] (it shone, it has shone) scheinen, glänzen, leuchten U3: 47
ship [ʃɪp] Schiff
ship container ['ʃɪpkənteɪnə] Schiffscontainer WF
shirt [ʃ3:t] Hemd WF
shocked [ʃɒkt] schockiert WF
shoe [ʃu:] Schuh
shone [ʃɒn] (→ shine): **it shone** es leuchtete, es hat geleuchtet U3: 47; **it has shone** es hat geleuchtet U3: 47
shook [ʃʊk] (→ shake): **I shook** ich schüttelte, ich habe geschüttelt
shoot [ʃu:t] (I shot, I've shot) schießen; werfen
shop [ʃɒp] **1** Laden, Geschäft; **2 shop for clothes** Kleidung kaufen WF
shop assistant ['ʃɒpəsɪstənt] Verkäufer/in
shoplifter ['ʃɒplɪftə] Ladendieb/in
shopper ['ʃɒpə] Käufer/in
shopping ['ʃɒpɪŋ] Einkaufen; **go shopping** einkaufen gehen
shopping centre ['ʃɒpɪŋsentə] Einkaufszentrum
short [ʃɔ:t] kurz; klein
shorts [ʃɔ:ts] Shorts, kurze Hosen
shot [ʃɒt] **1** Korbwurf; **2** (→ shoot) **I shot** ich schoss, ich habe geschossen; **I've shot** ich habe geschossen
should [ʃʊd, ʃəd]: **you should** du solltest, du müsstest; **When should I ...?** Wann soll ich ...?
shout [ʃaʊt] laut rufen, schreien; **she shouts something at him** sie ruft ihm etwas zu; **shout for help** um Hilfe rufen WF
show [ʃəʊ] **1** (I showed, I've shown) zeigen; **2** Show
shower ['ʃaʊə] Dusche U1: 18; **have a shower** duschen U3: 42
shown [ʃəʊn] (→ show): **I've shown** ich habe gezeigt
Shut up! [ʃʌt'ʌp] Halt den Mund!
shuttle ['ʃʌtl] Shuttle
shy [ʃaɪ] schüchtern
sick [sɪk] krank U1: 13; **it made me sick** es machte mich ganz krank WF
side [saɪd] Seite
sidewalk ['saɪdwɔ:k] (AE) Bürgersteig
sigh [saɪ] seufzen
sightseeing ['saɪtsi:ɪŋ] Besichtigungen
sign [saɪn] Schild; Zeichen
signal ['sɪgnəl] Zeichen, Signal
silk [sɪlk] Seide WF
silly ['sɪli] dumm, albern
silver ['sɪlvə] Silber WF
simple ['sɪmpl] einfach U1: 8; **simple past/present** einfache Vergangenheit/Gegenwart
since [sɪns] seit WF; **since then** seitdem WF
sing [sɪŋ] (I sang, I've sung) singen
Singapore ['sɪŋəpɔ:] Singapur
singer ['sɪŋə] Sänger/in
sir [s3:]: **Dear Sir/Madam, ...** Sehr geehrte Damen und Herren, ...
sister ['sɪstə] Schwester; **brothers and sisters** Geschwister
sit [sɪt] (I sat, I've sat) sitzen; sich setzen; **sit down** sich (hin)setzen U3: 46
size [saɪz] Größe
skateboard ['skeɪtbɔ:d] Skateboard
skateboarder ['skeɪtbɔ:də] Skateboarder/in
skate park ['skeɪtpɑ:k] Skatepark
skater ['skeɪtə] Skater/in
skiing ['ski:ɪŋ] Skifahren
skilled [skɪld] qualifiziert WF
skirt [sk3:t] Rock WF
sky [skaɪ] Himmel WF
slam [slæm] Slam *(Unfall beim Skateboarden)*
sleep [sli:p] (I slept, I've slept) schlafen
sleeping bag ['sli:pɪŋbæg] Schlafsack U2: 28
slept [slept] (→ sleep): **I slept** ich schlief, ich habe geschlafen; **I've slept** ich habe geschlafen
slim [slɪm] schlank
slip [slɪp] ausrutschen
slipper ['slɪpə] Hausschuh U4: 64
slippery ['slɪpəri] glatt WF
slogan ['sləʊgən] Slogan WF
slow [sləʊ] langsam
small [smɔ:l] klein
smart [smɑ:t] schick, elegant WF
smell [smel] Geruch WF
smile [smaɪl] **1** lächeln; **2** Lächeln
smog [smɒg] Smog

smoke [sməʊk] rauchen
smoked salmon [sməʊkt'sæmən] Räucherlachs
sneaker ['sni:kə] (AE) Sportschuh
snowboarder ['snəʊbɔ:də] Snowboarder/in
snow storm ['snəʊstɔ:m] Schneesturm WF
so [səʊ] so, also; daher
soccer ['sɒkə] Fußball
sock [sɒk] Socken WF
softball ['sɒftbɔ:l] Softball *(ähnlich wie Baseball)*
software ['sɒftweə] Software
sold [səʊld]**: it's sold to ...** er wird an ... verkauft WF
soldier ['səʊldʒə] Soldat/in
Somalia [sə'mɑ:liə] Somalia
some [sʌm] **1** einige, ein paar; **2** etwas; **See you again some time?** Sieht man sich mal wieder? U1: 10
somebody ['sʌmbədi] jemand
something ['sʌmθɪŋ] etwas; **something a bit different** etwas, das ein bisschen anders ist WF; **something different** etwas anderes
sometimes ['sʌmtaɪmz] manchmal
song [sɒŋ] Lied
soon [su:n] bald
sorry ['sɒri]**: Sorry./I'm sorry.** Tut mir leid. **I'm sorry I ...** Tut mir leid, dass ich ...; **feel sorry for me** mich bemitleiden
sort [sɔ:t]**: a sort of ...** eine Art ... U3: 41
soul [səʊl] Seele WF; **Great Soul** Große Seele WF
sound [saʊnd] **1** klingen, sich anhören; **2** Geräusch; **3 sound the alarm** Alarm auslösen WF
south [saʊθ] Süden; Süd-; südlich
South Africa [saʊθ'æfrɪkə] Südafrika U1: 6
South African [saʊθ'æfrɪkən] südafrikanisch; Südafrikaner/in U1: 8
southern ['sʌðən] Süd-, südlich WF
south-west [saʊθ'west]**: in south-west Africa** im Südwesten von Afrika
space [speɪs] Weltraum
Spain [speɪn] Spanien
Spanish ['spænɪʃ] spanisch; Spanisch; Spanier, Spanierin(nen)
speak [spi:k] (I spoke, I've spoken) sprechen; **speak to** sprechen mit
speaker ['spi:kə] Sprecher/in
special ['speʃl] besondere/r/s
special offer [speʃl'ɒfə] Sonderangebot
speech [spi:tʃ]**: (in)direct speech** (in)direkte Rede U2: 33
speeding ['spi:dɪŋ] rasend WF
spell [spel] buchstabieren
spelling ['spelɪŋ] Rechtschreibung
spend [spend] (I spent, I've spent) **1** ausgeben; **2** verbringen
spent [spent] (→ spend)**: I spent** ich gab aus/verbrachte, ich habe ausgegeben/verbracht; **I've spent** ich habe ausgegeben/verbracht
spider ['spaɪdə] Spinne
spoke [spəʊk] (→ speak)**: I spoke** ich sprach, ich habe gesprochen U1: 8
sponsored ['spɒnsəd] gesponsert
sport [spɔ:t] Sport, Sportart; **play sports** Sport treiben
sports centre ['spɔ:tssentə] Sportzentrum
sporty ['spɔ:ti] sportlich
spot [spɒt] **1** entdecken WF; **2 a spot on the face** ein Pickel im Gesicht WF
spread [spred] (I spread, I've spread) verbreiten; **I spread** ich verbreitete, ich habe verbreitet; **I've spread** ich habe verbreitet
spring [sprɪŋ] Frühling
spy [spaɪ] Spion/in
squash [skwɒʃ] Squash
stadium ['steɪdiəm] Stadion U1: 10
staff [stɑ:f] Personal
stage [steɪdʒ] Bühne; **on stage** auf der Bühne
stairs [steəz] Treppe U3: 46
stall [stɔ:l] (Verkaufs-)Stand
stamp [stæmp] Stempel
stand [stænd] (I stood, I've stood) **1** stehen; **stand in the way of people** Menschen im Weg stehen WF; **stand up** aufstehen WF; **2** sich stellen U1: 8; **3 I can't stand them** ich kann sie nicht ausstehen
star [stɑ:] **1** Stern U3: 47; **2** Star *(berühmte Persönlichkeit)*
start [stɑ:t] **1** anfangen, beginnen; **I started running/to run** ich begann zu rennen; **start a programme** eine Sendung ins Leben rufen; **I'll start my own business** ich werde mich selbstständig machen; **2** Start, Anfang
state [steɪt] (Bundes-)Staat, Land
statement ['steɪtmənt] Aussage U2: 29
station ['steɪʃn] Bahnhof; **at Exeter Station** im Bahnhof Exeter
statistics [stə'tɪstɪks] Statistik WF
statue ['stætʃu:] Statue; **Statue of Liberty** ['stætʃu:əv'lɪbəti] Freiheitsstatue
stay [steɪ] **1** bleiben; übernachten; **2** Aufenthalt, Besuch U1: 10
steal [sti:l] (I stole, I've stolen) stehlen
step [step] Stufe
stereotype ['steriətaɪp] Stereotyp, Klischee(vorstellung) U2: 26
still [stɪl] **1** (immer) noch; **2** trotzdem U4: 54
stink [stɪŋk] stinken WF
stole [stəʊl] (→ steal)**: I stole** ich stahl, ich habe gestohlen
stolen ['stəʊlən] (→ steal)**: I've stolen** ich habe gestohlen; **"Stolen Generations"** „Gestohlene Generationen"
stomach ['stʌmək] Magen WF
stone [stəʊn] Stein U1: 8
stood [stʊd] (→ stand)**: I stood** ich stand, ich habe gestanden U1: 8; **I've stood** ich habe gestanden U1: 8
stop [stɒp] **1** anhalten, stoppen; stehen bleiben; **2** aufhören; **stop using the Internet** aufhören, das Internet zu benutzen; **3** Halt; Haltestelle
store [stɔ:] (AE) Laden, Geschäft
story ['stɔ:ri] Geschichte
straight [streɪt]**: go straight on** geradeaus (weiter)gehen WF
strange [streɪndʒ] merkwürdig, seltsam
street [stri:t] Straße
street entertainer ['stri:tentəteɪnə] Straßenkünstler/in WF
streetmarket ['stri:tmɑ:kɪt] Straßenmarkt WF
stress [stres] **1** betonen; **2 able to deal with stress** belastbar WF
stressed [strest] gestresst
stressful ['stresfl] stressig WF
strict [strɪkt] streng
strong [strɒŋ] stark
student ['stju:dnt] **1** (ältere/r) Schüler/in; Student/in; **2** (AE) Schüler/in
studio ['stju:diəʊ] Studio
study ['stʌdi] **1** studieren WF; **2** untersuchen, erforschen WF
stuff [stʌf] Zeug, Kram
stupid ['stju:pɪd] dumm, blöd
style [staɪl] Stil WF
subject ['sʌbdʒɪkt] (Schul-)Fach

suburb ['sʌbɜ:b] Vorort
subway ['sʌbweɪ] (AE) U-Bahn
successful [sək'sesfl] erfolgreich
such [sʌtʃ] solch WF; **There's no such thing.** So etwas gibt es nicht.
suddenly ['sʌdnli] plötzlich
suit [su:t] **1** Anzug; Kostüm; **2 suit somebody** jemandem stehen WF
sum up [sʌm'ʌp] zusammenfassen U4: 61
summary ['sʌməri] Zusammenfassung
summer ['sʌmə] Sommer
sun [sʌn] Sonne
suncream ['sʌnkri:m] Sonnenkrem WF
Sunday ['sʌndeɪ, 'sʌndi] Sonntag
sung [sʌŋ] (→ sing): **I've sung** ich habe gesungen
sunglasses ['sʌnglɑ:sɪz] Sonnenbrille
sunny ['sʌni] sonnig
super ['su:pə] super, toll
supermarket ['su:pəmɑ:kɪt] Supermarkt
superstar ['su:pəstɑ:] Superstar
support [sə'pɔ:t] unterstützen U2: 30
suppose [sə'pəʊz] annehmen, vermuten U2: 30
sure [ʃʊə] sicher; **make sure (that) ...** dafür sorgen, dass ... U4: 60
surf [sɜ:f] surfen
surfboard ['sɜ:fbɔ:d] Surfbrett
surfer ['sɜ:fə] Surfer/in
surfing gear ['sɜ:fɪŋgɪə] **1** Surfkleidung, -klamotten; **2** Surfausrüstung
surf school ['sɜ:fsku:l] Surfschule
surname ['sɜ:neɪm] Nachname, Familienname
surprise [sə'praɪz] Überraschung; **it took me by surprise** es überraschte mich WF
surprised [sə'praɪzd] überrascht
surprising [sə'praɪzɪŋ] überraschend WF
survey ['sɜ:veɪ] Umfrage, Untersuchung
swam [swæm] (→ swim): **I swam** ich schwamm, ich bin geschwommen
sweatshop ['swetʃɒp] ausbeuterischer Betrieb WF
Sweden ['swi:dn] Schweden WF
swim [swɪm] (I swam, I've swum) schwimmen
swimmer ['swɪmə] Schwimmer/in
swimming ['swɪmɪŋ] Schwimmen; **go swimming** schwimmen gehen
swimming pool ['swɪmɪŋpu:l] Schwimmbad
swimming trunks ['swɪmɪŋtrʌŋks] Badehose WF
swimsuit ['swɪmsu:t] Badeanzug WF
Switzerland ['swɪtsələnd] Schweiz
symbol ['sɪmbl] Symbol

T

table ['teɪbl] **1** Tisch; **2** Tabelle
Table Mountain ['teɪblmaʊntən] Tafelberg WF
table tennis ['teɪbltenɪs] Tischtennis
tackle ['tækl] bewältigen, anpacken WF
tactics ['tæktɪks] Taktik WF
take [teɪk] (I took, I've taken) **1** nehmen; bringen; **2** wegnehmen; **2** dauern WF; **Take a jacket.** Nimm/Bring eine Jacke mit. **take an exam** eine Prüfung machen; **Take care.** Mach's gut. U1: 10; **take down** abnehmen, abmontieren WF; **take off** starten WF; **I take off my jacket** ich ziehe meine Jacke aus; **take out the rubbish** den Müll rausbringen; **take over** übernehmen WF; **take part (in)** teilnehmen (an), mitmachen (bei) U2: 28; **take photos** Fotos machen, fotografieren; **take place** stattfinden WF; **take risks** Risiken eingehen WF; **Can I take a message?** Kann ich (ihm/ihr) etwas ausrichten? **How long did it take you?** Wie lange hast du gebraucht? WF; **Which size do you take?** Welche Größe haben Sie? WF
takeaway ['teɪkəweɪ] Imbissstube; **take-away food/...** Essen/... zum Mitnehmen WF
taken ['teɪkən] **1** besetzt, belegt U3: 40; **2** (→ take) **I've taken** ich habe genommen
talent ['tælənt] Talent U1: 8
talk [tɔ:k] **1 talk (to)** reden (mit), sprechen (mit), sich unterhalten (mit); **It has been nice talking to you.** Es war nett, mit dir zu sprechen. U1: 10; **2** Vortrag
talk show ['tɔ:kʃəʊ] (AE) Talkshow
talk time ['tɔ:ktaɪm] Freiminuten WF
tall [tɔ:l] groß *(bei Personen)*
task [tɑ:sk] Aufgabe U2: 33
taste [teɪst] schmecken
tattoo [tə'tu:] Tätowierung, Tattoo
taught [tɔ:t] (→ teach): **I taught** ich unterrichtete, ich habe unterrichtet; **I've taught** ich habe unterrichtet
taxi ['tæksi] Taxi
tea [ti:] Tee
teach [ti:tʃ] (I taught, I've taught) unterrichten, beibringen
teacher ['ti:tʃə] Lehrer/in
team [ti:m] Team, Mannschaft
teamworker ['ti:mwɜ:kə]: **be a teamworker** teamfähig sein WF
techno ['teknəʊ] Techno *(Musikrichtung)*
technology [tek'nɒlədʒi] Technik, Technologie
teen [ti:n] Teenager
teenage ... ['ti:neɪdʒ] Teenager- U2: 22
teenager ['ti:neɪdʒə] Teenager
teeth [ti:θ] Zähne (→ tooth)
tell (about) [tel] (I told, I've told) erzählen (von); sagen
temple ['templ] Tempel WF
ten-seater ['tensi:tə] zehnsitzig WF
tennis ['tenɪs] Tennis
tense [tens] Zeit(form)
tent [tent] Zelt
terrace ['terəs] Terrasse WF
terrible ['terəbl] schrecklich, furchtbar
test [test] Test, Klassenarbeit; Prüfung; **have a test** einen Test machen lassen U1: 13
text [tekst] **1** Text; **2** SMS; **3** eine SMS senden, simsen
text bullying ['tekstbʊliɪŋ] SMS-Terror
text message ['tekstmesɪdʒ] SMS (Textnachricht)
than [ðæn, ðən]: **faster than** schneller als
thank [θæŋk] danken WF; **I want to thank you for being with me.** Ich möchte Ihnen dafür danken, dass Sie bei mir waren. U3: 47; **Thank God.** Gott sei Dank. WF; **Thank you.** Danke (schön).
Thanks. [θæŋks] Danke.
that [ðæt] **1** das; der, die, das (da); **2** dass; **3** der, die, das *(in Relativsätzen)*; **that evening** an diesem Abend; **That's OK.** Schon gut./Bitte. **That's why ...** Deshalb/Darum ...; **That's 2 pounds, please.** Das macht 2 Pfund, bitte.
the [ðə, ði] der, die, das; **The next day ...** Am nächsten Tag ...

theatre ['θɪətə] Theater
their [ðeə] ihr/e; **men in their 20s** Männer in den Zwanzigern WF
them [ðem] ihnen, sie
theme park ['θi:mpɑ:k] Themenpark
themselves [ðəm'selvz] sich (selbst); selbst
then [ðen] dann
there [ðeə] da, dort; dahin, dorthin; **there's (= there is)** da ist, es gibt/ist; **there are** da sind, es gibt/sind; **there was/were** da war(en), es gab/war(en)
these [ði:z] die (hier); diese
they [ðeɪ] sie; **they're (= they are)** sie sind
thick [θɪk] dick U3: 46
thing [θɪŋ] Ding, Sache; **the right/best/... thing** das Richtige/Beste/...; **There's no such thing.** So etwas gibt es nicht.
think [θɪŋk] (I thought, I've thought) denken, nachdenken; finden; **think of** denken an; **think of going/...** überlegen zu gehen/...; **I can't think of the right word.** Mir fällt das richtige Wort nicht ein. U3: 43; **What do you think of ...?** Was hältst du von ...?
thirsty ['θɜ:sti]**: I'm thirsty** ich habe Durst U3: 42
this [ðɪs] dies (hier), das (hier); diese/r/s; **this evening/...** heute Abend/...
thorough ['θʌrə] gründlich WF
those [ðəʊz] diese, jene, die (da)
thought [θɔ:t] (→ think)**: I thought** ich dachte, ich habe gedacht
thought bubble ['θɔ:tbʌbl] Gedankenblase
thousand ['θaʊznd] tausend
threw [θru:] (→ throw)**: I threw** ich warf, ich habe geworfen
through [θru:] durch, hindurch
throw [θrəʊ] **1** (I threw, I've thrown) werfen; **2** Wurf; **free throw** Freiwurf
thrown [θrəʊn] (→ throw)**: I've thrown** ich habe geworfen
Thursday ['θɜ:zdeɪ, 'θɜ:zdi] Donnerstag
ticket ['tɪkɪt] Eintrittskarte; Fahrkarte, Flugschein
ticket inspector ['tɪkɪtɪnspektə] Fahrkartenkontrolleur/in WF
tie [taɪ] Krawatte WF
tiger ['taɪgə] Tiger U1: 6
tightly ['taɪtli]**: It fits tightly.** Er/Sie/Es sitzt eng. WF
tights [taɪts] Strumpfhose WF
till [tɪl] bis WF
time [taɪm] **1** Zeit; Uhrzeit; **all the time** die ganze Zeit; **(for) a long time** lange; **on time** pünktlich; **What time is it?** Wie spät ist es? **2** Mal; **at a time** gleichzeitig WF
timetable ['taɪmteɪbl] Stundenplan
tip [tɪp] **1** Tipp; **2 rubbish tip** Müllkippe WF
tired ['taɪəd] müde; **I'm tired of my job** ich habe meine Arbeit satt
tiring ['taɪərɪŋ] ermüdend WF
title ['taɪtl] **1** Titel; **2** Anrede U4: 63
to [tu:, tu, tə] **1** zu, nach; an; **to the north of ...** nördlich von ... WF; **fall to the ground** auf den Boden fallen; **get to and from the airport** zum Flughafen und zurück gelangen WF; **go to bed** ins Bett gehen; **I've been to France.** Ich bin (schon einmal) in Frankreich gewesen. **it's 24–18 to North** es steht 24:18 für North; **He says goodbye to her.** Er sagt ihr auf Wiedersehen. **Welcome to London.** Willkommen in London. **2** bis; **It's five to ten.** Es ist fünf vor zehn. **3 they help you to read** sie helfen dir zu lesen; **I don't know what to say.** Ich weiß nicht, was ich sagen soll. U4: 54; **things to do** Sachen, die man machen kann; **to change things** um Dinge zu verändern; **To finish, ...** Um zum Ende zu kommen, ...
today [tə'deɪ] heute; **today's world** die heutige Welt WF
together [tə'geðə] zusammen
toilet ['tɔɪlət] Toilette U4: 56
told [təʊld] (→ tell)**: I told** ich erzählte, ich habe erzählt; **I've told** ich habe erzählt
tomato, tomatoes [tə'mɑ:təʊ, tə'mɑ:təʊz] Tomate, Tomaten
tomorrow [tə'mɒrəʊ] morgen
tonga ['tɒŋgə] *eine Art Pferdekutsche (in Indien)* WF
tongue twister ['tʌŋtwɪstə] Zungenbrecher
tonight [tə'naɪt] heute Nacht, heute Abend U2: 30
too [tu:] **1** auch; **2 too old** zu alt; **Too bad!** Schade!
took [tʊk] (→ take)**: I took** ich nahm, ich habe genommen; **it took me by surprise** es überraschte mich WF
tooth, teeth [tu:θ, ti:θ] Zahn, Zähne
top [tɒp] Spitze, oberes Ende; **at the top** ganz oben (auf), auf der Spitze
top up [tɒp'ʌp]**: top up a mobile** Handy-Guthaben aufladen U3: 42
topic ['tɒpɪk] Thema
touch [tʌtʃ] berühren, anfassen; **Let's keep in touch.** Wir hören voneinander. *(Lass uns in Verbindung bleiben.)* U1: 10
tough [tʌf] hart, zäh, stark
tour [tʊə] Tour; Rundgang, Führung
tourism ['tʊərɪzəm] Tourismus WF
tourist ['tʊərɪst] Tourist/in
tourist office ['tʊərɪstɒfɪs] Touristeninformation, Fremdenverkehrsbüro
towards [tə'wɔ:dz] auf ... zu, in Richtung
tower ['taʊə] Turm
town [taʊn] Stadt
town centre ['taʊnsentə] Stadtzentrum, Stadtmitte
township ['taʊnʃɪp] Township U1: 6
toy [tɔɪ] Spielzeug
track [træk] **1** Weg, Pfad; **2** Bahn, Laufbahn
tracker ['trækə] Fährtensucher/in
tractor ['træktə] Traktor
tradition [trə'dɪʃn] Tradition
traditional [trə'dɪʃənl] traditionell WF
traffic ['træfɪk] Verkehr
traffic light ['træfɪklaɪt] (Verkehrs-)Ampel
train [treɪn] **1** trainieren; **2** ausbilden WF; **3** eine Ausbildung machen; **4** Zug, Eisenbahn
train driver ['treɪndraɪvə] Lokomotivführer/in
trainee [treɪ'ni:] Auszubildende/r, Trainee WF
trainer ['treɪnə] **1** Trainer; **2** Sportschuh
training ['treɪnɪŋ] Ausbildung
tram [træm] Straßenbahn
transfer ['trænsfɜ:] Transfer WF
transfer [træns'fɜ:] versetzen WF
translate [træns'leɪt] übersetzen
transport ['trænspɔ:t] Beförderung, Transport WF
travel ['trævl] **1** reisen, fahren; **2** Reise-, Reisen
traveller ['trævələ] Reisende/r; Landfahrer/in
tray [treɪ] Tablett
treasure hunt ['treʒəhʌnt] Schatzsuche

treat [tri:t] Genuss, besonderes Vergnügen
tree [tri:] Baum
trend [trend] Trend WF
trip [trɪp] Ausflug, Reise
trouble ['trʌbl] Unruhe; **I'm in big trouble** ich stecke in großen Schwierigkeiten
troubled ['trʌbld] aufgewühlt WF
trousers ['traʊzəz] Hose WF
true [tru:] wahr; **True, ...** Es stimmt schon, ... WF
truly ['tru:li]: **Yours truly, ...** (AE) Mit freundlichen Grüßen ...
trust [trʌst] **1** vertrauen, trauen; **2** Stiftung WF
try [traɪ] versuchen, (aus)probieren; **try something on** etwas anprobieren WF
T-shirt ['ti:ʃɜ:t] T-Shirt
tube [tju:b]: **the tube** die (Londoner) U-Bahn
Tuesday ['tju:zdeɪ, 'tju:zdi] Dienstag
tuk-tuk ['tʊktʊk] *dreirädrige Autorikscha* WF
tunnel ['tʌnl] Tunnel
turbine ['tɜ:baɪn] Turbine U3: 50
Turkey ['tɜ:ki] Türkei
Turkish ['tɜ:kɪʃ] türkisch; Türkisch; Türke/Türkin
turn [tɜ:n]: **1 turn (to the left)** sich (nach links) drehen; **turn left/right (into Hill Street)** nach links/rechts (in die Hill Street) abbiegen; **2** werden WF
turn off [tɜ:n'ɒf] ausschalten
turn on [tɜ:n'ɒn] einschalten
TV ['ti:'vi:] Fernsehen; Fernsehgerät; **TV licence** Fernsehgebühr U4: 56
twice [twaɪs] zweimal WF
type [taɪp] Typ WF
typical ['tɪpɪkl] typisch U3: 43

U

umbrella [ʌm'brelə] Schirm
uncle ['ʌŋkl] Onkel
uncomfortable [ʌn'kʌmftəbl] unbequem, ungemütlich U4: 61
uncool [ʌn'ku:l] nicht cool, uncool
under ['ʌndə] unter
underground ['ʌndəgraʊnd] **1** unterirdisch; **2** U-Bahn
underground station ['ʌndəgraʊndsteɪʃn] U-Bahnhof
underground train ['ʌndəgraʊndtreɪn] U-Bahn-Zug
underline [ʌndə'laɪn] unterstreichen
underlined [ʌndə'laɪnd] unterstrichen
underneath [ʌndə'ni:θ] unter, darunter WF
understand [ʌndə'stænd] (I understood, I've understood) verstehen
understood [ʌndə'stʊd] (→ understand): **I understood** ich verstand, ich habe verstanden; **I've understood** ich habe verstanden WF
unemployed [ʌnɪm'plɔɪd] arbeitslos
unemployment [ʌnɪm'plɔɪmənt] Arbeitslosigkeit
unfair [ʌn'feə] unfair, ungerecht WF
unfortunately [ʌn'fɔ:tʃənətli] leider; unglücklicherweise U2: 24
unfriendly [ʌn'frendli] unfreundlich U1: 19
unhappy [ʌn'hæpi] unglücklich
unhealthy [ʌn'helθi] ungesund
uniform ['ju:nɪfɔ:m] Uniform
unimportant [ʌnɪm'pɔ:tnt] unwichtig WF
unit ['ju:nɪt] **1** Lektion; **2 TV/DVD unit** TV/DVD-Anlage WF
United Nations [ju'naɪtɪd'neɪʃənz] Vereinigte Nationen WF
university [ju:nɪ'vɜ:səti] Universität WF
unkind [ʌn'kaɪnd] unfreundlich, gemein
unscrupulous [ʌn'skru:pjələs] skrupellos WF
unusual [ʌn'ju:ʒuəl] ungewöhnlich WF
up [ʌp]: **up to ...** bis zu ... WF; **What's up?** Was gibt's?
upon [ə'pɒn]: **knock upon your door** an deine Tür klopfen WF
upstairs [ʌp'steəz] oben (im Haus); nach oben U4: 56
urgent ['ɜ:dʒənt] dringend
us [ʌs] uns
use [ju:z] benutzen, verwenden
use [ju:s] Gebrauch WF
useful ['ju:sfl] nützlich
usually ['ju:ʒuəli] meistens, normalerweise, gewöhnlich
utility room [ju:'tɪlətiru:m] Waschküche, Hauswirtschaftsraum WF

V

valid ['vælɪd] gültig WF
valley ['væli] Tal WF
VAT [vi:eɪ'ti:] Mehrwertsteuer WF
veg [vedʒ] *kurz für:* vegetable WF
vegetable ['vedʒtəbl] (ein) Gemüse
vegetarian [vedʒə'teəriən] Vegetarier/in, vegetarisch U3: 39
verb [vɜ:b] Verb, Zeitwort
verse [vɜ:s] Strophe
version ['vɜ:ʃn] Version, Fassung WF
very ['veri] sehr
vet [vet] Tierarzt/-ärztin
video ['vɪdiəʊ] Videofilm, Video
video game ['vɪdiəʊgeɪm] Videospiel
view [vju:] **1** betrachten WF; **2 view(s)** Aussicht, Sicht U4: 60
Viking ['vaɪkɪŋ] Wikinger, Wikinger-
village ['vɪlɪdʒ] Dorf
violence ['vaɪələns] Gewalt, Gewalttätigkeit
violent ['vaɪələnt] gewalttätig
virus ['vaɪrəs] Virus U1: 13
visit ['vɪzɪt] **1** besuchen; **2** Besuch U1: 19
visitor ['vɪzɪtə] Besucher/in, Gast
visitor centre ['vɪzɪtəsentə] Besucherzentrum
voice [vɔɪs] Stimme
volleyball ['vɒlibɔ:l] Volleyball
voluntary ['vɒləntri] freiwillig; ehrenamtlich U2: 22
volunteer [vɒlən'tɪə] Freiwillige/r
vote [vəʊt]: **vote for somebody** für jemanden stimmen WF
vulture ['vʌltʃə] Geier WF

W

wait (for) [weɪt] warten (auf); **I can't wait for it.** Ich kann es kaum erwarten. **Let's wait and see.** Warten wir's ab. **wait in line** (AE) Schlange stehen
wake up [weɪk'ʌp] (I woke up, I've woken up) aufwachen
Wales [weɪlz] Wales
walk [wɔ:k] gehen, laufen
walker ['wɔ:kə] Spaziergänger/in, Wanderer/Wanderin
walking ['wɔ:kɪŋ] Spazierengehen, Wandern
walking shoe ['wɔ:kɪŋʃu:] Wanderschuh

wall [wɔːl] Wand; Mauer
want [wɒnt] wollen; **want to go** gehen wollen; **they want you to do things** sie wollen, dass du Dinge tust
wanted ['wɒntɪd] gesucht
war [wɔː] Krieg
wardrobe ['wɔːdrəʊb] Kleiderschrank U4: 56
warm [wɔːm] warm
warning (against) ['wɔːnɪŋ] Warnung (vor) U1: 16
warning notice ['wɔːnɪŋnəʊtɪs] Warnhinweis WF
was [wɒz, wəz] war; **wasn't (= was not)** war nicht; **she was taken** sie wurde weggenommen; **they thought it was a good idea** sie dachten, es wäre eine gute Idee
wash [wɒʃ] waschen WF
wash up [wɒʃ'ʌp] abwaschen, spülen WF
washing ['wɒʃɪŋ] (Wäsche-)Waschen WF
washing machine ['wɒʃɪŋməʃiːn] Waschmaschine U4: 56
Washington State [wɒʃɪŋtən'steɪt] der Bundesstaat Washington
waste [weɪst] verschwenden; **a waste of time** Zeitverschwendung
watch [wɒtʃ] beobachten, sich anschauen; zusehen; **Watch me!** Pass auf! **watch TV** fernsehen
water ['wɔːtə] Wasser
wave [weɪv] Welle
way [weɪ] Weg; **she's on her way to winning** sie ist auf dem besten Weg zu gewinnen WF; **by the way** übrigens U1: 10; **give way** die Vorfahrt beachten WF
we [wiː] wir; **we're (= we are)** wir sind
wear [weə] (I wore, I've worn) tragen, anziehen
weather ['weðə] Wetter
webcode ['webkəʊd] Webcode
web page design ['webpeɪdʒdɪzaɪn] Webseiten-Design U4: 52
website ['websaɪt] Website
wedding ['wedɪŋ] Hochzeit
wedding day ['wedɪŋdeɪ] Hochzeitstag
Wednesday ['wenzdeɪ, 'wenzdi] Mittwoch
week [wiːk] Woche
weekend [wiːk'end] Wochenende
weigh [weɪ] wiegen
weight [weɪt] Gewicht; **lose weight** abnehmen, Gewicht verlieren
welcome ['welkəm] willkommen heißen WF; **Welcome to London.** Willkommen in London. **we aren't welcome** wir sind nicht willkommen; **You're welcome.** Nichts zu danken; Bitte schön.
well [wel] **1** gut; **Well done!** Gut gemacht! **2 Well, …** Nun/Tja, …; **be well** gesund sein WF; **be well over 24 years old** weit über 24 Jahre alt sein WF
well-paid [wel'peɪd] gut bezahlt WF
Welsh [welʃ] walisisch; Walisisch; Waliser/in(nen)
went [went] (→ go): **I went** ich ging, ich bin gegangen
were [wɜː] waren; warst; wart; **weren't (= were not)** waren/warst/wart nicht; **they were taken** sie wurden weggenommen; **If I were you, …** An deiner Stelle …
west [west] Westen; West-; westlich
Western Australia [westənɒ'streɪliə] Westaustralien *(austr. Bundesstaat)*
wet [wet] nass, feucht
wetsuit ['wetsuːt] Surf-/Tauch-(schutz)anzug
whale [weɪl] Wal
whale watching ['weɪlwɒtʃɪŋ] Walbeobachtung; **go whale watching** auf Walbeobachtungstour gehen
what [wɒt] **1** was; **What a …!** Was für ein/eine …! **What about you?** Und du?/Was ist mit dir? **What are they in German?** Wie heißen sie auf Deutsch? **What next?** Was nun? U4: 52; **What time is it?** Wie spät ist es? **What's that?** Was ist das? **What's your name?** Wie heißt du? **What's up?** Was gibt's? **2** welche/r/s
whatever [wɒt'evə]: **whatever the weather** egal, wie das Wetter ist
wheel [wiːl] Rad U3: 41
wheelchair ['wiːltʃeə] Rollstuhl; **he's in a wheelchair** er sitzt im Rollstuhl
when [wen] **1** wann; **2** wenn; **3** als
where [weə] wo; wohin; **Where are you from?** Woher kommst du?
wherever [weər'evə] wo (auch) immer WF
whether ['weðə] ob
which [wɪtʃ] welche/r/s
while [waɪl] während U2: 29
whisky ['wɪski] Whisky U2: 26
white [waɪt] weiß; **white bread** Weißbrot; **white people** Weiße
Whites [waɪts] Weiße WF
who [huː] **1** wer; **Who with?** Mit wem? U3: 44; **2** der, die, das *(in Relativsätzen)*
whole [həʊl] ganz WF
why [waɪ] warum, weshalb; **That's why …** Deshalb …, Darum …
Wi-Fi ['waɪfaɪ] *umgangssprachlich für:* Funknetzwerk (z.B. WLAN) U4: 56
wide [waɪd] **1** breit; **2** weit
wife [waɪf] Ehefrau WF
wild [waɪld] wild; wild lebend
wildlife ['waɪldlaɪf] Wildtiere und -pflanzen WF
will [wɪl]: **I'll (= I will) go** ich werde gehen
win [wɪn] (I won, I've won) gewinnen
wind [wɪnd] Wind WF
wind farm ['wɪndfɑːm] Windpark U3: 50
window ['wɪndəʊ] Fenster
windsurfing ['wɪndsɜːfɪŋ] Windsurfing WF
winner ['wɪnə] Gewinner/in
winter ['wɪntə] Winter
wishes ['wɪʃɪz]: **Best wishes, …** Viele Grüße …
witch [wɪtʃ] Hexe
with [wɪð] mit; bei; **with 57% living at home** wobei 57% zu Hause wohnen WF
without [wɪ'ðaʊt] ohne
woke up [wəʊk'ʌp] (→ wake up): **I woke up** ich wachte auf, ich bin aufgewacht
woken up [wəʊkən'ʌp] (→ wake up): **I've woken up** ich bin aufgewacht
woman, women ['wʊmən, 'wɪmɪn] Frau, Frauen
won [wʌn] (→ win): **I won** ich gewann, ich habe gewonnen; **I've won** ich habe gewonnen
won't [wəʊnt]: **I won't (= will not) go** ich werde nicht gehen
wonder ['wʌndə] sich fragen WF
wonderful ['wʌndəfl] wundervoll WF

wood [wʊd] **1** Wald; **2** **piece of wood** Holzstück WF
wooden ['wʊdn] hölzern WF
woollen hat [wʊlən'hæt] Wollmütze WF
word [wɜːd] Wort; **words (of a song)** (Lied-)Text
word order ['wɜːdɔːdə] Satzstellung
wore [wɔː] (→ wear): **I wore** ich trug, ich habe getragen
work [wɜːk] **1** arbeiten; funktionieren; **work out** sich (gut) entwickeln, (gut) laufen U4: 52; **2** Arbeit
worker ['wɜːkə] Arbeiter/in
work experience [wɜːkɪk'spɪəriəns] Berufserfahrung; **do work experience** ein Berufspraktikum machen
working language ['wɜːkɪŋlæŋgwɪdʒ] Arbeitssprache WF
work permit ['wɜːkpɜːmɪt] Arbeitserlaubnis WF
workplace ['wɜːkpleɪs] Arbeitsplatz
world [wɜːld] Welt; **in the world** auf der (ganzen) Welt
World Cup [wɜːld'kʌp] (Fußball-) Weltmeisterschaft WF
worried ['wʌrid]: **I'm worried (about)** ich mache mir Sorgen (um), ich bin beunruhigt (wegen)
worry ['wʌri]: **worry (about)** sich Sorgen machen (um); **I didn't want to worry her** ich wollte sie nicht beunruhigen
worse [wɜːs] schlechter; schlimmer
worst [wɜːst] schlechteste/r/s; schlimmste/r/s
would [wʊd]: **I'd (= I would)** ich würde; **I'd like to go/...** Ich möchte gehen/...; **I wouldn't (= would not) like to go/...** Ich möchte nicht gehen/...; **Would you like ...?** Möchtest du/Möchten Sie ...?
Wow! [waʊ] Wow! Wahnsinn!

write [raɪt] (I wrote, I've written) schreiben
writer ['raɪtə] Schriftsteller/in
written ['rɪtn] (→ write): **I've written** ich habe geschrieben
wrong [rɒŋ] falsch; **What's wrong?** Ist etwas nicht in Ordnung? **You're wrong.** Du hast Unrecht.
wrote [rəʊt] (→ write): **I wrote** ich schrieb, ich habe geschrieben

X

X-ray assistant ['eksreɪəsɪstənt] Röntgenassistent/in U4: 62

Y

yeah [jeə] ja *(besonders in wörtl. Rede)*
year [jɪə] Jahr; Jahrgangsstufe; **a 13-year-old girl** ein 13-jähriges Mädchen; **What year are you in? - I'm in year 7.** In welcher Jahrgangsstufe bist du? - Ich bin in der 7. Stufe.
yellow ['jeləʊ] gelb
yes [jes] ja
yesterday ['jestədeɪ, 'jestədi] gestern
yet [jet]: **not ... yet** noch nicht
yogurt ['jɒgət] Jogurt U3: 42
you [juː] **1** du; ihr; Sie; **2** dir, euch, Ihnen; dich, euch, Sie; **you're (= you are)** du bist; ihr seid; Sie sind; **I said you'd be in the shop tomorrow.** Ich habe gesagt, du wärst morgen im Laden.
young [jʌŋ] jung; **young kids** kleine Kinder
your [jɔː] dein/e; euer, eure; Ihr/e
yours [jɔːz]: **Yours faithfully, ...** Mit freundlichen Grüßen ...; **Yours truly, ...** (AE) Mit freundlichen Grüßen ...

yourself dir/dich (selbst); sich (selbst); selbst; **a picture of yourself** ein Bild von dir
yourselves [jɔː'selvz] euch (selbst); sich (selbst); selbst
youth [juːθ] Jugendliche/r WF
youth camp ['juːθkæmp] Jugendferienlager WF
youth club ['juːθklʌb] Jugendklub

Z

zebra ['zebrə] Zebra WF
zoo [zuː] Zoo U1: 16
zoom [zuːm] Zoom WF

Alphabetische Liste der Wörter aus den Bänden 1–6 (Deutsch – Englisch)

* = unregelmäßiges Verb; siehe auch *List of irregular verbs*, S. 190/191

A

abbiegen: nach links/rechts (in die Hill Street) abbiegen turn left/right (into Hill Street)
Abend evening
Abendessen dinner
abends in the evening; *(mit Uhrzeit)* p.m.
Abenteuer adventure
aber but
abfahren *leave
Abfall rubbish; *(auf der Straße)* litter
abfliegen *leave
abgeben: (im Internet) Kommentare abgeben post comments; **eine Meinung abgeben** *give an opinion
abholen pick up
ablesen *read out
abnehmen *lose weight
Abneigung dislike
abreisen *leave
Absatz paragraph
Abschlussball *(an einer Schule)* (school) prom
abschneiden: gut abschneiden *do well
abschreiben copy
abseits der Straße off-road
Abspielgerät player
Absprache arrangement; **eine Absprache treffen** *make an arrangement
Abteilung department
achten respect
Achterbahn roller coaster
Actionfilm action film
Adjektiv adjective
Adresse address
Adverb adverb
Afrika Africa
afrikanisch; Afrikaner/in African
aggressiv aggressive
Ägypten Egypt
Akte file
Aktion *(Kampagne)* campaign
Aktivität activity
Akzent accent
Alarmanlage alarm
albern silly
Alkohol alcohol
alle all (the); *(jeder)* everybody; **alle 5 Minuten** every 5 minutes
allein alone
alles everything
allgemein general
Alphabet alphabet
alphabetisch alphabetical
als **1** as; **2** *(Wann?)* when; **schneller als** faster than
also so
alt old
Alter age; **im Alter von 16 Jahren** at 16 (years old)
am: am 5. August on August 5th; **am Morgen/...** in the morning/...; **Am nächsten Tag ...** The next day ...; **am selben Ort** in the same place; **am Strand** on the beach; **am Telefon** on the phone; **24 Stunden am Tag** 24 hours a day
American Football American football
Amerika America
Amerikaner/in American
amerikanisch American; **amerik. Ureinwohner/in** Native American
Ampel traffic light
Amtssprache official language
amüsieren: ich amüsiere mich I enjoy myself
an **1** *(bei)* at; **2** *(nach)* to; **3** *(in der Nähe von, neben)* by; **4** *(eingeschaltet)* on; **an den Armen** by his arms; **an der Tafel** on the board; **an Schultagen** on school days; **denken an** *think of
anbauen: etwas anbauen *grow things
anbieten offer
andere other; **ein anderer/anderes, eine andere** another
andere/r/s, anders (als) different (from)
andererseits: Einerseits ... Andererseits ... On the one hand, ... On the other hand, ...
(sich) ändern change
Anfang start
anfangen start
anfassen touch
Angaben zur Person personal details
Angebot offer
angeln fish; **Angeln** fishing
Angola Angola
angreifen attack
angriffslustig aggressive
Angst haben (vor) be afraid (of); **ich habe Angst** I'm frightened
ängstlich nervous
anhalten stop
Anhänger/in fan
anhören: sich anhören sound; **sich die CD anhören** listen to the CD
ankommen arrive
Anlegestelle pier
annehmen *(vermuten)* suppose
Anrede title
Anruf phone call; **Danke für den Anruf.** Thanks for calling.
anrufen phone; call
anschauen: sich den Film anschauen watch the film
Anschlagbrett noticeboard
anschließen: sich einem Zirkus anschließen join a circus
Anschreiben cover letter
ansehen: (sich) das Bild ansehen look at the picture
Ansicht scene
Ansichtskarte postcard
Antwort answer; **u.A.w.g.** *(= um Antwort wird gebeten)* RSVP
antworten answer
Anweisung order; **Anweisungen geben** Giving orders
Anzeige advert
anziehen: (sich) anziehen dress; *(tragen)* *wear
Anzug suit; **Surf-/Tauch(schutz)anzug** wetsuit
Apartheid apartheid
Apfel apple
Apfelwein cider
April April
Arbeit work; job
arbeiten work
Arbeiter/in worker
Arbeitgeber/in employer
Arbeitsgemeinschaft *(Klub)* club
arbeitslos unemployed
Arbeitslosigkeit unemployment
Arbeitsplatz workplace
Arbeitsstelle job
Arbeitszeit(en) hours
Argument argument
Arm arm
arm poor; **Du Arme/r!** Poor you!
Armut poverty
Art: eine Art ... a sort of ...

Artikel article
Arzt/Ärztin doctor
Asiat/in Asian
asiatisch Asian
Asien Asia
Assistent/in assistant
Astronaut/in astronaut
Atlantik Atlantic Ocean
auch too; also
auf on; *(auf ... hinauf/herauf)* onto; **auf das Haus zu** towards the house; **auf dem Bild** in the picture; **auf dem Land** in the country; **auf dem Parkplatz** in the car park; **auf dem Schulhof** in the playground; **auf den Boden fallen** *fall to the ground; **auf der (ganzen) Welt** in the world; **auf der Straße** in the street; **auf Deutsch** in German; **auf die Straße (hinaus)** into the street; **Auf Wiedersehen.** Goodbye.
Aufenthalt stay
Aufgabe job; task
aufgeben *give up
aufgehen *(sich öffnen)* open
aufgeladen: es ist aufgeladen it's charged up
aufgeregt excited
aufheben pick up
aufhören (mit) finish; stop; **aufhören, das Internet zu benutzen** stop using the Internet
aufladen: Handy-Guthaben aufladen top up a mobile
aufmachen open
aufmerksam carefully
aufnehmen record
aufpassen auf look after; **Pass auf!** Watch me!
aufregend exciting
Aufruf: letzter Aufruf final call
Aufstand riot
aufstehen *get up
aufstellen: ein Zelt aufstellen *put up a tent
aufwachen *wake up
aufzeichnen record
Auge eye
Augenblick: Einen Augenblick. Just a minute.
Augenbraue eyebrow
August August; **20. August** August 20th
aus **1** from; *(hinaus/heraus)* out; *(aus ... hinaus/heraus)* out of; **aus der Schule zurück** back from school; **2** *(zu Ende)* over; **3 aus Metall/...** made of metal/...

ausbilden train
Ausbildung education; training; **eine Ausbildung machen** train
ausdenken: sich ausdenken *make up
Ausdruck expression; phrase
ausdrucken print out
Ausflug trip
ausfüllen fill in
Ausgang *(Flugsteig)* gate
ausgeben *spend
ausgehen *go out
Ausgleichssport exercise; **Ausgleichssport treiben** *do exercise
auslachen laugh at
Ausland: im/ins Ausland abroad
ausleihen *(mieten)* rent
ausprobieren try
ausrauben: eine Bank ausrauben rob a bank
ausräumen empty
Ausrede excuse
ausrichten: Kann ich (ihm/ihr) etwas ausrichten? Can I take a message?
Ausrüstung equipment; gear
ausrutschen slip
Aussage statement
ausschalten turn off
aussehen look; **Wie sieht sie aus?** What does she look like?
Außenpfosten outside post
„Außentor" behind
Außerdem ... Also, ...
außerhalb (von) outside
Äußerung comment
Aussicht view(s)
Aussprache pronunciation
Ausstattung equipment
ausstehen: ich kann sie nicht ausstehen I hate them; I can't stand them
(aus dem Auto/...) aussteigen *get out (of the car/...)
Ausstellung exhibition
aussuchen *choose; pick
Austausch- exchange
Australian Rules Football Australian/Aussie Rules
Australien Australia; *(Spitzname)* Oz
Australier/in(nen), australisch Australian
auswählen *choose
Auswärtsspiel away match
Ausweis pass
Ausweispapiere papers
auswendig: Lerne es auswendig. Learn it by heart.
Auszeichnung award

ausziehen: ich ziehe meine Jacke aus I *take off my jacket
Auto car
Autobahn *(in den USA)* freeway
Autofahrer/in driver
Autogramm autograph
Autorennen car racing

B

Baby baby
Bad, Badezimmer bathroom
Badminton badminton
Bahn *(Laufbahn)* track
Bahnhof (railway) station; **im Bahnhof Exeter** at Exeter Station
Bahnsteig platform
bald soon
Ball ball
Banane banana
Band *(Musikgruppe)* band
Bande gang
Bandit/in outlaw
Bank *(Sparkasse)* bank
Bankkonto bank account
Bär bear
Bart beard
Baseball baseball
Basketball basketball
Batterieladegerät charger
bauen *build
Bauer/Bäuerin farmer
Bauernhof farm
Baum tree
Beachtung attention
beängstigend frightening
beantworten answer
bedeuten *mean
Bedeutung meaning
bedienen serve
beeilen: Beeil dich! Hurry up!
beenden finish
Befehl order; **Befehle erteilen** Giving orders
Befehlsform imperative
befragen question
begehen: ein Verbrechen begehen commit a crime
begeistert excited
beginnen start; **ich begann zu rennen** I started running/ I started to run
Begleitbrief (AE) cover letter
behalten *keep
behilflich: Kann ich Ihnen behilflich sein? Can I help you?
behindert disabled
bei **1** *(an)* at; **2** *(mit)* with; **bei Tim (zu Hause)** at Tim's house

beibringen *teach
Bein leg
beinahe almost; nearly
Beispiel example; **zum Beispiel** for example
beitreten: einem Klub beitreten join a club
bekommen *get; receive
belebt busy
belegt *(Platz)* taken
Belgien Belgium
beliebt popular
bemerken notice
bemitleiden: mich bemitleiden *feel sorry for me
benutzen use
beobachten watch
bequem comfortable
beraten *give (some) advice
Berater/in counsellor
bereit ready
Berg mountain
Bericht report
berichtigen correct
Beruf job; **Beruf, Berufs-** career
Berufserfahrung work experience
Berufspraktikum: ein Berufspraktikum machen *do work experience
Berufsschule college
berühmt famous
berühren touch
beschädigt damaged
beschäftigt busy
Beschäftigung activity; *(im Freien)* outdoor activity
Bescheid: geben Sie mir Bescheid let me know
beschimpfen: sie beschimpften mich they called me names
beschließen decide
beschreiben describe; **Beschreibe sie deinem Partner/deiner Partnerin.** Describe them to your partner.
Beschreibung description
beschweren: sich beschweren complain
besetzt *(Platz)* taken
Besichtigungen sightseeing
Besitzer/in owner
besondere/r/s special
Besprechung *(Rezension)* review
besser better
beste/r/s best; **am besten** best
bestehen pass
bestellen order
Besuch visit; *(Aufenthalt)* stay
besuchen visit
Besucher/in visitor
Besucherzentrum visitor centre
betonen stress
Betrieb business
Bett bed
beunruhigen worry
beunruhigt: ich bin beunruhigt (wegen) I'm worried (about)
Bevölkerung(szahl) population
bevor before
(sich) bewegen move
bewerben: sich bewerben (um/bei) apply (for/to)
Bewerbung application
Bewerbungsformular application form
Bewerbungsschreiben letter of application
bewölkt cloudy
bezahlen *pay
bezahlt paid
Bezahlung pay
bezeichnen call
Beziehung relationship
Bezirk district
Biber beaver
Bibliothekar/in librarian
Bier beer
Bild picture
bilden: Gruppen bilden *make groups
Bildschirm screen
Bildung education
billig cheap
bin: ich bin I'm (= I am)
Birne pear
bis to; **bis zum 15. Mai** by May 15th; **Bis dann.** See you. **Bis morgen/...** See you tomorrow/...
bisschen: ein bisschen a bit (of)
bist: du bist you're (= you are); **Bist du schon einmal ...? - Ja./Nein.** Have you ever ...? - Yes, I have./No, I haven't.
bitte please; **Hier, bitte.** Here you are. **Bitte.** *(Schon gut.)* That's OK. **Bitte schön.** *(Nichts zu danken.)* You're welcome.
bitten um ask for
Blase bubble
blass pale
blau blue
bleiben stay
Bleistift pencil
blöd stupid
Blödsinn nonsense
Blog blog
Bloggen blogging
Blogger/in blogger
blond blonde
bloß only
Blut blood; **Blut spenden** *give blood
Board *(Brett)* board
Boden floor; ground; **am Boden zerstört** devastated
Bombe bomb
Boot boat
Bordkarte boarding pass
böse (auf) angry (with)
Boss boss
Bote/Botin courier
Botschaft message
Boutique boutique
Brand fire
brauchen need
braun brown
breit wide
Brett board; **Schwarzes Brett** noticeboard
Brief letter
Brille glasses
bringen *bring; *take; **in die richtige Reihenfolge bringen** *put in the right order
Brite/Britin British
britisch British
Broschüre brochure
Brot bread; **belegtes Brot** sandwich
Brötchen roll
Brücke bridge
Bruder brother
Buch book
Bucheinband, -umschlag book cover
buchen book
Bücherei library
Buchhandlung, Buchladen bookshop
Büchse can
Buchstabe letter
buchstabieren spell
Budget budget
Bühne stage; **auf der Bühne** on stage
Bundesstaat state; **der Bundesstaat Washington** Washington State
Burg castle
Bürgerkrieg civil war
Bürgersteig pavement; (AE) sidewalk
Burka burka
Büro office
Büroleiter/in office manager
Bus bus
Busch: der (australische) Busch the bush
Busfahrer/in bus driver
Bushaltestelle bus stop

C

Café cafe
Callcenter call centre
Camping camping
Campingplatz campsite; (AE) campground
Cartoon cartoon
CD CD
Cent cent
Chatroom *(im Internet)* chat room
Checkliste checklist
Chef/in boss
Chor choir
Clique gang
Coach coach
Cola cola
Computer computer
Computerprogramm computer program
Computerprogrammierer/in computer programmer
cool cool; **nicht cool** uncool
Cousin/e cousin
„Cybermobber/in" cyberbully
„Cybermobbing" cyberbullying

D

da: da(hin) there; **da ist** there's; **da sind** there are; **da war/waren** there was/were; **da drüben** over there; **Ich bin wieder da!** I'm back!
Dach roof
dafür und dagegen for and against
dagegen: dafür und dagegen for and against; **Haben Sie etwas dagegen, wenn ich mich hier hinsetze?** Do you mind if I sit here?
daheim at home
daher so
Dame: Sehr geehrte Damen und Herren, ... Dear Sir/Madam, ...
daneben treffen/gehen miss
Dänemark Denmark
Danke (schön). Thank you./Thanks.
danken: Ich möchte Ihnen dafür danken, dass Sie bei mir waren. I want to thank you for being with me. **Nichts zu danken.** You're welcome.
dann then
darauf: ich freue mich darauf, von Ihnen zu hören I'm looking forward to hearing from you
darum that's why
das the; *(das da)* that; *(das hier)* this; *(in Relativsätzen)* that; who; **Das ist ...** That's ...
dass that; **Tut mir leid, dass ich ...** I'm sorry I ...
dasselbe the same
Datum date
dauern *take
Daumen: Ich drücke dir die Daumen. I'll keep my fingers crossed for you.
davor before that
decken: den Tisch decken *lay the table
Definition definition
dein/e your
Delfin dolphin
denken (an) *think (of); **daran denken** remember
Denkmal monument
deprimiert depressed
der the; *(der da)* that; *(in Relativsätzen)* that; who
derselbe the same
deshalb that's why
Design design
Detail detail
Detektiv/in detective
deutlich clear
deutsch; Deutsch; Deutsche/r German
Deutschland Germany
Dezember December
Diagramm diagram
Dialog dialogue
dich you; *(dich selbst)* yourself
Dichter/in poet
dick thick; *(bei Personen)* fat
die the; *(die da; Einzahl)* that; *(die da; Mehrzahl)* those; *(die hier; Mehrzahl)* these; *(in Relativsätzen)* that; who; **Männer, die Spiele spielen** men playing games
Diele entrance hall
Dienstag Tuesday
dies (hier) this
diese *(Mehrzahl)* these; *(diese da)* those
diese/r/s this; **an diesem Abend** that evening
dieselbe the same
Digital-; digital digital
Ding thing
dir you; *(dir selbst)* yourself; **ein Bild von dir** a picture of yourself
direkte Rede direct speech
Discjockey (DJ) DJ
Disko club
Diskussion discussion
doch: du kannst doch noch Urlaub machen you can have your holiday after all
Dollar dollar ($)
dolmetschen interpret; **Dolmetschen** interpreting
Donnerstag Thursday
Dorf village
dort(hin) there
Dose can
draußen *(im Freien)* outdoors; **da draußen** out there
drehen: sich drehen turn; **sich nach links drehen** turn to the left
dringend urgent
drinnen: (nach) drinnen inside; *(in der Halle)* indoors
Droge drug
drüben: da/dort drüben over there
Druck pressure
drücken push; **Ich drücke dir die Daumen.** I'll keep my fingers crossed for you.
Drucker printer
du you
Dubliner/in Dubliner
dumm silly; stupid
dunkel dark
durch *(hindurch)* through
durchdrehen panic
durcheinander bringen *(mischen)* mix up
Durchsage announcement
dürfen can; **ich darf gehen** I'm allowed to go; **nicht dürfen** mustn't
Durst: ich habe Durst I'm thirsty
Dusche shower
duschen *have a shower
DVD DVD
DVD-Player DVD player

E

echt real
Ecstasy ecstasy
egal: Das ist mir egal. I don't mind. **Ist doch egal!** Who cares? **egal, wie das Wetter ist** whatever the weather
Ehe marriage
Ehemann husband
ehrenamtlich voluntary
Ei egg
eifersüchtig (auf) jealous (of)
eigen: mein eigenes Zimmer my own room
Eigenschaft quality

Eigenschaftswort adjective
eigentlich actually; *(wirklich)* really
Eigentümer/in owner
ein/e a; an; *(Zahl)* one
Einband cover
eindringen: in einen Computer eindringen hack into a computer
eine/r/s one; **eines Tages** one day
Einerseits ... Andererseits ... On the one hand, ... On the other hand, ...
einfach easy; simple; *(nur)* just; **einfache Gegenwart/Vergangenheit** simple present/past
Einfall idea
einfallen: Mir fällt das richtige Wort nicht ein. I can't think of the right word.
einfügen *put in
eingeschaltet on
einheimisch local
einige some
Einkaufen shopping
einkaufen gehen *go shopping
Einkaufszentrum shopping centre; (AE) mall
einladen (zu) invite (for)
Einladung invitation
einmal once
einpacken pack
einsam lonely
einschalten turn on
einschließlich including
einschüchtern bully
Einsteigekarte boarding pass
einsteigen: in ein Flugzeug/... einsteigen *get on a plane/...
Eintrag entry
Eintrittskarte ticket
Eintrittspreis entrance fee
Einwanderer/Einwanderin immigrant
Einzelheit detail
Einzimmerwohnung one-bedroom apartment
Eis *(Speiseeis)* ice cream
Eisenbahn train
Eisenbahnstrecke railway line
Elefant elephant
Elektriker/in electrician
elektrisch electric
Elektrizität electricity
elektronisch electronic
elend miserable
Eltern, Elternteil parents, parent
E-Mail e-mail
Empfangschef/-dame receptionist
empfehlen recommend
Ende end; **Ende gut, alles gut.** All's well that ends well. **oberes Ende** top; **Um zum Ende zu kommen, ...** To finish, ...; **zu Ende** over
endlich at last
Energie energy
eng narrow
Engländer/in(nen): er ist Engländer he's English
England England
englisch; Englisch English
Englischlehrer/in English teacher
Enkelkinder grandchildren
(im Preis) enthalten included (in the price)
entlang along; **die Straße entlang** along the street
(sich) entscheiden decide
Entscheidung decision; **eine Entscheidung treffen** *make a decision
entschuldigen: sich entschuldigen *say sorry; **Entschuldigen Sie, ...** Excuse me, ...
Entschuldigung excuse
(sich) entspannen relax
entspannt relaxed
enttäuscht disappointed
entweder ... oder either ... or
entwickeln: sich (gut) entwickeln work out
er he; *(nicht bei Personen)* it
Erdkunde geography
Erdteil continent
Ereignis event
erfahren: etwas über London erfahren learn about London; **von ... erfahren** hear about ...
Erfahrung experience
erfinden *make up
erfolgreich successful
erforderlich required
ergeben: sich ergeben *come up
Ergebnis result
erhalten receive
erinnern: sich erinnern (an) remember
erkennen *(sich klar werden über)* realize
erklären explain; **ihr etwas erklären** explain something to her; **ich erkläre mich bereit, ihr zu helfen** I agree to help her
erlauben allow
erleichtert relieved
ermuntern, ermutigen encourage
ernst, ernsthaft serious
erraten guess
Ersatz replacement
erschüttert devastated
erst only
erstaunlich amazing
erste/r/s first; **erste Hilfe** first aid
erstens firstly
Erwachsene/r adult
erwarten expect; **sie erwarten von Teenagern, dass sie ...** they expect teenagers to ...; **Ich kann es kaum erwarten.** I can't wait for it.
erwischen *catch
erzählen (von) *tell (about)
erzielen *(Punkte)* score
es it; **es ist/gibt** there's; **es sind/gibt** there are; **es war(en)/gab** there was/were
essen *eat; **ein Eis essen** *have an ice cream; **essen gehen** *eat out; **zu essen geben** *feed
Essen food; *(Mahlzeit)* meal
Esszimmer dining room
Etikett label
etwas something; **etwas anderes** something different; **etwas Schokolade** some chocolate; **etwas gern tun** *be happy to do something
euch you; *(euch selbst)* yourselves
euer/eure your
Euro euro (€)
Europa Europe
Europäer/in; europäisch European
Expedition expedition
Experiment experiment
Experte/Expertin expert
explodieren explode
extra extra
Extremist/in extremist

F

Fabrik factory
Fach *(Schulfach)* subject
Fach(hoch)schule college
Fachmann/-frau expert
Fahne flag
„Fahrattraktion" *(im Vergnügungspark)* ride
Fähre ferry
fahren *go; *(ein Auto/einen Bus)* *drive; *(reisen)* travel; **Mountainboard/Rad fahren** *ride a mountain board/bike
Fahren: Quadfahren/Trikkefahren/... quad/Trikke/... riding
Fahrer/in driver

Fahrgast passenger
Fahrgeschäft ride
Fahrkarte ticket
Fahrrad bike; **Fahrrad fahren** *ride a bike
Fahrstunde driving lesson
Fahrt journey; ride
Fährtensucher/in tracker
fair fair| **Fair Play** fair play
Faktensammlung factfile
fallen *fall; **auf den Boden fallen** *fall to the ground
falls if
falsch wrong; false
Familie family
Familienname family name; surname
Fan fan
fangen *catch
fantastisch fantastic
Farbe colour
Farbige/r coloured
Farm farm
fassen *catch
fast almost; nearly
Fastfood fast food
faul lazy
Favorit/in favourite
Februar February
Federball(spiel) badminton
Federmäppchen pencil case
Feedback feedback
fehlen: es fehlt it's missing
fehlend: die fehlenden Wörter the missing words
Fehler mistake
Feinkostgeschäft und -imbiss (AE) deli
Feld field
Fels rock
Felsen *(Klippe)* cliff
Fenster window
Ferien holiday/s
fernhalten: von den Farmen fernhalten *keep out of the farms
fernsehen watch TV
Fernsehen, Fernsehgerät TV
Fernsehgebühr TV licence
Fernsehkarriere career in TV
fertig ready; **ich bin fertig** I'm finished
Fest; Festival festival
Festbeleuchtung illuminations
fettleibig obese
Fettleibigkeit obesity
feucht wet
Feuer fire
Feuerwehrfrau/-mann firefighter
Feuerwerk fireworks
Figur *(Person)* character
Film film; (AE) movie
Filmtrailer, -vorschau film trailer
Finanz-, finanziell financial
finden *find; *think
Firma company
Fisch, Fische fish
fischen fish; **Fischen** fishing
fit fit
Fitnessstudio gym
Flagge flag
Fleisch meat
flexibel flexible
fliegen *fly; *go
fliehen escape
fließendes Wasser running water
flüchten escape
Flug flight
Flugbegleiter/in flight attendant
Flughafen airport; **am Flughafen Exeter** at Exeter Airport
Flugschein (plane) ticket
Flugsteig gate
Flugzeug plane
Fluss river
Folge result
folgen follow
Förderunterricht extra classes
Form form
Formel formula
formlos informal
Formular form
forschen *do research
fort away
Foto photo; picture; **Fotos machen** *take photos
Fotoapparat camera
Fotograf/in photographer
fotografieren *take photos
Fotosession, Fotoshooting photo shoot
Foul foul
Frage question; **eine Frage stellen** ask a question
Fragebogen questionnaire
fragen ask; **sie nach etwas fragen** ask them about something
Frankreich France
Franzose(n)/Französin(nen); französisch; Französisch French
Frau, Frauen woman, women; *(Anrede allgemein)* Ms; *(Anrede für verheiratete Frauen)* Mrs
Freak freak
frei free; **im Freien** outdoors; **Beschäftigung im Freien** outdoor activity
Freiheit freedom
Freiheitsstatue Statue of Liberty
Freitag Friday
freiwillig voluntary
Freiwillige/r volunteer
Freiwurf free throw
Freizeit free time
Fremdenverkehrsbüro tourist office
Fremdsprache; fremdsprachig foreign language
fressen *eat
freuen: ich freue mich darauf, von Ihnen zu hören I'm looking forward to hearing from you; **ich freue mich für sie** I'm happy for her
Freund/in friend; *(feste/r Freundin/Freund)* boyfriend/girlfriend
freundlich friendly; kind; **Mit freundlichen Grüßen ...** Yours faithfully, ...; (AE) Yours truly, ...
Freundschaft/en schließen *make friends
Frieden peace
friedlich peaceful
Friseur/in hairdresser
Frisieren hairdressing
froh happy
Früchte fruit
früh early
früher once
Frühling spring
Frühstück breakfast
frühstücken *have breakfast
(sich) fühlen *feel
führen *go; *lead
Führer/in leader; *(für Sehenswürdigkeiten)* guide
Führerscheinprüfung driving test
Führung *(Rundgang)* tour
Füller pen
Funknetzwerk (z.B. WLAN) *(umgangssprachlich)* Wi-Fi
funktionieren work
für for; **es steht 24:18 für North** it's 24-18 to North
furchtbar awful; terrible
furchterregend frightening
Fürwort pronoun
Fuß *(Längenmaß)* foot, feet
Fuß, Füße foot, feet
Fußball football; soccer
Fußballweltmeisterschaft World Cup
Fußboden floor
füttern *feed

G

Gälisch Gaelic
Gang **1** *(Bande)* gang; **2** *(Fahrrad/Auto/...)* gear; **3** *(Korridor)* passage

ganz full; **das ganze Wochenende** all weekend; **die ganze Zeit** all the time
ganztags, Ganztags- full-time
gar nichts nothing
Garten garden
Gärtner/in gardener
Gas gas
Gast guest; visitor
Gebäude building
geben *give; **geben Sie mir Bescheid** let me know; **Gib Tim das Buch.** Give the book to Tim. **eine Party geben** *have a party; **Was gibt's?** What's up?
Gebiet district
Gebirge: im Gebirge in the mountains
geboren: ich wurde ... geboren I was born ...
Gebrauchsanweisung instructions
Geburtsdatum/-land date/country of birth
Geburtstag birthday
Gedankenblase thought bubble
Gedicht poem
gefährlich dangerous
gefallen: Es gefällt mir. I like it. **Wem gefällt es am besten?** Who likes it best?
gefälscht fake
Gefängnis prison; **im/ins Gefängnis** in prison; **ins Gefängnis kommen** *go to prison
Gefriertruhe, -schrank freezer
Gefühl feeling
gegen against
Gegend area; neighbourhood
Gegenteil opposite
gegenüber (von) opposite
Gegenwart: einfache Gegenwart simple present
gehängt: er wurde gehängt he was hanged
Gehalt pay
gehen *go; walk; **ans Telefon gehen** answer the phone; **mit jemandem gehen** *go out with somebody; **sie geht zur Schule** she's at school; **Wie geht's?** How are you?
Gehsteig pavement
Geist ghost
Gelände: im Gelände off-road
Geländer railings
gelangen *get
gelangweilt bored
gelb yellow
Geld money
Geldautomat ATM; cash machine
Geldschein note
gemein unkind
Gemüse vegetable/s
Generation generation
genießen enjoy
genug enough
Genuss treat
geöffnet open
Geografie geography
Gepäckabfertiger/in baggage handler
gerade just
Gerät machine
Geräusch noise; sound
gerecht fair
gern haben/tun **1** *(mögen)* like; **Ich laufe (nicht) gern.** I (don't) like walking. **2** *(genießen, Spaß haben an)* enjoy; **gern arbeiten** enjoy working; **3** *(sehr mögen)* **Ich lese sehr gern.** I love reading. **ich würde sehr gern ...** I'd love to ...
Geschäft **1** business; **2** *(Laden)* shop; (AE) store
Geschäftsführer/in manager
geschehen happen
Geschenk present
Geschichte **1** *(Erzählung)* story; **2** *(Schulfach)* history
geschieden: sie waren geschieden they were divorced
Geschirrspülmaschine dishwasher
Geschlecht gender
geschlossen closed
Geschwister brothers and sisters
Gesicht face
Gespenst ghost
gesponsert sponsored
Gespräch conversation; dialogue
gestatten allow
gestern yesterday
„Gestohlene Generationen" "Stolen Generations"
gestresst stressed
gesucht wanted
gesund healthy
Getränk drink
Gewalt(tätigkeit) violence
gewaltfrei non-violent
gewalttätig violent
Gewicht weight
Gewinn prize
gewinnen *win; **im Lotto gewinnen** *win the lotto
Gewinner/in winner
gewöhnlich ordinary; *(normalerweise)* usually
Gitarre guitar; **Gitarre spielen** play the guitar
glänzen *shine
glänzend brilliant
Glas glass
Glaube religion
glauben believe
gleich: der/die/das gleiche the same
Gleis **1** *(Bahnsteig)* platform; **2** *(Eisenbahnstrecke)* railway line
Glück: ich habe Glück I'm lucky; **Nächstes Mal hast du bestimmt mehr Glück!** Better luck next time! **Viel Glück!** Good luck!
glücklich happy
Glückliche/r: Der/Die Glückliche! Du Glückliche/r! Lucky thing!
glücklicherweise luckily
Glückwunsch: Herzlichen Glückwunsch! Congratulations! *(zum Geburtstag)* Happy birthday!
Golf golf
Gondel car
Gospel(musik) gospel
Grab grave
Grad degree
Gras grass
grau grey
Graubrot brown bread
Grenze border
Grill; Grillfest barbecue
groß big; large; *(bei Personen)* tall; **er ist einsfünfundachtzig groß** he's six feet one (inch)
großartig great; brilliant
Großbritannien Britain
Größe **1** size; **2** *(Körpergröße)* height
Großeltern grandparents
Großmutter grandmother; *(Oma)* grandma
Großstadt city
Großvater *(Opa)* grandad
grün green
Grund reason
Gruppe group
Grüße: Mit freundlichen Grüßen ... Yours faithfully, ...; (AE) Yours truly, ...; **Viele Grüße ...** Best wishes, ...; **(Viele) Liebe Grüße ...** (Lots of) Love, ...
grüßen: Grüße Dawn, bitte. Say hi to Dawn, please.
gut good; fine; *(schon gut)* OK; **gut aussehend** good-looking; **gut in** good at; **gut kennen/...** know/... well; **Gut gemacht!** Well done! **Gute(n) Abend/Morgen/Nacht** Good evening/morning/night; **Guten Tag.** Hello.

Wie geht's? - Danke, gut. How are you? - I'm fine, thanks. **Mach's gut.** Take care.
Guthaben credit; **Ich habe kein Guthaben mehr auf meinem Handy.** I'm out of credit.

H

Haar, Haare hair
haben *have; **Ich habe Geburtstag.** It's my birthday. **ich habe viel Spaß** I enjoy myself; **Welche Farbe hat dein Zimmer?** What colour is your room?
Hähnchen chicken
halb: halb zwei/... half past one/...; **dreieinhalb** three and a half; **eine halbe Stunde** half an hour; **mein halbes Frühstück** half my breakfast
Halbzeit half-time
Halle: in der Halle indoors
Hallo. Hello./Hi.
Halloween Halloween
Halt stop
halten *hold; *keep; **Halt den Mund!** Shut up! **sich an die Spielregeln halten** play by the rules; **einen Vortrag halten** *give a talk; **Was hältst du von ...?** What do you think of ...?
Haltestelle stop
Hamburger hamburger
Hamster hamster
Hand hand
handeln: Der Text handelt von ... The text is about ...
Handlung action
Handy mobile (phone); (AE) cellphone; **Handy-Guthaben aufladen** top up a mobile
Handzeichen hand signal
Happy End happy ending
hart hard; tough
Haschisch cannabis
Hase rabbit
hassen hate
hast: Hast du schon einmal ...? - Ja./Nein. Have you ever ...? - Yes, I have./No, I haven't.
hätte: Ich hätte gern ... I'd like ...
Haupt- main ...; **Hauptsatz** main clause
Hauptstadt capital
Haus house; **nach Hause gehen** *go home; **zu Hause** at home; **bei Tim zu Hause** at Tim's house; **Gehen wir zu mir nach Hause.** Let's go to my house.
Hausarrest: ich habe Hausarrest I'm grounded
Hausaufgaben homework
Hausaufgabenheft homework diary
Häuserblock block
Hausflur entrance hall
Hausschuh slipper
Haustier pet
Havanna Havana
heben: Heb(t) die Hand. Put up your hand.
Heft book
Heim home
heimatlos homeless
Heimwerkermarkt DIY store
heiraten *get married
heiß hot
heißen: Ich heiße Sarah. I'm Sarah. **Wie heißt du?** What's your name? **Wie heißen sie auf Deutsch?** What are they in German?
Heizkörper radiator
hektisch busy
Held/in, Held(inn)en hero, heroes
helfen help
Helfer/in helper
Helm helmet
herausfinden *find out
herausfordernd provocative
herbeirufen call
Herbst autumn
Herd cooker
hereinkommen *come in
Herr *(Anrede)* Mr; **Sehr geehrte Damen und Herren, ...** Dear Sir/Madam, ...
herstellen *make; produce
herüber across
herum around
herumhängen *hang around
herunterladen download
herzlich: Herzlichen Glückwunsch! Congratulations! *(zum Geburtstag)* Happy birthday!
heute today; **heute Morgen/...** this morning/...; **heute Abend/Nacht** tonight
Hexe witch
hier(her) here; **Hier, bitte.** Here you are. **Hier spricht Sarah.** It's Sarah.
Hilfe help; **erste Hilfe** first aid
hinab/herab down
hinaus/heraus out
Hindi Hindi
Hindu Hindu
hinein in; **hineingehen** *go in; **hineinkriechen** crawl in
hinsetzen: sich hinsetzen *sit down
hinten im Buch at the back of the book
hinter behind; **hinter einem Ball her** after a ball
Hintergrund background
hinüber across
hinunter/herunter down
hinwegkommen: über etwas hinwegkommen *get over something
hinzufügen *put in
Hirsch, Hirsche deer
hispanisch; Hispano-Amerikaner/in Hispanic
Hit hit
Hobby hobby
hoch high
Hochgefühl kick
hochheben pick up
Hochsprung (the) high jump
Hochzeit wedding
Hochzeitstag wedding day
Hockey hockey
Hof *(Bauernhof)* farm
hoffen hope; **Das hoffe ich.** I hope so.
höflich polite
Höhe height
holen *get
hören *hear; *(sich anhören)* listen to; **von ... hören** *hear about ...; **Wir hören voneinander.** Let's keep in touch.
Horror horror
Hose: kurze Hosen shorts
Hotel hotel
House house
Hüfte hip
Hügel hill
Huhn chicken
Hund dog
hundert hundred
Hunger: Ich habe Hunger. I'm hungry.
hungrig hungry
Hurling hurling
hurra rufen cheer
Hütte cabin

I

ich I; **Dies bin ich.** This is me.
Idee idea
Identität identity
If-Satz if-clause
ihm, ihn him; *(nicht bei Personen)* it
ihnen them

Ihnen you
ihr 1 *(Wer?)* you; 2 *(Wem?)* her; *(nicht bei Personen)* it
ihr/e 1 *(Einzahl)* her; *(nicht bei Personen)* its; 2 *(Mehrzahl)* their
Ihr/e your
illegal illegal
im: im April in April; **im Bahnhof Exeter** at Exeter Station; **im Bus** on the bus; **im Fernsehen** on TV; **im Internet** on the Internet; **im Jahre 1971** in 1971; **im Norden** in the north; **im Sonderangebot** on special offer; **im Vordergrund/Hintergrund** in the foreground/background; **im Urlaub** on holiday; **im Winter** in winter; **im Südwesten von Afrika** in south-west Africa
Imbissstube takeaway
immer always; *(jederzeit)* at all times
Immigrant/in immigrant
Imperativ imperative
in in; at; inside; *(in ... hinein/herein)* into; **in Dartmoor** on Dartmoor; **in den Urlaub fahren** *go on holiday; **in der Dean Road** in Dean Road; **in der Nacht** at night; **in der Schule** at school; **in die Mannschaft kommen** *get on the team; **in einer Reservation** on a reservation; **In welcher Jahrgangsstufe bist du? – Ich bin in der 7. Stufe.** What year are you in? – I'm in year 7. **ins Bett gehen** *go to bed; **eine Sendung ins Leben rufen** start a programme; **Willkommen in London.** Welcome to London. **Ich bin (schon einmal) in Frankreich gewesen.** I've been to France.
Inder/in, indisch Indian
Indianer/in Indian; *(amerik. Ureinwohner/in)* Native American
Indien India
indirekte Rede indirect speech
Indonesien Indonesia
Industrie industry
Informationen, Informations- information
informell informal
Inliner, Inlineskate in-line skate
innerhalb (von) inside
Insel island
insgesamt all in all
Installateur/in plumber
instand halten: Motorräder instand halten service motorbikes
interessant interesting
Interesse interest
interessiert (an) interested (in)
Internat boarding school
international international
Internet Internet; **im Internet** on the Internet
Internet-Kiosk Internet kiosk
Interview interview
Ire(n)/Irin(nen); irisch; Irisch Irish
irgendwelche any
Irland Ireland
irre (AE) awesome
ist is
Italien Italy

J

ja yes; *(besonders in wörtl. Rede)* yeah
Jacke jacket
jagen hunt
Jäger/in hunter
Jahr year; **ein 13-jähriges Mädchen** a 13-year-old girl
Jahreszeit season
Jahrgangsstufe year; **In welcher Jahrgangsstufe bist du?** What year are you in?
Jahrmarkt funfair
Januar January
Jeans jeans
jede/r/s each; every
jeder *(alle)* everybody
jederzeit at all times
jemals ever
jemand somebody
jene *(Mehrzahl)* those
jetzt now
joggen jog
Jogger/in jogger
Jogging jogging
Jogurt yogurt
Journalist/in journalist
jubeln cheer
Judo judo
Jugendferienlager youth camp
Jugendklub youth club
Jugendliche/r kid
Juli July
jung young
Junge boy
Juni June
Junior-Ranger junior ranger

K

Kajak kayak
Kajakfahren kayaking
Kalifornien California
Kalorie calorie
kalt cold
Kamera camera
Kampagne campaign
kämpfen *fight; **um etwas kämpfen** *fight for something
Kanal canal
Kaninchen rabbit
kaninchensicher rabbit-proof
Kanu canoe
Kanufahren canoeing
Kappe cap
Kapstadt Cape Town
kaputt broken
Kapuzensweatshirt/-jacke hoody
Karikatur cartoon
Karneval carnival
Karriere career
Karte card; *(Landkarte)* map
Karteikarte file
Kartoffel, Kartoffeln potato, potatoes
Kartoffelchips crisps; (AE) potato chips
Käse cheese
Kassierer/in cashier
Kasten box
Katastrophe disaster
Katze cat
kaufen *buy
Käufer/in shopper
Kaufhaus department store
Kaution deposit
kein/e no; not ... any
kennen *know; **kennen lernen** *meet; **Schön, dich/Sie kennen zu lernen.** Nice to meet you.
Kick *(Hochgefühl)* kick
kicken kick
Kilogramm kilogram
Kilometer kilometre
Kilt *(Schottenrock)* kilt
Kind, Kinder child, children; kid, kids
Kinderbetreuung, Kinderpflege childcare
Kinderheim home
Kino cinema
Kirche church
Kirmes funfair
Kirsche cherry
Kiste box
Klamotten gear
Klapphandy flip phone

klar: sich klar werden über realize
Klasse class; (AE) grade
Klassenarbeit test
Klassenlehrer/in class teacher
Klassenzimmer classroom
Klavier piano
Kleid dress
Kleider, Kleidung clothes; *(Klamotten)* gear
Kleiderschrank wardrobe
klein little; short; small; **kleine Kinder** young kids
Klempner/in plumber
Kletterer/Kletterin (rock) climber
klettern climb; **auf einen Hügel klettern** climb a hill; **Klettern** (rock) climbing
Klingelton ringtone
klingen sound
Klinik clinic
Klippe cliff
Klischee(vorstellung) stereotype
Klub club
klug clever
Knopf button
Koala(bär) koala
Koch/Köchin cook
kochen cook
Kolonie colony
Kolumbien Colombia
komfortabel comfortable
komisch funny
kommen *come; *(gelangen)* *get; **Ich komme aus London.** I'm from London. **Er kommt zu spät.** He's late. **ins Gefängnis kommen** *go to prison; **Komm schon!** Come on!
Kommentar comment
Komödie comedy
Königin queen
können can; **ich kann nicht kommen** I'm not able to come
konnte: ich konnte (nicht) I could(n't)
könnte: ich könnte I could
Kontext context
Kontinent continent
Konto account
kontrollieren check
Konzert concert
Kopf head
Kopfsprung: einen Kopfsprung machen dive
kopieren copy
Korb *(Basketball)* hoop
Korbwurf shot
Körper body
korrekt correct
Korridor passage
korrigieren correct
kosten *(Geld)* *cost; **Was kostet/kosten ...?** How much is/are ...?
kostenlos free
Kostüm suit
Kraft energy
Kram stuff
krank ill; sick
Krankenhaus hospital
Krankenpfleger/-schwester nurse
Krankheit illness
Kricket cricket
kriechen crawl
Krieg war
Kriminelle/r criminal
Krokodil crocodile
Küche kitchen
Kuchen cake
Kuh cow
Kühlschrank fridge
Kultur culture
„Kummerkastentante" agony aunt
kümmern: sich kümmern um look after; **sich um Taschen kümmern** *deal with bags
Kumpel buddy
Kunde/Kundin customer
Kunst art
Künstler/in artist
Kurier/in courier
Kurs *(Lehrgang)* course
kurz short; **kurz (be)vor** just before
küssen, sich küssen kiss
Küste coast; *(Strand)* seashore
Kwaito kwaito

L

lächeln smile; **Lächeln** smile
Lachs salmon
Ladegerät charger
Laden shop; (AE) store
Ladendieb/in shoplifter
Lagerfeuer campfire
Lampe light
Land country; *(Staat)* state; land; **auf dem Land** in the country
landesweit national
Landfahrer/in traveller
Landkarte map
lang: 14 Jahre lang for 14 years
lang/e long
lange (for) a long time; **lange bleiben** stay for long
langsam slow
langweilen: ich langweile mich I'm bored
langweilig boring
Laptop laptop
Lärm noise
lassen: Lasst uns aufhören. Let's finish. **stehen/liegen lassen** *leave; **sich scheiden lassen** *get divorced
Lauch(stange) leek
Laufbahn **1** *(Bahn)* track; **2** *(Karriere)* career
laufen *run; walk; **(gut) laufen** work out; **Laufen** running
Läufer/in runner
laut loud
leben live
Leben life, *(Mehrzahl)* lives
Lebenslauf CV (curriculum vitae); (AE) résumé
Lebensmittel food
leer empty
leeren empty
legen *put
Lehre apprenticeship
Lehrer/in teacher
Lehrgang course
leicht easy
Leichtathletik athletics
leid: Tut mir leid. I'm sorry. / Sorry.
leider unfortunately; **Leider ...** I'm afraid ...
leihen: sich einen Füller (aus)leihen borrow a pen
leitende/r Bibliothekar/in chief librarian
Leiter/in des Vorstellungsgesprächs interviewer
Lektion unit
lernen learn; **Lerne es auswendig.** Learn it by heart. **für eine Prüfung lernen** revise for an exam
lesen *read
Leser/in reader
Lesewoche reading week
„Letterboxing" letterboxing
letzte/r/s last; **letzter Aufruf** final call; **eine Entscheidung in letzter Minute** a last-minute decision
letztendlich in the end
leuchten *shine
Leute people; **Hallo Leute.** (AE) Hi you guys.
Licht light
Lichtschalter light switch
lieb: Liebe/r ... Dear ...; **(Viele) Liebe Grüße ...** (Lots of) Love, ...
Liebe love
lieben love
Liebesfilm/-roman romance

Lieblings- favourite
Lied song
liegen *lie
Limonade lemonade
Lineal ruler
Linie line
Link link
links left; **auf der linken Seite** on the left; **links (von Ihnen)** on your left
Lippe lip
Liste list
locker *(informell)* informal
Lohn pay
Lokomotivführer/in train driver
löschen *(Computer)* delete
Lösung (eines Problems) answer (to a problem)
Lotto lotto
Löwe lion
Lücke gap
lügen lie
lustig funny
Luxemburg Luxembourg
Luxuslimousine limo

M

machen *do; *make; **eine Lehre machen** *do an apprenticeship; **ein Picknick machen** *have a picnic; **eine Prüfung machen** *take an exam; **einen Test machen lassen** *have a test; **Das macht zwei Pfund, bitte.** That's two pounds, please. **Es macht Spaß.** It's fun. **Ich mache Hausaufgaben.** I *do my homework. **Mach dir Notizen.** *Make notes. **Mach(t)/Machen Sie nur.** Go ahead. **Mach's gut.** Take care. **sie macht Urlaub** she's on holiday; **Was machst du (da)?** What are you doing?
Macht power
Mädchen girl
Mahlzeit *(Essen)* meal
Mai May
Make-up make-up
Mal time
mal: Sieht man sich mal wieder? See you again some time?
Mama mum; (AE) mom
Manager/in manager
manchmal sometimes
Mango, Mangos mango, mangoes
Mann, Männer man, men
männlich male
Mannschaft team
Marke brand
Markt market
Marsch march
März March
Maschine machine
Massaker massacre
Mathe(matik) maths
Mauer wall
Maus *(Computer)* mouse
Mechaniker/in mechanic
Medien: die Medien the media
Medizin-; medizinisch medical
Meer sea; ocean
mehr more
Meile mile
mein/e my
meinen *mean
Meinung opinion; **eine Meinung abgeben** *give an opinion; **meiner Meinung nach** in my opinion; **ich ändere meine Meinung** I change my mind; **Ich bin derselben Meinung (wie du).** I agree (with you).
meiste/n: der/die/das meiste, die meisten most; **die meisten Gäste** most of the guests
meistens usually
Mensch person; **Menschen** people
merken *(bemerken)* notice
merkwürdig strange
Messer knife, knives
Metal metal
Metall metal
Meter metre
Mexiko Mexico
mich me; *(mich selbst)* myself
mieten rent; *(Fahrrad/...)* hire
Milch milk
militärisch military
Milliarde billion
Million million
Millionär/in millionaire
mindestens at least
Mindmap mind map
Ministerpräsident/in prime minister
Minute minute
mir me; *(mir selbst)* myself
mischen mix up
mit with; **mit 16 (Jahren)** at 16 (years old); **mit dem Rad/Bus/Auto/...** by bike/bus/car/...; **Mit wem?** Who with?
mitbringen *take
Mitglied in einem Klub werden join a club
Mitleid: mit mir Mitleid haben *feel sorry for me
mitmachen (bei) *take part (in); join in (with)
mitnehmen *take
Mittagessen lunch
Mittagspause lunch break; lunchtime
Mittagszeit lunchtime
Mitteilung message
Mittelpfosten centre post
Mittelwort der Vergangenheit past participle
Mitternacht midnight
Mittwoch Wednesday
„Mobber/in" bully
Mobbing bullying
Möbel furniture
Mobiltelefon mobile (phone); (AE) cellphone
Mode fashion
Modell model
modern modern
mögen like; **sehr mögen** love; **Ich möchte (gehen/...)** I'd like (to go/...); **Ich möchte nicht gehen/...** I wouldn't like to go/...; **Möchtest du/Möchten Sie ...?** Would you like ...?
Moment moment; **im Moment** at the moment
Monat month
Mond moon
Monster monster
Montag Monday
Moor *(Hochmoor)* moor
morgen tomorrow
Morgen morning; **Montagmorgen** Monday morning
morgens in the morning; *(mit Uhrzeit)* a.m.
Moskito mosquito
Motor motor
Motorrad motorbike
Mountainbike mountain bike
Mountainbikefahren mountain biking
Mountainboard mountain board
Mountainboardfahren mountain boarding
MP3-Player MP3 player
müde tired
Muffin muffin
Müll rubbish
multikulturell multicultural
Mund mouth; **Halt den Mund!** Shut up!
Muschel seashell
Museum museum
Musik music
Musiker/in musician
Musikinstrument musical instrument
Muslim/in Muslim

müssen *have to; must; **Ich muss ...** I've got to ...; **Ich kann nicht anders, ich muss lachen.** I can't help laughing. **du müsstest** you should
mutig brave
Mutprobe dare
Mutter mother
Muttersprache first language
Mutti mum; (AE) mom

N

nach 1 *(Wann?)* after; **nach der Schule** after school; **fünf nach zehn** five past ten; **Viertel nach elf** quarter past eleven; 2 *(zu)* to; **nach Hause gehen** *go home; **nach oben** upstairs; 3 **sie nach etwas fragen** ask them about something
Nachbar/in neighbour
nachdem after
nachdenken *think
Nachmittag afternoon
nachmittags in the afternoon; *(mit Uhrzeit)* p.m.
Nachname family name; surname
Nachricht 1 *(Mitteilung)* message; 2 **Nachricht(en)** news
nachschlagen,-sehen look up
nachsprechen repeat
nächste/r/s: der nächste Flughafen the nearest airport; **nächste Woche** next week
Nacht night
nachts at night
Nähe: in der Nähe von by; near
Name name
Nase: Ich habe die Nase voll. I'm fed up.
nass wet
Nation nation
national national
Nationalhymne national anthem
Nationalität nationality
Nationalmannschaft national team
Nationalpark national park
natürlich of course
Naturwissenschaft science
neben by; next to
negativ negative
nehmen *take; **Ich nehme ...** *(Bestellung)* I'll have ...
neidisch (auf) jealous (of)
nein no
nennen call
nerven: Eltern nerven! Parents are a pain!
nervös nervous
nett nice; kind; **Es war nett, mit dir zu sprechen.** It has been nice talking to you.
Netz network
neu new
Neu-Delhi New Delhi
neueste/r/s latest
Neuigkeit(en) news
nicht not; **Iss nicht.** Don't eat.
nichts nothing; not ... anything
nie never
Niederlande Netherlands
niemals never
niemand nobody; not ... anybody
nirgendwo(-hin/-her) not ... anywhere
noch: (immer) noch still; **noch ein/eine/einer/eins** another; **noch einmal** again; **noch nicht** not ... yet; **noch nie** never
Nomen noun
Nord- north; northern
Nordamerika North America
Norden north; **im Norden** in the north
Nordirland Northern Ireland
nördlich north; northern
Nordosten: im Nordosten von Afrika in north-east Africa
Nordwesten north-west
normal ordinary
normalerweise usually
Note mark
Notiz note
November November
Nummer number
nun now; **Was nun?** What next? **Nun, ...** Well, ...
nur only; *(einfach)* just
nützlich useful

O

ob if; whether
obdachlos homeless
oben: oben (im Haus) upstairs; **ganz oben (auf)** at the top
Oberschule *(USA)* high school
Obst fruit
Obstgarten orchard
Obstpflücker/in fruit picker
obwohl although
oder or
offen open
offensichtlich obviously
(sich) öffnen open
oft often
ohne without
ohnehin anyway
Ohr ear
okay OK
Oktober October
olympisch: die Olympischen Spiele the Olympics
Oma grandma
Onkel uncle
online online
Opa grandad
Orange orange
ordnen organize
Ordnung: in Ordnung OK; **Ist alles in Ordnung bei dir?** Are you OK? **Ist etwas nicht in Ordnung?** What's wrong?
Organisation organization
organisieren organize
Orkan hurricane
Ort place
örtlich local
Osten; Ost- east
Österreich Austria
Ostküste east coast
östlich east
oval oval
Ozean ocean

P

paar: ein paar some; a few
packen pack
Paddeln canoeing
Panik: in Panik geraten panic
Papa dad
Papier paper
Papiere papers
Park park
Parkplatz car park
Partizip Perfekt past participle
Partner/in partner
Party party
Passagier/in passenger
passieren happen
Passiv passive
Pause break
peinlich embarrassing
Pence pence (p)
perfekt perfect
Person person; *(Figur)* character
Personal staff
Pfad track
Pferd horse
Pfirsich peach
Pflaume plum
pflücken pick
Pfosten post
Pfund *(Gewichtseinheit)* pound; *(brit. Währung)* pound (£)
Picknick picnic
piepsen beep

Pier pier
Piercing piercing
pink pink
Pirat/in pirate
Pizza pizza
Pizzeria pizzeria
Plan plan; *(Karte)* map
planen plan; **die Zukunft planen** look ahead
Planer/in planner
Platz **1** *(Ort)* place; **2** *(Sitz)* seat; **3** *(Spielfeld)* court
plaudern chat
plötzlich suddenly
Podcast podcast
Pole/Polin Polish
Polen Poland
Polizei, Polizei- police
Polizeibeamter/-beamtin, Polizist/in police officer
polnisch; Polnisch Polish
Pommes frites chips
Pony pony
Popcorn popcorn
Pop(musik) pop
Porree(stange) leek
Portfolio portfolio
Portion: eine Portion Obst a serving of fruit
positiv positive; **HIV-positiv sein** be HIV positive
Post(amt) post office
Poster poster
Postkarte postcard
Postleitzahl postcode
Präposition preposition
präsentieren present
Präsident/in president
Preis **1** *(Kaufpreis)* price; **2** *(Gewinn)* prize; **3** *(Auszeichnung)* award
preiswert cheap
Premierminister/in prime minister
Prioritätenliste priority list
pro per; **24 Stunden pro Tag** 24 hours a day
probieren try
Problem problem
produzieren produce
Programmierer/in programmer
Projekt(arbeit) project
Prominente/r celebrity
Pronomen pronoun
Protektor protector
Protest protest
Protestmarsch march
provozierend provocative
Prozent per cent
Prüfung exam; test; **eine Prüfung machen** *take an exam
Puma (AE) cougar
Punk(musik) punk
Punkt point
pünktlich on time
Punktzahl score
putzen clean

Q

Quad quad (bike)
Quiz quiz

R

Rad **1** wheel; **2** *(Fahrrad)* bike; **Rad fahren** *ride a bike
Radfahren cycling
Radiergummi rubber
Radio radio
Rand *(südafrikanische Währung)* rand
Ranger ranger
Rangliste priority list
Rap(musik) rap
Rapper/in, Rapsänger/in rapper
Rasen grass
Rat(schläge) advice; **Rat(schläge) geben** *give (some) advice
raten guess
Ratte rat
rauchen smoke
Räucherlachs smoked salmon
Raum room
Raumpfleger/in cleaner
raus: Ich muss hier raus. I have to get out of this place.
rausbringen: den Müll rausbringen *take out the rubbish
R & B(-Musik) R & B
reagieren (auf) react (to)
Rechner computer
recht quite
Recht right; **Du hast Recht.** You're right.
rechts right; **auf der rechten Seite** on the right; **rechts (von Ihnen)** on your right
Rechtschreibung spelling
Rede speech
reden (mit) talk (to)
Referenz reference
Regal, Regale shelf, shelves
Regel rule
Regenbogen rainbow
Regierung government
Regisseur/in director
regnen rain
reich rich
Reihe *(Serie)* series
Reihenfolge order
(sich) reimen (auf) rhyme (with)
Reise journey; trip; **Reise-** travel
reisen travel; **Reisen** travel
Reisende/r traveller
Reiten horse riding
Religion religion
rennen *run; **Rennen** *(Wettrennen)* race
Rennfahrer/in racing driver
reparieren fix; repair
Reporter/in reporter
Reservat(ion) reservation
reservieren (lassen) book
respektieren respect
Restaurant restaurant
retten save
Rettungssanitäter/in paramedic
Rezension review
Rhein Rhine
Rhythmus rhythm
richtig right; correct; *(echt)* real; **das Richtige/Beste/...** the right/best/... thing
Richtung: in Richtung Haus towards the house
Rindfleisch beef
„ritzen" *cut
Rolle role
Rollen(spiel)karte role card
Rollstuhl wheelchair; **er sitzt im Rollstuhl** he's in a wheelchair
Rom Rome
romantisch romantic
Röntgenassistent/in X-ray assistant
rosa pink
rot red
Rubrik heading
Rucksack rucksack
rufen call; *(laut rufen)* shout
Rugby rugby
ruhig quiet
Rundgang tour
Rupie rupee

S

Sabotage sabotage
Sache thing; **Sachen, die man machen kann** things to do
Saft juice
sagen *say; *tell; **ihr etwas sagen** say something to her; **Er sagt ihr auf Wiedersehen.** He says goodbye to her.
Salat salad; *(Kopfsalat)* lettuce
Salz salt
sammeln collect
Samstag Saturday

samstags on Saturdays
sandboarden sandboard
Sandwich sandwich
Sänger/in singer
satthaben: ich habe meine Arbeit satt I'm tired of my job
Satz sentence
Satzstellung word order
sauber clean
sauber machen clean
schade: Schade! Too bad! **Das ist schade.** That's a pity.
schämen: ich schäme mich wegen ... I'm embarrassed about ...
Schaf, Schafe sheep
Schatzsuche treasure hunt
schauen look
Schauspieler/in actor
scheiden: sich scheiden lassen *get divorced
scheinen seem; *(glänzen)* *shine
schematische Darstellung diagram
Scherz joke
scheußlich horrible
schicken *send
Schiedsrichter/in referee
schiefgehen *go wrong
schießen *shoot; *(Tor)* score
Schiff boat; ship
Schikanieren bullying
Schild sign
Schildchen label
Schinken ham
Schirm umbrella
Schlafanzug pyjamas
schlafen *sleep
Schlafsack sleeping bag
Schlafzimmer bedroom
schlagen *hit
Schlagzeile headline
Schlange *(Warteschlange)* queue; (AE) line; **Schlange stehen** queue (up); (AE) wait in line
schlank slim
schlau clever
schlecht bad
schlechter worse
schlechteste/r/s worst
schließen close
Schließfach locker
schließlich at last; in the end
schlimm bad
schlimmer worse
schlimmste/r/s worst
Schloss castle
Schluss ending; **(mit ihm) Schluss machen** *break up (with him)
Schlüssel key
Schlüsselwort keyword
schmal narrow
schmecken taste
Schmerzen pain
schmutzig dirty
Schneesturm snow storm
schneiden *cut
schnell fast; quickly
Schnellimbiss *(für Fisch/Pommes frites)* fish and chip shop
Schokolade chocolate
schon already; **schon einmal** ever; **Schon gut.** *(Bitte.)* That's OK. **schon wieder** again
schön beautiful; fine; nice; **(Einen) Schönen Tag noch!** (AE) Have a nice day!
Schotte(n)/Schottin(nen) Scottish
Schottisch *(engl. Dialekt)* Scots
Schottland Scotland
Schrank cupboard
schrecklich awful; terrible
schreiben *write
Schreibetui pencil case
schreien scream; shout
Schriftsteller/in writer
schüchtern shy
Schuh shoe
Schularbeiten homework
Schule school
Schüler/in **1** pupil; *(ältere/r Schüler/in)* student; **2** (AE) student
Schülerkalender homework diary
Schulheft exercise book
Schulhof playground; **auf dem Schulhof** in the playground
Schultag school day
Schultasche bag
schütteln *shake; **sie schüttelt den Kopf** she shakes her head
Schützer protector
schwanger pregnant
schwarz black
Schwarze black people; Blacks
Schwein pig
Schweiz Switzerland
schwer hard; *(schwierig)* difficult
Schwerpunkt main point
Schwester sister
schwierig difficult
Schwierigkeiten: ich stecke in großen Schwierigkeiten I'm in big trouble
Schwimmbad swimming pool
Schwimmbecken pool
schwimmen *swim; **schwimmen gehen** *go swimming; **Schwimmen** swimming
Schwimmer/in swimmer
See *(Binnensee)* lake
sehen look; *see; **Sieht man sich mal wieder?** See you again some time?
sehr a lot; very; (very) much; **Sehr geehrte Damen und Herren, ...** Dear Sir/Madam, ...
seid: ihr seid you're (= you are)
Seilbahn cable car
sein *be
sein/e his; *(nicht bei Personen)* its
Seite side; *(Buch, Heft)* page; **ein Land auf der anderen Seite der Erde** a land down under
Sekunde second
selbst *(je nach Person)* myself/yourself/himself/herself/itself/ourselves/yourselves/themselves; **selbst gemacht** home-made
Selbstbedienungscafé coffee shop
Selbstbeherrschung self-control
selbstsicher confident; self-confident
selbstständig: ich werde mich selbstständig machen I'll start my own business
selbstverständlich of course
Selbstvertrauen self-confidence
seltsam strange
senden *send
Sendung *(Radio, Fernsehen)* programme
September September
Serie series
Sessel chair
setzen: sich (hin)setzen *sit (down)
seufzen sigh
Sex sex
Shorts shorts
Show show
Shuttle shuttle
sich (selbst) *(je nach Person)* yourself/himself/herself/itself/yourselves/themselves
sicher sure; *(in Sicherheit)* safe
Sicherheitsausrüstung safety gear
Sicherheitskontrolle security check
Sicht view(s)
sie **1** *(Wer?)* she; *(nicht bei Personen)* it; *(Mehrzahl)* they; **2** *(Wen?)* her; *(nicht bei Personen)* it; *(Mehrzahl)* them
Sie you

Sieger/in winner
Signal signal
simsen text
sind are
Singapur Singapore
singen *sing
Sitz seat
sitzen *sit; **er sitzt im Rollstuhl** he's in a wheelchair
Skandal scandal
Skateboard skateboard
Skateboarder/in skateboarder
Skatepark skate park
Skater/in skater
Skifahren skiing
Slam slam
Smog smog
SMS text (message); **eine SMS senden** text
SMS-Terror text bullying
Snowboarder/in snowboarder
so **1** so; **2** like that/this; **so bald wie möglich** asap (= as soon as possible); **so ein Job** a job like that/this; **So etwas gibt es nicht.** There's no such thing. **so viele/... wie** as many/... as
soeben just
Softball softball
Software software
sogar even; **Es war sogar besser.** In fact, it was better.
Soldat/in soldier
sollen: Wann soll ich ...? When should I ...? **Ich weiß nicht, was ich sagen soll.** I don't know what to say. **du solltest** you should
Somalia Somalia
Sommer summer
Sonderangebot special offer
Sonnabend Saturday
Sonne sun
Sonnenbrille sunglasses
sonnig sunny
Sonntag Sunday
sorgen: dafür sorgen, dass ... *make sure (that) ...
Sorgen: sich Sorgen machen (um) worry (about); be worried (about)
sorgfältig carefully
sowieso anyway
Spanien Spain
Spanier/in(nen); spanisch; Spanisch Spanish
spanischsprachig Hispanic
spannend exciting
sparen save
Spaß fun; **Es macht Spaß.** It's fun. **Spaß haben an** enjoy; **Spaß am Arbeiten haben** enjoy working; **ich habe viel Spaß** I enjoy myself
spät, zu spät late; **Er kommt zu spät.** He's late. **Wie spät ist es?** What time is it?
später later
Spazierengehen walking
Spaziergänger/in walker
Speicherkarte memory card
speichern *(MP3-Player)* *hold
Speiseeis ice cream
Speisekarte menu
spenden: Blut spenden *give blood
Spiegel mirror
Spiel game; *(Wettkampf)* match
spielen play; *(in einem Film/Theaterstück)* act; **Gitarre spielen** play the guitar; **Spielt das Gespräch nach.** Act the dialogue.
Spieler/in player
Spielfeld court
Spielhalle amusement arcade
Spielregel: sich an die Spielregeln halten play by the rules
Spielstand score
Spielzeug toy
Spind locker
Spinne spider
Spion/in spy
Spitze top; **auf der Spitze** at the top
Sport, Sportart sport; **Sport treiben** play sports
sportlich sporty
Sportschuh trainer; (AE) sneaker
Sportzentrum sports centre
Sprache language
Sprechanlage intercom
sprechen (mit) *speak (to); talk (to); **Hier spricht Sarah.** It's Sarah. **Es war nett, mit dir zu sprechen.** It has been nice talking to you.
Sprecher/in speaker
Sprichwort saying
springen jump
sprudelnd fizzy
Squash squash
Staat state
Staatsbürgerschaft nationality
Stadion stadium
Stadt town; *(Großstadt)* city
Stadtmitte, -zentrum town centre
Stand *(Verkaufsstand)* stall
Star star
stark strong; *(hart, zäh)* tough
Stärke power
Start start
statt instead of
Statue statue
Stechmücke mosquito
stehen *stand; **es steht 24:18 für North** it's 24-18 to North; **Wie steht's?** What's the score? **stehen bleiben** stop
stehlen *steal
Stein stone; *(Fels)* rock
Stelle place; **An deiner Stelle ...** If I were you, ...
stellen *put; **sich stellen** *stand
Stempel stamp
sterben die
Stereotyp stereotype
Stern star
Steward/ess flight attendant
Stichwort keyword
Stimme voice
Stockwerk floor
stoppen stop
Strand beach; *(Küste)* seashore; **am Strand** on the beach
Strandpromenade boardwalk
Straße road; street
Straßenbahn tram
Streit argument; **Streit haben** *have an argument
streiten: sich streiten *fight
streng strict
Strom electricity
Stromkabel power cable
Strophe verse
Stubenarrest: ich habe Stubenarrest I'm grounded
Stück piece
Student/in student
Studio studio
Stufe step; *(Jahrgangsstufe)* year; **Ich bin in der 7. Stufe.** I'm in year 7.
Stuhl chair
Stunde hour; *(Unterrichtsstunde)* lesson
Stundenplan timetable
suchen look for
Suchmaschine search engine
Südafrika South Africa
Südafrikaner/in; südafrikanisch South African
Süden; Süd-; südlich south
super super
Supermarkt supermarket
Superstar superstar

Surfausrüstung surfing gear
Surfbrett surfboard
surfen surf
Surfer/in surfer
Surfkleidung, -klamotten surfing gear
Surfschule surf school
Surf(schutz)anzug wetsuit
Symbol symbol
Szene scene

T

Tabelle table
Tablett tray
Tafel board
Tafelberg Table Mountain
Tag day
Tagebuch diary
Talent talent
Talkshow chat show; (AE) talk show
Tante aunt
tanzen dance; **tanzen gehen** *go dancing
Tänzer/in dancer
tapfer brave
Tasche bag; *(Kleidung)* pocket
Taschengeld pocket money
Tasse cup; **eine Tasse Tee** a cup of tea
Tastatur keyboard
Taste button
Tätowierung tattoo
Tatsache fact
Tattoo tattoo
taub deaf
Tauch(schutz)anzug wetsuit
Tausch- exchange
tausend thousand
Taxi taxi
Team team
Technik technology
Techno techno
Technologie technology
Tee tea
Teenager teenager, teen; **Teenager-** teenage ...
Teil part
teilen: sich ein Zimmer teilen share a room
teilnehmen (an) *take part (in)
Teilzeit, Teilzeit- part-time
Telefon phone; **am Telefon** on the phone; **ans Telefon gehen** answer the phone
telefonieren phone
telefonisch Hilfe holen phone for help
Telefonnotiz phone message
Tennis tennis
Termin *(Verabredung)* appointment
Terminkärtchen appointment card
Terror: SMS-Terror text bullying
Test test; **einen Test machen lassen** *have a test
teuer expensive
Text text; *(Liedtext)* words (of a song)
Theater theatre
Thema topic
Themenpark theme park
Tier animal; *(zahmes Tier, Haustier)* pet
Tierarzt/-ärztin vet
Tierhandlung pet shop
Tierrechte, Tierschutz- animal rights
Tiger tiger
Tipp tip
Tisch table
Tischtennis table tennis
Titel title
Tja, ... Well, ...
Tochter daughter
Toilette toilet
toll brilliant; cool; great; super; (AE) awesome
Tomate, Tomaten tomato, tomatoes
Tor **1** gate; **2** *(Sport)* goal
töten kill
Tour tour
Tourist/in tourist
Touristeninformation tourist office
Township township
Tradition tradition
tragen **1** carry; **2** *(anziehen)* *wear
Trainer trainer
trainieren train; practise
Traktor tractor
trauen *(vertrauen)* trust
Traum dream
träumen dream
traurig sad
treffen *hit; **sich treffen (mit)** *meet; **eine Absprache treffen** *make an arrangement; **eine Entscheidung treffen** *make a decision
Treffpunkt: ein Treffpunkt a place to meet
Treppe stairs
Tretboot pedal boat
treten kick
trinken *drink; **eine Cola trinken** *have a cola
trotzdem still
Tschechische Republik Czech Republic
Tschüs. Bye.
T-Shirt T-shirt
tun *do; *(an einen Platz tun)* *put
Tunnel tunnel
Tür door
Turbine turbine
Türke/Türkin Turkish
Türkei Turkey
türkisch; Türkisch Turkish
Turm tower
Turnhalle gym
Tut mir leid. I'm sorry./Sorry.
Tüte bag
Typ type
typisch typical
Tyrann bully
tyrannisieren bully

U

U-Bahn underground; (AE) subway; **die (Londoner) U-Bahn** the tube
U-Bahnhof underground station
U-Bahn-Zug underground train
üben practise
über **1** above; **2** *(über die Straße)* across (the road); **3** about; on; **über die Sprechanlage** on the intercom
überall(-hin/-her) everywhere; **überall in/auf** all over
übergewichtig overweight
überlegen zu gehen/... *think of going/...
übernachten stay
überprüfen check
überrascht surprised
Überraschung surprise
Überschrift heading
übersetzen translate
übrig: ich habe nicht viel dafür übrig I'm not keen on it; **Was bleibt von dir übrig?** What's left of you?
übrigens by the way
Übung exercise
Uhr clock; **um acht Uhr/zwanzig Uhr** at eight o'clock
Uhrzeit time
um *(herum)* around; **um acht/zwanzig Uhr** at eight o'clock; **um Dinge zu verändern** to change things; **um etwas kämpfen** *fight for something
umarmen: jemanden umarmen *give somebody a hug

umbringen kill
Umfrage survey
Umgebung environment
umgehen: mit Problemen umgehen *deal with problems
umschauen: sich umschauen look around
Umschlag cover
umsonst for free
Umstandswort adverb
umsteigen change
umtauschen: Geld umtauschen change money
Umwelt environment
umziehen move
Umzug removal
unabhängig independent
Unabhängigkeit independence
unbequem uncomfortable
und and; **Und du?** What about you? **Na und?** Who cares?
unecht fake
Unfall accident
unfreundlich unfriendly; unkind
ungefähr about
ungemütlich uncomfortable
ungesetzlich illegal
ungesund unhealthy
unglaublich amazing
unglücklich unhappy; *(elend)* miserable
unglücklicherweise unfortunately
Uniform uniform
Unrecht: Du hast Unrecht. You're wrong.
Unruhe trouble
uns us; *(uns selbst)* ourselves
unser/e our
Unsinn nonsense
unten below
unter under; **anrufen/eine SMS schicken unter 071...** phone/text on 071...
unterhalb (von) below
unterhalten: sich unterhalten (*have a) chat; **sich unterhalten (mit)** talk (to)
Unterhaltung conversation
unterirdisch underground
Unterkunft accommodation
Unternehmen company
unterrichten *teach
Unterrichtsstunde lesson
unterstreichen underline
unterstrichen underlined
unterstützen support
Untersuchung *(Umfrage)* survey
unterwegs out and about; on the road
unwahr false
Urbevökerung: zur Urbevölkerung zählend Aboriginal
Urlaub holiday/s; **in den Urlaub fahren** *go on holiday; **sie macht Urlaub, sie ist im Urlaub** she's on holiday

V

Vater father
Vati dad
Vegetarier/in, vegetarisch vegetarian
Verabredung date; *(Termin)* appointment
verabschieden: sich von ... verabschieden *say goodbye to ...
(sich) verändern change
verängstigt aussehen look frightened
Veranstaltung event
verantwortlich responsible
Verantwortung responsibility
verärgert annoyed
Verb verb
verbieten ban; prohibit
verbinden (mit) link (to/with)
Verbindung link; **in Verbindung bringen (mit)** link (to/with); **Lass uns in Verbindung bleiben.** Let's keep in touch.
verblüfft puzzled
verboten prohibited
Verbrechen crime
Verbrecher/in criminal
verbreiten *spread
verbringen *spend
verdienen earn
Verein club
verfolgen follow
Verfügung: zur Verfügung stellen provide
Vergangenheit past
vergessen *forget; *(stehen/liegen lassen)* *leave
vergleichen compare
Vergnügen: besonderes Vergnügen treat
verhalten: sich verhalten behave
Verhältnis relationship
Verhältnisse conditions
Verhältniswort preposition
verheiratet married
verhören question
verirren: sich verirren *get lost
verkaufen *sell
Verkäufer/in shop assistant; (AE) sales clerk
Verkehr traffic
Verkehrssicherheit road safety
verlassen *leave
Verlaufsform der Gegenwart present progressive
Verlaufsform der Vergangenheit past progressive
verlegen embarrassed
verletzen *hurt; **ich habe mir die Hand verletzt** I hurt my hand
verletzt hurt
verlieren *lose
vermieten hire
vermissen miss
vermitteln mediate
vermuten suppose
verpassen, versäumen miss
verschieden different
verschwenden waste
verschwinden disappear
Versicherung insurance
verspätet late
verstehen *understand; **..., verstehst du?** ..., you see.
Versuch experiment
versuchen try
vertrauen trust
vervollständigen complete
verwenden use
verwundert puzzled
Video(film) video
Videospiel video game
viel a lot; lots of; much; **eine viel befahrene Straße** a busy road; **Viel Glück!** Good luck!
viele lots of; many; **Viele Grüße ...** Best wishes, ...
vielleicht maybe; perhaps
Viertel neighbourhood
Viertel vor/nach eins quarter to/past one
Virus virus
Visagist/in make-up artist
Vogel bird
voll full; **Ich habe die Nase voll.** I'm fed up.
vollendete Vergangenheit past perfect
Volleyball volleyball
vollkommen perfect
vollständig complete; full
von **1** of; **2** from; **3** *(vom/von ... herab/herunter)* off; **4** *(durch)* by
vor **1** *(Wo?)* in front of; *(außerhalb von)* outside; **2** *(Wann?)* before; **vor zwei Jahren** two years ago; **fünf vor zehn** five to ten
vorausschauen look ahead
vorbei **1** *(zu Ende)* over; **2** **am Haus vorbei** past the house

(sich auf etwas) vorbereiten prepare (for something)
Vordergrund foreground
voreingenommen: gegen jemanden voreingenommen sein be biased against somebody
vorhaben plan
vorlesen *read (out); **ihr etwas vorlesen** read something to her
Vorlieben und Abneigungen likes and dislikes
Vormittag morning
vormittags *(mit Uhrzeit)* a.m.
Vorname first name
Vorort suburb
Vorschrift rule; **Vorschriften für das Verhalten im Brandfall** fire instructions
vorsichtig careful
Vorsingen audition
Vorsitzende/r chairperson
Vorsprechen audition
vorstellen: sich (etwas) vorstellen imagine; **Stell dir vor!** Guess what!
Vorstellungsgespräch (job) interview
Vortrag talk
Vorwand excuse
vorziehen prefer

W

Wachfrau/-mann security guard
wachsen *grow
Wagen car
Wahl choice
wählen *choose; pick
Wahnsinn! Wow!
wahr true; *(echt)* real
während during; while
wahrscheinlich probably
Wal whale
Walbeobachtung whale watching; **auf Walbeobachtungstour gehen** *go whale watching
Wald wood; *(Waldgebiet)* forest
Wales Wales
Waliser/in(nen); walisisch; Walisisch Welsh
Wand wall
Wanderer/Wanderin walker; hiker
wandern hike
Wandern walking
Wanderschuh walking shoe
Wanderung hike
wann when
war was
wäre: sie dachten, es wäre eine gute Idee they thought it was a good idea
waren, warst, wart were
warm warm
Warnung (vor) warning (against)
wärst: Ich habe gesagt, du wärst morgen im Laden. I said you'd be in the shop tomorrow.
warten (auf) wait (for); **Warten wir's ab.** Let's wait and see.
Warteschlange queue; (AE) line
warum why
was what; **Was für ein/e ...!** What a ...! **Was für Sendungen?** What kind of programmes? **Was gibt's?** What's up? **Was ist das?** What's that? **Was ist mit dir?** What about you? **Was nun?** What next?
Waschmaschine washing machine
Wasser water
Webcode webcode
Webseiten-Design web page design
Website website
wechseln: die Schule wechseln change schools; **Geld wechseln** change money
Wecker alarm clock
weg away
Weg way; *(Pfad)* track
wegen: ich schäme mich wegen ... I'm embarrassed about ...
weggehen 1 *(ausgehen)* *go out; 2 **weggehen (von)** *leave
wegnehmen *take
wehtun *hurt
weiblich female
Weihnachten Christmas
weil because
weinen cry
weiß white
Weißbrot white bread
Weiße white people; Whites
weit far; *(Ausdehnung)* wide
weiter further
weitere 1 *(mehr)* more; 2 *(andere)* other
weiterleiten forward
welche/r/s what; which; **Welche Farbe hat dein Zimmer?** What colour is your room?
Welle wave
Welt world; **auf der (ganzen) Welt** in the world
Weltmeisterschaft *(Fußball)* World Cup
Weltraum space
wenig: ein wenig a bit (of)
weniger less
wenigstens at least
wenn if; when
wer who
werden 1 *become; 2 *get; **ich werde gehen** I'll (= I will) go; **ich werde nicht gehen** I won't (= will not) go; **ich werde gewinnen, ich gewinne** I'm going to win; **Ich werde Ranger.** I'm going to be a ranger. **Erste/r werden bei ...** *come first in ...
werfen *throw; *shoot
weshalb why
West- west
Westaustralien Western Australia
Westen west
westlich west
Wettbewerb competition
Wetter weather
Wettkampf match
Whisky whisky
wichtig important
wie 1 how; **Wie geht's?** How are you? **Wie heißen sie auf Deutsch?** What are they in German? **Wie heißt du?** What's your name? **Wie nennt/bezeichnet man ...?** What do you call ...? **Wie spät ist es?** What time is it? **wie man uns findet** how to find us; 2 *(so wie)* like; **wie das Buch ist** what the book is like; **Wie sieht sie aus?** What does she look like?
wieder again; **Ich bin wieder da!** I'm back!
Wiedersehen. Bye.
wiegen weigh
Wiese field
Wikinger Viking
wild wild
Wildtiere und -pflanzen wildlife
willkommen: wir sind nicht willkommen we aren't welcome; **Willkommen in London.** Welcome to London.
Wind wind
Windpark wind farm
Winter winter
wir we
wirklich really
Wirtschaft economy
wissen *know
Wissenschaftler/in scientist
Witz joke; **Du machst wohl Witze.** You must be joking.
wo where

Woche week
Wochenende weekend
woher: Woher kommst du? Where are you from?
wohin where
wohnen live
Wohnung flat; (AE) apartment
Wohnwagen *(Standwohnwagen)* mobile home
Wohnzimmer living room
Wolke cloud
wollen want; **gehen wollen** want to go; **sie wollen, dass du Dinge tust** they want you to do things
Wort word
Wörterbuch, -verzeichnis dictionary
Wortnetz, Wörternetz network
Wow! Wow!
wunderschön beautiful
wurde/n: sie wurde/n weggenommen she was/they were taken
würde: ich würde I'd (= I would)
Wurf throw
Wurst, Würstchen sausage
wütend (auf) angry (with)
Wurzel root

Z

zäh tough
Zahl number
zahlen *pay
zahmes Tier pet
Zahn, Zähne tooth, teeth
Zahnarzt/-ärztin dentist
Zaun fence
Zeichen sign; signal
zeichnen *draw
zeigen *show
Zeile line
Zeit time; *(Zeitform)* tense
Zeitschrift magazine
Zeitung newspaper
Zeitverschwendung a waste of time
Zeitwort verb
Zelt tent
Zeltplatz campsite; (AE) campground
Zensur mark
Zentimeter centimetre
Zentrum centre
zerbrochen broken
Zeug stuff
Zeugnis reference
ziemlich quite
Ziffer number
Zigarette cigarette
Zimmer room; **Zimmer im ersten Stockwerk** first floor room
Zirkus circus
Zitat quote
Zoo zoo
Zoohandlung pet shop
zu **1** to; **sie helfen dir zu lesen** they help you to read; **zu Fuß** on foot; **zu Hause** at home; **2** for; **3** **zu alt** too old; **zu spät** late; **4** *(geschlossen)* closed
zuerst first
Zug train
Zuhause home
zuhören listen
zujubeln cheer
Zukunft future
zulassen allow
zum: zum Beispiel for example; **zum Frühstück/Mittagessen** for breakfast/lunch
zumachen close
zunächst at first
Zungenbrecher tongue twister
zuordnen match
zur: sie geht zur Schule she's at school; **Er kommt zu spät zur Schule.** He's late for school.
zurück back
zurückrufen call/phone back
zurücktreten (von ...) stand clear (of ...)
zurufen: sie ruft ihm etwas zu she shouts something at him
zurzeit at the moment
zusammen together
zusammenfassen sum up
Zusammenfassung summary
Zusammenhang context
zusätzlich extra
zusehen watch
Zustände conditions
zustimmen: Ich stimme (dir) zu. I agree (with you).
zuversichtlich confident
zweit-: der/die/das zweitgrößte/... the second largest/...; **Englisch als Zweitsprache** English as a Second Language
zwingen force; **keiner kann mich dazu zwingen, dies zu essen** nobody can make me eat this; **wenn man mich zwänge** if they made me
zwischen between

Girls/Women

Alison ['ælɪsn]
Amina [ə'mi:nə]
Amisha [ə'mi:ʃə]
Amy ['eɪmi]
Anna ['ænə]
Becca ['bekə]
Charlotte ['ʃɒ:lət]
Clare [kleə]
Corinna [kə'rɪnə]
Dominique [dɒmɪ'ni:k]
Ella ['elə]
Emily ['emɪli]
Emma ['emə]
Flo [fləʊ]
Hasina [hə'si:nə]
Jessica ['dʒesɪkə]
Kala ['kɑ:lə]
Karen ['kærən]
Kathryn ['kæθrɪn]
Kirsty ['kɜ:sti]
Kylie ['kaɪli]
Lalita [lə'li:tə]
Latika [lə'ti:kə]
Livvy ['lɪvi]
Lizzy ['lɪzi]
Loren ['lɔ:rən]
Mandiso [mæn'di:səʊ]
Mary ['meəri]
Miriam ['mɪriəm]
Natalie ['nætəli]
Petra ['petrə]
Polly ['pɒli]
Sadie ['seɪdi]
Sal [sæl]
Sarah ['seərə]
Saruga [sə'ru:gə]
Sophie ['səʊfi]
Sue [su:]
Susan ['su:zən]
Thembi ['tembi]

Boys/Men

Adam ['ædəm]
Alex ['ælɪks]
Brian ['braɪən]
Carl [kɑ:l]
Connor ['kɒnə]
Darren ['dærən]
Dave [deɪv]
David ['deɪvɪd]
Delani [də'lɑ:ni]
Dinkar ['dɪŋkɑ:]
Dodo ['dəʊdəʊ]
Hal [hæl]
Hugh [hju:]
Jacob ['dʒeɪkəb]
Jamal [dʒə'mɑ:l]
Javed [dʒɑ:'ved]
Jim [dʒɪm]
Jo, Joe [dʒəʊ]
Josh [dʒɒʃ]
Lalit [læ'lɪt]
Maman [mæ'mɑ:n]
Michael ['maɪkəl]
Mike [maɪk]
Melikhaya [melɪ'kɑ:jə]
Paul [pɔ:l]
Peter ['pi:tə]
Rolihlahla [rəʊli'lɑ:lə]
Rollo ['rɒləʊ]
Rory ['rɔ:ri]
Salim [sæ'li:m]
Steve [sti:v]
Terry ['teri]
Thomas ['tɒməs]
Trevor ['trevə]
Tsotsi ['tsɒtsi]
Vikram ['vɪkrʌm]
William ['wɪljəm]
Zack [zæk]

Families

Bai [baɪ]
Blake [bleɪk]
Elliott ['elɪət]
Hemmings ['hemɪŋz]
Jackson ['dʒæksən]
Jones [dʒəʊnz]
Logmore ['lɒgmɔ:]
Mathebula [mætə'bu:lə]
MacLeod [mə'klaʊd]
Malik ['mælɪk]
Owen ['əʊɪn]
Patel [pə'tel]
Philpott ['fɪlpɒt]
Rao [raʊ]
Saban [sæ'bæn]
Sinclair ['sɪnkleə]
Smith [smɪθ]
van Tonder [væn'tɒndə]
van Wyk [væn'wɪk]
Watson ['wɒtsən]

People

Alfred Mercier ['ælfrəd'mɜ:siə]
Angela Loughran ['ændʒələ'lɒfrən]
Ashley Qualls ['æʃli'kwɔ:lz]
Carole King ['kærəl'kɪŋ]
Charles Causley ['tʃɑ:lz'kɔ:sli]
Duke of Edinburgh ['dju:kəv'edɪnbərə]
Eleanor Roosevelt ['elɪnə'rəʊzəvelt]
Goolam Rajah ['gu:ləm'rɑ:dʒə]
Indira Gandhi [ɪn'dɪərə'gændi]
Jane Walker ['dʒeɪn'wɔ:kə]
Katrina Kaif [kə'tri:nə'kaɪf]
Lungile Mfeka [lʊn'gi:ləmə'fekə]
Mahatma Gandhi [mə'hætmə'gændi]
Makhaya Ntini [mə'kɑ:jənə'ti:ni]
Maryelen Loughran [meəri'elən'lɒfrən]
Meenal Dave ['mi:nəl'deɪv]
Mike Jubb ['maɪk'dʒʌb]
Nelson Mandela ['nelsnmæn'delə]
Ralph Waldo Emerson ['rælf'wɔ:ldəʊ'eməsən]
Presley Chweneyagae ['prezli'tʃwenəjə'gɑ:eɪ]
Tenzing Norgay ['tenzɪŋ'nɔ:geɪ]
Terry Pheto ['teri'petəʊ]
Zola ['zəʊlə]

Places

Addo Elephant National Park ['ædəʊ'elɪfənt'næʃnəl'pɑ:k]
Agra Cantonment ['ɑ:grəkæn'tɒnmənt]
Ahmedabad ['ɑ:mədəbæd]
Bangalore [bæŋgə'lɔ:]
Bewerly Park Centre ['bju:əli'pɑ:k'sentə]
Bhopal [bəʊ'pɑ:l]
Birmingham ['bɜ:mɪŋəm]
Blesberg Mountain ['blesbɜ:g'maʊntən]
Blossom Street ['blɒsəmstri:t]
Botton ['bɒtən]
Boulders Bay ['bəʊldəz'beɪ]
Brighton ['braɪtən]
Calne [kɑ:n]
Cape Peninsula National Park ['keɪpə'nɪnsjələ'næʃnəl'pɑ:k]
Chennai ['tʃenaɪ]
Coventry ['kɒvəntri]
Detroit [də'trɔɪt]
Earl Street ['ɜ:lstri:t]
Glasgow ['glɑ:zgəʊ]
Hangklip Mountain ['hæŋklɪp'maʊntən]
Isle of Mull ['aɪləv'mʌl]
Istanbul [ɪstæn'bʊl]
Johannesburg [dʒəʊ'hænɪsbɜ:g]
Kendriya [ken'dri:jə]
Kirti Mandir ['kɪətimæn'diə]
Kolkata [kɒl'kætə]
Kruger National Park ['kru:gə'næʃnəl'pɑ:k]
Lake District ['leɪkdɪstrɪkt]
Leamington Spa [lemɪŋtən'spɑ:]
Liverpool ['lɪvəpu:l]
Manhattan [mæn'hætən]
Manila [mə'nɪlə]
Mount Everest ['maunt'evərest]
Mumbai [mʊm'baɪ]
Nairobi [naɪ'rəʊbi]
Nepal [nɪ'pɔ:l]
Newcastle ['nju:kɑ:sl]
North Yorkshire ['nɔ:θ'jɔ:kʃə]
Nottingham ['nɒtɪŋəm]
Oban ['əʊbən]
Pakistan [pɑ:kɪ'stɑ:n]
Porbandar ['pɔ:bændə]
Port Elizabeth [pɔ:tɪ'lɪzəbəθ]
Pretoria [prɪ'tɔ:riə]
Qunu ['ku:nu:]
Ringwood Road ['rɪŋwʊd'rəʊd]
Robben Island ['rɒbən'aɪlənd]
Scafell Pike ['skɔ:fel'paɪk]
Sharpeville ['ʃɑ:pvɪl]
Sheffield ['ʃefi:ld]
Soweto [sə'wetəʊ]
Surat ['sʊərət]
Vikas Marg ['vi:kəs'mɑ:g]
Wolverhampton [wʊlvə'hæmptən]

Other names

Afrikaans [æfrɪ'kɑ:ns]
Akshardham Temple [ækʃə'dɑ:m'templ]
Arsenal ['ɑ:sənl]
Bhopal Shatabdi Express [bəʊ'pɑ:lʃə'tæbdiik'spres]
Berg-en-Dal Camp ['bɜ:gəndæl'kæmp]
Bollywood ['bɒliwʊd]
Dreamz Murphy [dri:mz'mɜ:fi]
Fairtrade [feə'treɪd]
Eiffel Tower ['aɪfəl'taʊə]
Grand Hotel ['grændhəʊ'tel]
Grange School ['greɪndʒ'sku:l]
Hari's Cafe ['hɑ:riz'kæfeɪ]
Lincoln Park High School ['lɪŋkənpɑ:k'haɪsku:l]
Lipizzaner [lɪpɪ'tsɑ:nə]
Magic Campsite ['mædʒɪk'kæmpsaɪt]
Metro ['metrəʊ]
National Exhibition Centre ['næʃnəleksɪ'bɪʃnsentə]
Newlands Stadium ['nju:ləndz'steɪdiəm]
Quivvers ['kwɪvəz]
Red Fort ['red'fɔ:t]
Royal Hotel ['rɔɪəlhəʊ'tel]
Slumdog Millionaire ['slʌmdɒgmɪljə'neə]
Tata Nano ['tɑ:tɑ:'nɑ:nəʊ]
Taj Mahal ['tɑ:dʒmə'hɑ:l]
The Camphill Village Trust [ðə'kæmphɪl'vɪlɪdʒtrʌst]
Ubulongwe [u:bu:'lɒŋgwi]
UNICEF ['ju:nɪsef]
Value Click Media ['vælju:'klɪk'mi:diə]
Warwick Road School [wɒrɪk'rəʊd'sku:l]
Xhosa ['kɔ:sə]
Zulu ['zu:lu:]

IRREGULAR VERBS

Infinitive form (Grundform)	Simple past form (Einfache Vergangenheit)	Present perfect form (Vollendete Gegenwart)	
be	I was, you were, she was	I've been	sein
have	I had	I've had	haben
do	I did	I've done [dʌn]	tun, machen
beat	I beat	I've beaten	schlagen
become	I became	I've become	werden
begin	I began	I've begun	beginnen
blow	I blew	I've blown	blasen
break up	I broke up	I've broken up	Schluss machen
bring	I brought	I've brought	bringen
build	I built	I've built	bauen
buy	I bought	I've bought	kaufen
catch	I caught	I've caught	fangen; fassen
choose	I chose	I've chosen	(aus)wählen, aussuchen
come	I came	I've come	kommen
cost	it cost	it has cost	(Geld) kosten
cut	I cut	I've cut	schneiden
deal	I dealt [delt]	I've dealt [delt]	sich kümmern
draw	I drew	I've drawn	zeichnen
drink	I drank	I've drunk	trinken
drive	I drove	I've driven ['drɪvn]	fahren
eat	I ate [et]	I've eaten	essen
fall	I fell	I've fallen	fallen
feed	I fed	I've fed	füttern
feel	I felt	I've felt	(sich) fühlen
fight	I fought	I've fought	kämpfen; sich streiten
find	I found	I've found	finden
fly	I flew	I've flown	fliegen
forget	I forgot	I've forgotten	vergessen
get	I got	I've got	bekommen; holen
give	I gave	I've given	geben
go	I went	I've gone [gɒn]	gehen; fahren
grow	I grew	I've grown	wachsen
hang around	I hung around	I've hung around	herumhängen
hear	I heard [hɜːd]	I've heard [hɜːd]	hören
hit	I hit	I've hit	schlagen; treffen
hold	I held	I've held	halten
hurt	I hurt	I've hurt	verletzen
keep	I kept	I've kept	halten, behalten
know	I knew	I've known	wissen; kennen
lay the table	I laid the table	I've laid the table	den Tisch decken
lead	I led	I've led	führen
leave	I left	I've left	verlassen; (liegen) lassen
lie	I lay	I've lain	liegen
lose	I lost	I've lost	verlieren
make	I made	I've made	machen
mean	I meant [ment]	I've meant [ment]	meinen; bedeuten

Infinitive form (Grundform)	**Simple past form** (Einfache Vergangenheit)	**Present perfect form** (Vollendete Gegenwart)	
meet	I met	I've met	treffen; kennen lernen
pay	I paid	I've paid	zahlen, bezahlen
put	I put	I've put	stellen, legen, tun
read	I read [red]	I've read [red]	lesen, vorlesen
ride	I rode	I've ridden	(Rad/Quad) fahren
run	I ran	I've run	rennen
say	I said [sed]	I've said [sed]	sagen
see	I saw	I've seen	sehen
sell	I sold	I've sold	verkaufen
send	I sent	I've sent	senden
shake	I shook	I've shaken	schütteln
shine	I shone [ʃɒn]	I've shone [ʃɒn]	scheinen, glänzen
shoot	I shot	I've shot	schießen; werfen
show	I showed	I've shown	zeigen
sing	I sang	I've sung	singen
sit	I sat	I've sat	sitzen; sich setzen
sleep	I slept	I've slept	schlafen
speak	I spoke	I've spoken	sprechen
spend	I spent	I've spent	ausgeben; verbringen
spread	I spread	I've spread	verbreiten
stand	I stood	I've stood	stehen; (sich) stellen
steal	I stole	I've stolen	stehlen
swim	I swam	I've swum	schwimmen
take	I took	I've taken	nehmen; bringen
teach	I taught	I've taught	unterrichten, beibringen
tell	I told	I've told	erzählen; sagen
think	I thought	I've thought	(nach)denken; finden
throw	I threw	I've thrown	werfen
understand	I understood	I've understood	verstehen
wake up	I woke up	I've woken up	aufwachen
wear	I wore	I've worn	tragen, anziehen
win	I won	I've won	gewinnen
write	I wrote	I've written	schreiben

Test yourself (S.21–65)

Unit 1, S.21:
Test 1: 1 g); 2 h); 3 b); 4 a); 5 d); 6 f).
Test 2: 1 win; 2 keep; 3 Throw; 4 join; 5 spend; 6 text.
Test 3: 1 in; 2 for; 3 brilliantly; 4 in; 5 water; 6 during.
Test 4: 1 you mind; 2 Do, to; 3 name, by; 4 've got; 5 's been; 6 you, some.
Test 5: 1 had worked; 2 had had; 3 had fought; 4 had been; 5 had become; 6 had stopped.
Test 6: 1 Dear Sir or Madam, ... 2 I'd like to / want to complain. 3 The TV was broken. 4 The shower didn't work. 5 The manager said that I should write to you. 6 Yours faithfully, ...

Unit 2, S.35:
Test 1: 1 hoodies (They're not for proms.) or limos (They're no clothes.); 2 responsible (It isn't bad/negative.) 3 beautiful (It isn't a colour.); 4 broken (It isn't good/positive.); 5 train (It isn't on the road.); 6 cupboard (It isn't for camping.).
Test 2: 1 do; 2 take; 3 commit; 4 take; 5 pass; 6 support.
Test 3: 1 sorry; 2 unfortunately; 3 pity; 4 change; 5 kind; 6 already.
Test 4: 1 around; 2 outside; 3 at; 4 in; 5 with; 6 against.
Test 5: 1 don't enjoy; 2 went; 3 hired; 4 met; 5 are meeting; 6 'm looking.
Test 6: My two friends Kirsty and Anna went hiking last week. They carried rucksacks with food, their tent and their sleeping-bags. One evening, when they were quite tired, they stopped near a river. They put up their tent and started to cook. But suddenly it started to rain, so they went into the tent, where they slept. The next morning, when they looked outside, they were very surprised. There was water everywhere and their tent was on a little island! They felt stupid a bit frightened too. But actually they were very lucky.

Unit 3, S.51:
Test 1: 1 Bollywood; 2 New Delhi; 3 Mumbai; 4 Hindi; 5 Taj Mahal; 6 1.2 billion.
Test 2: 1 d); 2 e); 3 a); 4 f); 5 b); 6 c).
Test 3: 1 from; 2 in; 3 about; 4 in; 5 over; 6 than.
Test 4: 1 programmer; 2 industries; 3 wind; 4 railway; 5 cash; 6 call.
Test 5: 1 don't like; 2 flew; 3 wasn't; 4 found; 5 was; 6 would/'d stay.
Test 6: 1 Is it OK / Do you mind if I go swimming / go to the swimming pool / use your swimming pool? 2 Is it OK / Do you mind if I have a shower? 3 Is it OK / Do you mind if I have a drink / drink something? 4 Is it OK / Do you mind if I top up my mobile? 5 Is it OK / Do you mind if I go to bed / sleep (a bit)? 6 Is it OK / Do you mind if I use your phone / phone home / phone (to) Germany?

Unit 4, S.65:
Test 1: 1 call centre; 2 dining room; 3 entrance hall; 4 away match; 5 washing machine; 6 alarm clock.
Test 2: 1 Mr; 2 Smith; 3 April 15th, 1993; 4 Germany; 5 male; 6 CV23 7LU.
Test 3: 1 upstairs; 2 radiator; 3 wardrobe; 4 cooker; 5 fridge; 6 freezer.
Test 4: 1 spent; 2 flew; 3 chose; 4 found; 5 bought; 6 didn't cost.
Test 5: 1 Sir, Madam; 2 for, your; 3 'd, apply; 4 last, reference (for me); 5 work, until; 6 Yours faithfully, ...
Test 6: 1 Did you get the job in the shop? 2 No, I didn't. The interview went well / I did well in the interview. 3 But I still didn't get the job. And you? 4 I've applied for an apprenticeship. 5 The people there seem nice. 6 I hope it works out for me.

Check your points for each test:

6 points	Excellent!
5 points	Very good. Keep working hard.
4 points	Good. Try and learn the things that you forgot.
3 points	OK, but you can do better.
2 points	You can do much better. You should do some revision.
0–1 point	Study the answers and try the test again.

Vocabulary (S.130–139)

S.130: Test yourself 1: a) choose; b) simple; c) already; d) stadium; e) choir; f) informal; g) receive; **2:** 1 b); 2 c); 3 a); 4 b); **3:** 1 map; 2 meet; 3 choose; 4 action

Do you remember? a) brave, dirty, frightened, poor, self-confident, stressed, surprised, unemployed; b) competition, hit, match, player, soccer, team, throw, win

Lerntipp 2 (1) right; (2) wrong; (3) wrong; (4) wrong; (5) right

S.133: Test yourself 1: a) aggressive; b) unfortunately; c) stereotype; d) journey; e) awful; f) luckily **2:** 1 relaxed; 2 unfortunately; 3 kind; 4 below; 5 outside; 6 positive; **3:** 1 b); 2 b); 3 a); 4 b); 5 a)

Do you remember? 1 ground; 2 expect; 3 suit; 4 wet; 5 gym; 6 illegal

Lerntipp 3 1: biased, enough, mosquito, mouse, positive, roof, space, stadium, while, young; **2:** nation; virus; slow; tonight; unfortunately; spread; **3:** 1 accent, 2 act, 3 action, 4 actually, 5 aggressive, 6 already, 7 although, 8 amazing, 9 argument, 10 artist

S.136: Test yourself 1: 1 Indian; 2 marriage; 3 build; 4 fly; 5 empty; 6 peace; **2:** 1 millionaire; 2 billion; 3 vegetarian; 4 gas; 5 husband; 6 salt; **3:** 1 This is the second best film by this director. 2 I can't think of the right word at the moment. 3 They thanked the guests for coming. 4 The story was so sad, I couldn't help crying.

Do you remember? 1 shake; 2 carry; 3 strong; 4 annoyed; 5 platform; 6 seat

S.139: Test yourself 1: 1 My sister lives abroad. 2 My brother works in a DIY store. 3 Your friend seems to be nice. 4 You can't be serious! 5 The hurricane was a disaster. 6 I want to learn Polish. **2:** 1 I tried hairdressing, but it didn't work out. 2 I'm really fed up. 3 Don't worry – you'll get over it. 4 If you notice a fire, you have to phone for help. 5 My teacher will be happy to talk to you. 6 My country of birth is Portugal. **3:** 1 cooker/freezer/fridge; 2 dining room/DIY store/entrance hall; 3 date of birth/gender/postcode; 4 embarrassing/perfect/uncomfortable

Do you remember? a) accident, address, apprenticeship, barbecue, beautiful, brochure, competition, equipment, experience, receive, successful, support; b) 1 Quick, please! There was an accident in Hill Street. I don't know the full address. 2 My brother took part in a skiing competition last winter. He was quite successful. 3 Did you receive the holiday brochure that I sent you last month? 4 The weather is beautiful today. Let's get our swimming equipment and go to the lake.

Bildquellen

123RF Limited (S.79 F: Anneke Schram; S.90 H: Cathy Yeulet); **action press**, Hamburg (S.61: Olycom S.p.a.; S.82: South West News Service; S.92: Bernd Heinz); **adpic**, Bonn (S.43/112 A: R. Brenner); **Africa Media Online**, Pietermaritzburg. S.A. (S.100 Bild 1: Roger de la Harpe, S.101 Bild 9: Graeme Williams/South Photographs); **Agentur Focus**, Hamburg (S.39 E: Adrian Fisk); **agratravelguide.com** (S.41 C und D); **akg-images**, Berlin (S.100 Bild 3 und 5: africanpictures); **Alamy**, Abington, UK (S.6–7 C: Photodisc; S.6 A: Celia Mannings, F: Eitan Simanor; S.7 I: Gallo Images, K: Deryck Dillon; S.8 u.: Eric Nathan; S.14 o. re.: Gallo Images/City Press, u. re.: Gallo Images; S.19: Arco Images GmbH; S.22 A: Angela Hampton Picture Library, B: Photofusion Picture Library, C: Janine Wiedel Photolibrary; S.23 E: MBI, F: acumenimages.com, G: ImageState; S.24: Blend Images; S.25 o. re.: Alex Segre; S.33: ACE STOCK LIMITED; S.34: Nick Gregory; S.42: Tomas Kopecny; S.55 u.: Martin Jenkinson; S.57 Bild 1: Vicky Skeet; S.71 u.: Images Source Black; S.73: Jack Picone; S.74: AfriPics.com; S.77 u.: Picture Partners; S.78 u.: Blend Images; S.84: Dinodia Images; S.85: Aflo Foto Agency; S.90 o.: terry harris just greece photo library, C: Tim Hill; S.91: David Pearson; S.93: ImageSelect; S.99 u.: NRT-Helena; S.108: Johnny Greig Portraits; S.116 M. li.: Timothy Large; S.117 u. li.: Modern Landscapes; S.121: RubberBall); **American Red Cross** (S.58 A); **The Associated Press** (S.8 o.: AP Photo/Rick Rycroft; S.101 Bild 10: AP Photo/NTB); Courtesy **arrivealive.co.za** (S.71 A); **Farley Baricuatro**, Cebu City (S.16 B); **Bigstock.com**, New York (S.38 Charlotte: barsik); Courtesy **City of Bristol College** (S.92 u. Logo); **Axel Bührmann**, S.A. (S.69 M.); Courtesy of the **Camphill Village Trust** (S.59 Bild 1); **Chardé** (S.71 B); Courtesy of the **Children's Commissioner for England**, London (S.30 u. Buzz Off Logo); **Cinetext Bild- und Textarchiv**, Frankfurt/M (S.20 o. und A: Kinowelt; S.36 A: Bildarchiv, S.104 o.: Allstar); **Colin Neighbourhood Partnership**, Belfast (S.26 u.); **Colourbox**, Berlin (S.17 M.); **Corbis**, Düsseldorf (S.12 B: Bettmann, C: William Campbell/Sygma; S.14 M. re.: Yves Forestier/Sygma; S.17 u.: Gideon Mendel; S.36 C: Brian Lee; S.39 B: Stringer/India/Reuters; S.75 u.: David Turnley); **Department of Health**, London (S.58 B); **Dreamstime**, Brentwood (S.87: Martyn Unsworth; S.90: Sunil Lal); Courtesy **The Duke of Edinburgh's Award** (S.28); **Claire L. Evans**, Portland (S.26 o.); **Fotex Medien Agentur**, Hamburg (S.96: Susa); **Fotolia.de** (S.43/112 F: photoparfum; S.56 B: Kevin Penhallow; S.72 M.: Klaus Rose, u.: Martin; S.86 u.: Paul Hill); **Chris Freeland**, St. Louis (S.16 C); **Getty Images**, München (S.6 D: Apic/Hulton Archive, Reproduction authorised by the **South African Reserve Bank**; S.7 H: John Macdougall/AFP; S.9: Quinn Rooney; S.10: Per-Anders Pettersson; S.12 A: Rolls Press/Popperfoto; S.13 o.: Per-Anders Pettersson; S.14 o. M.: De Agostini; S.20 C: Jeff Vespa/WireImage; S.25 A: Comstock Images; S.92 M.: Erik Isakson; S.94 o.: Scott Stulberg/Photographer's Choice); **Bonnie Glänzer**, Berlin (S.106 u. li.); **graphic@eastcoastproductions.tv** (S.27); **ipnstock**, New York (S.47 o.: Clay McLachlan/IPN); **iStockphoto**, Calgary (S.6 *elephant*: Hansjoerg Richter; S.12 u.: Henrique NDR Martins; S.38 *Anna*: Eileen Hart, *Brian*: Kim Gunkel, *David*: Wilson Valentin, *Emily*: Jess Wiberg; S.39 A: Hrvoje Tomic; S.54: Terry J Alcorn; S.56 A: Andy Medina; S.57 Bild 2: Alan Crawford, Bild 3: johnnyscriv, Bild 5: Linda Steward, Bild 6: AtWaG; S.58 E: Kenn Wislander, *Darren*: Jason Stitt, *Connor*: MoniqueRodriguez, *Anna*: Claudia Dewald, *Mr Watson*: Catherine Lane; S.79 E (Bildschirm): Marc Fischer; S.86 o.: Anandha Krishnan, M.: Vikram Raghuvanshi; S.90 D: Linda & Colin McKie; S.94 u. re.: Roman Sigaev; S.109: Liudmila Chernova; S.111: Lidia Ryzhenko; S.116 *man with tie*: Justin Horrocks, *anorak*: SteveStone, *socks*: kycstudio, *cardigan*: zorani, *swimsuits*: Steve Cole; S.117 *land*: Chad Thomas, *ticket inspector*: Bojan Tezak, *pilot*: bojan fatur, *motorway*: Edward Shaw; S.118 *utility room*: Ross Chandler, *chimney*: ilbusca, *garage*: Kelvin Jay Wakefield, *balcony*: lillisphotography, *ceiling*: Günay Mutlu, *terrace*: jean frooms, *attic*: Stefan Klein; S.122: Dean Mitchell; S.124: Leslie Banks; S.137 M.: Pavel Pospisil); **Jason John** (S.49 li.); Courtesy **Keep Britain Tidy**, Wigan (S.58 D); The **Kobal Collection**, London (S.20 B: Moviworld/MK2/Miramax; S.104 M. und u., S.105 o. und M.: Film 4/Celador Films/Pathe International); **laif Agentur für Photos & Reportagen**, Köln (S.17 o.: Kost); **Eugene Manalastas** (S.98); **MediaClubSouthAfrica.com** (S.7 J: Graeme Williams; S.14: Nelson Mandela Bay Municipality); **Newsland Rugby Stadium** (S.11 o.); **Photolibrary**, London (S.52–53: Katzer Katzer/Mauritius; S.60: Image Source; S.79 E (ohne Computerbild): Ulrich Niehoff; S.90 B: Joy Skipper); **Photosindia**, Gurgaon (S.37 G: Dinodia); **Picture-alliance**, Frankfurt/M (S.17 *cell*: Jaakko_Avikainen / dpa; S.29 *mosquito device*: Friso Gentsch / dpa/lni; S.43/112 C: Klaus Franke / dpa – Report, D: Bernd Wüstneck/dpa – Bildarchiv, G: Armin Weigel / dpa – Report, H: Matthias Hiekel / ZB-Funkregio Ost; S.69 u.: Pressefoto Ulmer; S.81: Manfred Kötter/Sander; S.99 o.: Photoshot; S.100 Bild 2: dpa – Bildarchiv; S.101 Bild 11: dpa – Fotoreport; S.106: MCT_/Landov / dpa); **Press Association Images**, London (S.30 o.: Barry Batchelor / PA Archive; S.101 Bild 8: PA/PA Archive); **Radio Diaries**, New York (S.13 u.: Melikhaya Mpumela); Courtesy **Road Safety Team**, Leicestershire (S.58 C); **Werner Schulz**, Redhill (S.40 u.); **Shutterstock images**, New York (S.11 A li.: Taavi Toomasson, A re.: Inginsh; S.14 o. li.: Ewan Chesser, M.: Michael Roeder; S.23 o. li.: Shpak Anton; S.25 *Grange School* (Montage): deedl; S.29 *teenager*: Robert Kneschke; S.36 *map* (Montage): AridOcean, Stasys Eidiejus, *flag*: Huebi, D: Oleg_Mit; S.37 E: Craig Hanson, F: Jeremy Richards, H:

jorisvo; S.39 C: Paul Prescott, D: Studio 1One; S.40 o. *icon*: Goran Paunovic, M.: Paul Prescott; S.41 A: Paul Prescott, B: Socrates, u.: Aleksandar Todorovic; S.43 Bild 1: Arkady, Bild 2: Kanwarjit Singh Boparai, Bild 3: Dmitry Remesov, Bild 4: Andrey Chmelyov, Bild 5: Hal_P, Bild 6: Andre Blais, E: anweber; S.50 o. und M.: Kharidehal Abhirama Ashwin; S.57 Bild 4: Luis Santos, Bild 8: David William Taylor; S.59 *climbing*: Marilyn Barbone, *sailing*: PhotoSky 4t com; S.66 o. li.: Sylvaine Thomas, u.: musicman; S.68 u.: TebNad; S.70 M.: Sean Bolt, u.: pjcross; S.71 re. (Montage): Jennie Endriss; S.72 o.: Sam Chadwick; S.76: Monkey Business Images; S.77 o.: Galina Barskaya; S.78 o.: Elke Dennis; S.79 A: senai aksoy, B: Diego Cervo, C li.: Sandra Kemppainen, C re.: Brian and Vildan Chase, D: Melissa King; S.80 o.: Yuri Arcurs, u.: Stephen Mcsweeny; S.83: Alexander Gitlits; S.88: Paul Prescott; S.90 A und G: Monkey Business Images, F: Matka_Wariatka; S.94 Bild 1: StephanScherhag, Bild 2: David Peta, Bild 3: Jbor, Bild 4: Chrislofoto, Bild 5: Jonathan Larsen; S.102 o. li.: yxowert, o. re.: Triff, *crown*: Valdis Torms, *house*: Viktoria, u. li.: suravid; S.103: Olga Semicheva; S.110: Monkey Business Images; S.115 *antelope*: Chris Kruger, *buffalo*: senai aksoy, *eagle*: avid Peta, *giraffe*: Chris Kruger, *gorilla*: Styve Reineck, *hippo*, *hyena*: EcoPrint, *jackal*, *vulture*: Lukas Maton, *leopard*: Stuart Taylor, *rhino*: Brooke Whatnall, *zebra*: Pal Teravagimov; S.116 o.: Konstantin Sutyagin, *coat*: Eduard Stelmakh, *hoody*: sint, *sweaters*: Losevsky Pavel; S.117 *take off*: devi, *comfortable*: Kristian Sekulic, *crowded*: RexRover; S.118 *roof*: Fotaw, *cellar*: Photobank.ch; S.127 o.: Antony McAulay, M.: Glenn R. McGloughlin, u.: Mario Lopes; S.128 u.: Chris Jenner; S.129 *broken cup*: Joey Bruno, *keyboard*: Jayson Ross; S.131 *limo*: Alexus, *hoodies*: Jason Vandehey, *keys*: Olga Mitsova; S.132 o.: Vinicius Tupinamba, M.: ronfromyork; S.134 o.: Pavel V Mukhin, u.: jovannig; S.135 *sun*: oriontrail, *wind farm*: Brian A Jackson; S.137 u.: Visaro; S.138: Edwin Verin; S.139 *alarm clock*: Koksharov Dmitry; S.140 o.: BlueOrange Studio, M.: Johnny Lye, u.: Dmitry Naumov); **South Africa Tours and Travel.com** (S.100 Bild 6); **Still Pictures** (S.6–7 G: Paul Springett); **Superbild**, Berlin (S.69 o.: Bernd Ducke); **theimagefile.com** (S.36 B: Massimo Usai); Courtesy **TransFair e.V.**, Köln (S.89); **Transit-Archiv**, Leipzig (S.97: Sylvia Pollex); **Ullstein Bild**, Berlin (S.49 re.: NMSI/Science Museum; S.70 o.: dpa; S.100 4: AP; S.101 Bild 7: Keith; S.105 u.: TopFoto); **Unicef** (S.6 E: NYHQ2007-0143/Nesbitt; S.81 o.); **Martynka Wawrzyniak**, New York (S.107); Courtesy **York College** (S.53 re. u.).

u.= unten, o. = oben, re. = rechts, li. = links, M. = Mitte

Titelbild: Shutterstock images, New York (sf2301420max)

Textquellen

S.14 u., Data source: Statistics South Africa
S.26 u., Data source: *Attitudes to Crime and Criminal Justice: Findings from the 1998 British Crime Survey (2000)* Home Office Research Study 200, London: Home Office
S.46–47: Excerpt (adapted) from "Nightmare" by Meenal Dave. From: *Katha: Short Stories by Indian Women* by Urvashi Butalia (editor). London: Telegram Books, 2008
S.96, Data source: Office for National Statistics. Crown Copyright material is reproduced with the permission of the Office of Public Sector Information (OPSI)
S.82: "Teenager with one hand could become catwalk model". Adapted from: www.dailymail.co.uk/news/article-1166994/Teenager-born-hand-kidneys-set-catwalk-model-htlm
S.102: "Give me a house" by Charles Causley. From: *Selected Poems for Children*, Macmillan, London 1997
S.102: "Secret Love" by Mike Jubb. From: *Read Me 2 – A poem for every day of the year*, Macmillan London 1999, p. 81
S.106–107: *How to be a teenage millionaire* by Susan Abbey, Nenagh, Irland

Liedquellen

S.103: *(You've got a friend) When you're down*, lyrics by Carole King, copyright 1971 by Screen Ems-EMI Music inc. Für D/A/CH/Osteuropäische Länder: EMI Publishing Germany GmbH, Hamburg

PRESENTATION PHRASES

How to start	Wie man beginnt
I want to tell you about ...	Ich möchte euch etwas über ... erzählen.
I'm going to talk about ...	Ich werde über ... sprechen.
In this talk, we're going to look at ...	In diesem Vortrag werden wir uns mit ... befassen.
Our presentation is about ...	Unser Referat ist über ...

How to link ideas	Wie man Gedanken verbindet
Firstly ... / Secondly ... / Thirdly ...	Erstens ... / Zweitens ... / Drittens ...
Next ...	Als Nächstes ...
In addition ...	Außerdem/Zusätzlich ...
So ...	Also/Daher ...
For example ...	Zum Beispiel ...

How to explain things	Wie man Dinge erklärt
Look at the board/poster/transparency.	Schaut an die Tafel / auf das Poster / auf die Folie.
This picture/photo shows ...	Dieses Bild/Foto zeigt ...
Look, here it is on the map.	Schaut, hier ist es auf der Karte.
It's on the board.	Es steht an der Tafel.
The word ... means ...	Das Wort ... bedeutet ...
We picked this because ...	Wir haben uns dafür entschieden, weil ...
We learned/found out that ...	Wir haben herausgefunden, dass ...
Did you know that ...	Wusstet ihr, dass ...

When you're stuck	Wenn man feststeckt
Just a minute.	Einen Augenblick.
What's the word? ...	Wie heißt das Wort? ...
What I'm trying to say is ...	Was ich versuche zu sagen, ist ...
It's something like ...	Es ist so etwas Ähnliches wie ...
Sorry, I mean ...	Entschuldigung, ich meine ...

How to end	Wie man zum Schluss kommt
So on the whole I'd say ...	Im Großen und Ganzen würde ich sagen, ...
So to finish I'd like to say ...	Zum Abschluss möchte ich sagen, ...
That's the end of my presentation.	Das ist das Ende meines Referats.
Thank you for listening.	Danke fürs Zuhören.
I hope you liked my presentation.	Ich hoffe, mein Referat hat euch gefallen.
Do you have any questions?	Habt ihr irgendwelche Fragen?

Giving feedback	Wie man Feedback gibt
I think your talk was very interesting.	Ich denke, dein Vortrag war sehr interessant.
You used words that I can understand.	Du hast Worte verwendet, die ich verstehen kann.
You spoke slowly and clearly.	Du hast langsam und deutlich gesprochen.
You looked at the class.	Du hast die Klasse angeschaut.

CLASSROOM PHRASES

You and your teacher

Sorry, I'm late.	Entschuldigung, dass ich zu spät komme.
Sorry, I've forgotten my book.	Entschuldigung, ich habe mein Buch vergessen.
I haven't done my homework.	Ich habe meine Hausaufgaben nicht gemacht.
Can I go to the toilet, please?	Darf ich bitte zur Toilette gehen?
Can I open/close the window, please?	Kann ich bitte das Fenster öffnen/schließen?
I didn't understand what you said.	Ich habe nicht verstanden, was Sie gesagt haben.

You need help

Can you help me, please?	Können Sie mir bitte helfen?
Can you write it on the board, please?	Können Sie es bitte an die Tafel schreiben?
Can you explain it to me, please?	Können Sie es mir bitte erkären?
Can you spell "...", please?	Können Sie bitte „..." buchstabieren?
Sorry, I can't find it.	Entschuldigung, ich kann es nicht finden.
What page?	Auf welcher Seite?
Which line/paragraph, please?	Welche Zeile / Welcher Absatz, bitte?
Could you say that again, please?	Könnten Sie das bitte wiederholen?
Could you speak louder, please?	Könnten Sie bitte lauter sprechen?
Could you speak more slowly, please?	Könnten Sie bitte langsamer spechen?
Can we listen to it again, please?	Können wir es bitte noch einmal hören?
What's "..." in English / in German?	Was heißt „..." auf Englisch / auf Deutsch?
Is "..." the right word for ...?	Ist „..." das richtige Wort für ...?
Can I say it in German?	Kann ich es auf Deutsch sagen?

Homework and exercises

Can we work together, please?	Können wir bitte zusammenarbeiten?
Can we make notes?	Können wir uns Notizen machen?
Can I read the next sentence?	Kann ich den nächsten Satz lesen?
Can we act the dialogue?	Können wir den Dialog spielen?
Can I borrow your ruler/pencil/..., please?	Kann ich mir bitte dein Lineal / deinen Bleistift /... ausleihen?
I can't do number 3.	Ich kann Nummer 3 nicht lösen.
I don't understand this exercise.	Ich verstehe diese Übung nicht.
I don't know. / I'm not sure.	Ich weiß es nicht. / Ich bin nicht sicher.
Pardon?	Wie bitte?
Is this right?	Ist das richtig?
Sorry, I haven't finished yet.	Entschuldigung, ich bin noch nicht fertig.
What's the homework?	Was haben wir (als Hausaufgabe) auf?
It's my turn.	Ich bin an der Reihe.
Can I take ... 's part, please?	Kann ich bitte ... s Teil/Rolle übernehmen?
Where can I find more information about this?	Wo kann ich mehr Informationen dazu finden?

Canada
United States of America
Bermuda
Bahamas
Puerto Rico
Belize
Jamaica
St Kitts and Nevis
Antigua and Barbuda
Dominica
St Lucia
St Vincent and the Grenadines
Barbados
Grenada
Trinidad and Tobago
Guyana
Pacific Ocean
Atlantic Ocean
Ireland
United Kingdom
Malta
Gambia
Sierra Leone
Liberia
Ghana
Nigeria
Cameroon
Suda
Ugand
Rwanda
Tanzani
Zambia
Zimbabwe
Namibia
Botswana
South Africa
Lesotho
English spoken as a first language
English used as an official language

Pacific
Ocean
Indian
Ocean
Pakistan
India
Bangla-
desh
Philippines
Micronesia
Marshall
Islands
Palau
Nauru
Kiribati
Kenya
Singapore
Papua
New
Guinea
Seychelles
Solomon
Islands
Tuvalu
Malawi
Mauritius
Vanuatu
Fiji
Islands
Tonga
adagascar
Australia
waziland
New
Zealand

South Africa
ZIMBABWE
BOTSWANA
NAMIBIA
MOZAMBIQUE
LESOTHO
SWAZI-LAND
Francistown
Windhoek
Gaborone
Maputo
Mbabane
Maseru
Kalahari Desert
Namib Desert
Gemsbok National Park
Kalahari-Gemsbok National Park
GREAT LIMPOPO TRANSFRONTIER PARK
Gonarezhou National Park
Zinave National Park
Banhine National Park
Limpopo National Park
Kruger National Park
Save
Limpopo
Molopo
Olifants
Vaal
River Orange
Caledon
Tugela
Gr. Kei
Gr. Fish
Sondags
Touws
Breede
Limpopo
Pietersburg
Phalaborwa
Nelspruit
Mpumalanga
Sun City
Pretoria
Gauteng
Krugersdorp
Johannesburg
Sharpeville
Mafikeng & Mmabatho
North West
Welkom
Free State
Kwazulu-Natal
Upington
Kimberley
Bloemfontein
Pietermaritzburg
Durban
Drakensberg Mountains
to Eastern Cape
Kokstad
Northern Cape
De Aar
Umtata
Eastern Cape
East London
Alexander Bay
Port Nolloth
Western Cape
Robben Island
Cape Town
Table Mountain National Park
Cape of Good Hope
Boulders Beach
Seal Island
Hermanus
Cape Agulhas
Port Elizabeth
Atlantic Ocean
Indian Ocean
0
100
200
300
400
500 km